WAGGY'S TALES

DAVE WAGSTAFFE'S FOUR DECADES AT MOLINEUX

WAGGY'S TALES

DAVE WAGSTAFFE'S FOUR DECADES AT MOLINEUX

DAVE WAGSTAFFE

breedon **books**
P U B L I S H I N G

First published in Great Britain in 2008 by
The Breedon Books Publishing Company Limited
Breedon House, 3 The Parker Centre,
Derby, DE21 4SZ.

ISBN: 978-1-85983-621-7

Printed and bound by Cromwell Press, Trowbridge, Wiltshire.

Contents

Foreword

This book has been solely written by myself in its entirety. Why did I write it? Because I wanted to share with you some of the untold stories from behind the scenes during my time at Molineux. As well as the humorous side of things I also wanted to put the record straight on some of the more serious incidents that arose. I have also tried to show you how life as a professional footballer was not all it was made out to be. It certainly was a wonderful career, but as you will discover it was a very bumpy ride at times. As with any job there were many ups and downs, but as a footballer you could have more than 30,000 people watching you when you were on a downer. I have endeavoured to share with you many of these highs and lows and tales of our travels throughout Europe and across the world. My life at Wolverhampton Wanderers spanned four decades and I am sure that you will be surprised to read of some of the interesting happenings during that period.

I have written over 100,000 words freehand and would like to thank Steve Gordos for the many hours he spent typing it out for me.

Dave Wagstaffe

April 2008

Maine Road to Molineux

How did I get from Maine Road to Molineux? I suppose it all started on Saturday 15 December 1962. Wolves visited City, the match ending in a thrilling 3–3 draw, and I had one of my better games.

My display that day did not make it a happy occasion for Wolves's young full-back Johnny Harris. He had played a couple of games in August 1961 but broke his leg in the second one against Villa. This was his return to the first team after a 15-month battle to regain his form and fitness and he was unfortunate enough to find me in good form for once. On the hour Wolves switched full-backs so that Bobby Thomson, who would be capped by England the following year, was marking me. I then switched to the right wing, but Bobby merely followed me. I did not fare as well against him as I had done against young Harris, but I had still had a good match. I should have had a goal too, but Fred Davies made a flying leap to keep out my shot just after half-time. That would have made it 4–1 and it was a crucial save.

Sitting in the big bath after the match, I was aware of someone through the steam, a man in a suit and wearing spectacles. He was asking for me. I stuck up my hand and declared 'I'm here'. He leaned over the edge of the bath and shook hands with me. 'Very well played, young man,' he kept repeating. 'Well done,' he said as he disappeared from view in a cloud of steam.

The man in the suit turned out to be Wolves director John Ireland. Impressed with my performance, he vowed that he would one day sign me for his club. He did, but it took two years to come about, by which time he had become chairman. Wolves always did well at Maine Road in those days. This was their eighth successive visit without losing. If my shot had not been met by that superb save from Fred Davies, we might have put a stop to that sequence. Goals were pretty rare for me. I had played in every City League game the previous season, but managed to hit the back of the net just once. However, I was still fairly pleased with life. I was not yet 20, having got into the City side at the age of 17.

Now fast-forward two years. It was 5pm on Christmas Eve 1964. I had just arrived from town in Manchester. 'There's been a telephone call for you from George Poyser,' my mother said. Poyser was the City manager at the time and my mother added 'You've got to ring him back straight away.'

'Have you any idea what he wanted?' I inquired. 'No,' she replied, 'but it must be important because he insisted you ring the moment you came home.'

George Poyser had taken over from Leslie McDowall who, after a long spell as manager, had resigned in May 1963 when City got relegated. Les had not had fantastic results at Manchester City, apart from the 1956 FA Cup Final win over Birmingham City, but they had been a reasonable First Division team for many years. He was not a household name as a manager, but I suppose he will always be remembered in football circles for his invention of the 'Revie Plan' – playing Don Revie as a deep-lying centre-forward. In the early 1960s the team began to slide and Les paid the price when they went down. George Poyser, who had been his chief scout and assistant, took over.

I had been at the club for five years, joining them on leaving school to become a ground-staff boy and eventually moving through the ranks to become a first-team regular. I had played 144 League games for City by this time and I was becoming very disillusioned with the way the club was being run and the lowly position they were in. It was bad enough living in the shadow of United all the time, but now it seemed the club were going nowhere fast. Who could have forecast that Joe Mercer and Malcolm Allison would breeze into Maine Road and take City to the Second Division title, the First Division title, the FA Cup, League Cup and European Cup-Winners' Cup? I had let my feelings be known to the management towards the end of 1964 and suggested that my future in football might be better elsewhere. Little did I know that this was to be sooner rather than later.

I rang the number that George Poyser had left with my mother. It turned out to be his home number, which was a novelty in itself; it was unheard of for a player to have the manager's home number. George answered. 'Hello,' I said, 'you left a message for me to ring you.'

'Yes,' he replied. 'Now listen carefully.' George always spoke with a dour, unexciting voice and went on 'Wolves want you.'

'Oh,' I stammered, quite taken aback.

'Meet me at Maine Road, 10 o'clock Boxing Day morning,' he continued. 'Pick up your boots then we'll drive to Wolverhampton. If you sign you play for them; if you don't, you come back and play for us. Don't be late.'

The phone went down and I thought 'Merry Christmas to you too, George.' He had just spoken to me as though I was off to play for some Sunday morning football team.

As you can imagine, Boxing Day 1964 meant there was virtually no traffic on the M6 at 10am, so we made good time down to Junction 13, which at that time was where the motorway ended. We turned off and approached Wolverhampton via Penkridge, Gailey and Fordhouses and I remember thinking what a pleasant area it was. However, the closer we came to Molineux, through Dunstall and up the hill under the railway bridges towards Stafford Street, the worse the surroundings became. Looking back, I can see now why people from the north had a terrible opinion of Wolverhampton, because anybody at that time travelling south had to follow the A449, which went straight past Molineux. In those days everything along that route was virtually falling down. Still, I was not there to admire the view: I had some serious business to attend to.

Our journey to Molineux took about an hour and 15 minutes and I remember being surprised by the number of fans that were strolling about around the ground at that time in the morning. The significance of this I would realise later. I had played at Molineux before, so I was no stranger to the ground, and two of those occasions came to mind immediately. The first was some years earlier when Wolves' reserves had won the Central League Championship. In those days it was customary for the champions to play a team selected from the rest of the Central League teams. I was lucky enough to be selected and I still have the commemorative tankard that was presented to each player after the match.

The other occasion was not such a happy one. It was the opening day of the 1962–63 First Division season and Manchester City had to visit Molineux. We were absolutely annihilated and lost 8–1. There was a bright note for me, however, or so I thought. I reckon I scored our only goal that day, the ball going straight in from a corner. That's how I saw it, but records have it as an own-goal, suggesting that the ball glanced off George Showell's head. Ted Farmer scored four goals that day, which helped wipe out the memory of what had happened in the corresponding game the previous year. There was some history between Farmer and City's stalwart German goalkeeper Bert Trautmann. When Wolves scored the only goal of the game, Farmer stood over Trautmann, mocking him by applauding. Wolves's skipper Bill Slater ran almost the length of the field to pull Farmer away, if I recall it right.

George Poyser and I went through the main entrance at Molineux into the office reception area to be met by Andy Beattie. To be perfectly honest, until I was introduced to him I had not a clue that Andy Beattie was caretaker manager with Wolves. I was aware, though, that the legendary Stan Cullis had been sacked earlier in the season. The reason for my lack of knowledge about Wolves was the fact that national daily newspapers' sports sections were all regionalised. The northern sections carried the match reports and ins and outs of only the likes of United, City, Liverpool and Everton. It took a major happening to be reported in all the national sporting sections. The introductions over, George Poyser was off to the boardroom for a drink. Before he went he reminded me of his remark two days before. 'Don't forget, if you sign you play here. If you don't, you play at Maine Road and in both cases the kick-off is 3 o'clock, so don't take too long about it.'

In those days you were allowed to sign and play on the same day, unlike the present system, under which you have to sign by 5pm the Thursday before a Saturday game — something I still do not understand.

Andy Beattie ordered a pot of tea and we went into the manager's office to be joined by Jack Howley, the Wolves secretary and general manager. Before anything else was discussed, Andy Beattie sat me down and said 'Now, David, let me put you in the picture. I am nothing whatsoever to do with this transfer; I am here purely as caretaker manager. If you sign for Wolverhampton Wanderers, then for a short time you will be under my jurisdiction as a player in the team. All I ask of you is that you play to the system that I am playing at the moment until the new manager arrives. I shan't be taking part in any negotiations so I shall leave you with Mr Howley.'

I looked over the desk at Jack Howley. He was dressed like someone from the 1930s in an old-fashioned suit with a waistcoat, thick horn-rimmed glasses and his hair plastered down with Brylcreem and parted down the middle. He looked a formidable figure, just like you would picture a Lancashire mill owner. 'What happens now, Mr Howley?' I asked, having never been in such a situation.

'Well, David,' he replied, 'what wages are you on at Manchester City?' As if he didn't know!

'Twenty-seven and eight,' I replied, which meant my basic pay was £27 and I received an extra £8 when playing in the first team.

'Hmm, and what are you looking for from us?'

'Er, 40 and five,' I gabbled as quickly as I could, trying not to make it sound so much.

'WHAT!' exclaimed Howley. 'We've got internationals here that don't earn that.'

I did not have a clue what to say next because the situation was totally foreign to me. I decided the best thing to do was take the initiative.

'Well, what about a signing-on fee then?' I managed to get out.

'And how much had you in mind?' he asked, rather sarcastically.

'Two thousand,' I coughed.

Silence. Then he suddenly looked at his watch, leaned forward, looked over his glasses at me and said 'Just excuse me for a few moments.'

As he left the room I glanced at my own watch. It was five minutes past 12. I began to wonder where I would be playing that day and did not relish the thought of going back to Maine Road to play against Bury. It was then that I decided that whatever he offered me I would sign and to hell with the consequences. Jack Howley came back into the room and sat at the desk directly opposite me. I was relaxed now and he did not seem to be such an imposing figure.

'OK, David,' he said, 'the best we can offer you is £35 and five with a signing-on fee of £1,250, which will have to be taxed. I'll give you 15 minutes to think about it. The phone is over there should you wish to call anybody.'

'No need for 15 minutes,' I replied, 'just give me the forms and I'll sign them.' I did take up the offer to use the phone to speak to my dad, giving him time to drive down from Manchester to watch the game.

Looking back I realise that I was so naïve. I know I should have bargained for a much better signing-on fee (before tax) and at least £10 a week more on my wage. I know this now because of an incident that happened just 15 or so months later. A new signing asked me to accompany him to town and show him where the building societies were. 'Come on, we'll go in this one,' he said when we reached the town centre. We wandered inside and he said 'I'd like to open an account.' When the cashier asked him how much he would like to open the account with, he answered '£6,500' and promptly opened the briefcase he had with him before pouring the amount in notes onto the counter. I do not know who was more amazed, me or the cashier. £6,500 in 1965 could buy you three nice houses.

Sitting in the office on Boxing Day 1964, waiting for the forms to be typed up, I was puzzled. Andy Beattie had already told me that he was nothing to do with my transfer and the only person I had dealt with was the secretary-general manager. So who had instigated the deal? Suddenly it came back to me: the man who had emerged from a cloud of steam about two years before. I wondered where John Ireland was that day and was to learn later that he had over-celebrated Christmas a little and left negotiations to Jack Howley. That was unlucky for me. I might have struck a better deal with a hung-over chairman.

By 12.30 I had signed the forms and was strolling up Molineux Alley with Andy Beattie to meet the rest of the squad, who were having a pre-match meal at the Molineux Hotel. 'By the way,' I inquired, 'who are we playing today?'

'Aston Villa. It's a local derby,' said Beattie in that wonderfully soft Scottish accent of his. 'We're expecting a good crowd.'

I was embarrassed when we reached the Molineux Hotel and he introduced me to the squad of 20 players and I did not know any of them personally. The only contact I had had with any of them was when I had played against them. I knew for sure that I was not going to be flavour of the month with one of the 20 – the one whose place I was about to take. In the programme for the game little Scottish winger Pat Buckley was down to wear the number-11 shirt. That apart, my biggest problem was that in two hours I had to play a First Division derby game with teammates I had only just met before a crowd of 30,000. This was a trial in itself, but a worse scenario was to come.

We finished our pre-match meal, then had a team-talk and strolled back down to the ground to prepare for the game. All players, whether playing home or away, have a walk out on to the pitch before the game and naturally we did so when we entered the ground.

To my horror I realised that the pitch was frozen solid, absolutely rock hard, the worst conditions that I would ever want to play on. My game was based on speed, balance, touch and turn — everything that the pitch was against. To cap it all, I had brought only my match boots with me, normal run-of-the mill studded boots. There was no way I was going to be able to play in my usual footwear.

I was in a dilemma so I asked either Jack Dowen or Joe Gardiner, the trainers, if they could fix me up with some kind of footwear to cope with the conditions. A large sack was produced and tipped up in the middle of the dressing room. Out tumbled a mish-mash of various kinds of footwear — plimsolls, trainers, flats, baseball boots, the lot. After rummaging through the state-of-the-art footwear I found that the only thing that would fit me was a pair of baseball boots. Remember those? They came just above your ankle and had a rubber disc either side of your ankle bone.

I could not help but think 'What am I doing here? Three hours ago I was a Manchester City player but now there's a new club, a frozen pitch, a 30,000 crowd, nobody knows me except for my dad, and I'm going out to make a debut in a pair of baseball boots.' As I ran onto the pitch the teams were being announced over the Tannoy system. After 'Number 11, Wagstaffe' was announced I could hear mutterings from all over the ground of who, what and where from. Don't forget that for two days there had been no newspapers and in those days there was no local radio or midday sports round-up as we have now. So until my arrival on the pitch nobody but the officials and players of the club knew of my signing or, in some cases, of my existence. For the record, we lost 1–0. I wasn't very pleased with my performance but on reflection I suppose I gave a reasonable account of myself under the circumstances. Villa included Barry Stobart, an ex-Wolves man, who had left City a few weeks before me. The line up that day:

Wolves: Davies, Thomson, G. Harris, Flowers, Woodfield, Miller, Wharton, Broadbent, Crawford, Kemp, Wagstaffe.

Villa: Withers, Lee, Aitken, Wylie, Sleeuwenhoek, Pountney, Baker, Stobart, Hateley, Woosnam, Macleod.

Scorer: Baker.

Referee: M. Fussey (Retford).

Attendance: 30,829.

That was my first game for Wolverhampton Wanderers, and it was to be the last game for Wolves of a great favourite of the fans, Peter Broadbent, who was soon transferred to Shrewsbury. This was also the day I was to embark on a 30-year relationship with Wolves.

The programme for that Boxing Day game does not include my name, of course. Pat Buckley was down to play outside-left, but it does contain an item of interest in the shape of an article written by Ivan Sharpe. He was a distinguished football writer and as an amateur player had won an Olympic gold medal in 1912. Sharpe always wrote a feature in the Wolves programme in those days, headed 'Today's Topical Talk'. In the programme for the Villa match one of the things he talked about was how the game could be made more attractive, including his own pet idea – banning the back pass to the goalkeeper.

Sharpe wrote 'The originator of the pass was J.T. Robertson, the Scottish international wing-half-back and first manager of Chelsea FC. Now everybody's doing it and it kills attractive forward play by taking the easy way out. Make defenders pit their wits against attackers and play constructively – this would reduce boredom and reward brainy forward play.'

Ivan was ahead of his time. It's a pity it took so many years before the back-pass law was finally changed.

Back in Manchester after my Molineux debut, I went for a drink with my fiancée Barbara in the evening. I related to her the events of the previous 12 hours; because everything that day had happened so quickly, we had not been able to sit down and discuss any plans for the future.

Barbara had recently got herself a good job as a receptionist at Kennedy Street Enterprises, which was a newly-formed theatrical agency, in the centre of Manchester. The agency had just signed up such promising acts as Freddie and the Dreamers, Herman's Hermits, Wayne Fontana and Dave Berry, to name but a few. With the boom in pop music at the time, the future looked very good indeed. As it turned out, the agency went on to become one of the biggest in the North West many years later. With a new job and a good home in Manchester, where she had lived all her life, would Barbara want to go and live in Wolverhampton? I also had been born and lived all my life in Manchester, but because I had signed those forms at Molineux I had no choice but to move to Wolverhampton. I had not given a thought to the non-playing side of things when I had signed but now I had to face up to the future.

For the first few days I was allowed to travel back and forth to training sessions but the question still had to be answered: where was I going to live? Jack Howley's door was ajar as I knocked on it and through the crack I could see another figure seated opposite him and a part-empty bottle of Scotch on the desk. Jack did not answer. Instead he walked to the half-open door and peered round. 'Oh, it's you David,' he said cheerfully. 'Come on in.' I followed him in. 'This is George Noakes, our chief scout. We were just having a chat.'

'And a drink,' I thought to myself, as it was clear to me that the two old pals were having a festive tipple together. I exchanged a few pleasantries with George and he said that he had seen me play many times and he wished me all the best at Molineux.

'Do you want me to leave?' he said.

'No. I just wanted to ask Mr Howley something,' I replied. I could not have picked a better time. I remember thinking 'Johnnie Walker's put Jack in the right mood to ask for anything.'

'First of all,' I said politely, 'what about my expenses, travelling to and from Manchester?'

'No problem,' he replied, much to my delight. 'See Jack Robinson in the office next door and tell him how much you need.'

'Well, that was easily taken care of,' I thought. Now for my next question. 'Mr Howley, where am I going to live?'

Remember, things had taken place so quickly that no mention of expenses or places to live had ever been discussed at our initial meeting. There was a short silence. 'Are you married?' he said, still in a jovial mood.

'No, but I'm going to be,' was my reply.

'That's a pity,' he said.

'What is? – that I'm getting married?' I said, puzzled.

'No,' he replied, and he and George had a good laugh. 'No, the fact that you're not married at the moment, because you would have been able to have a club house,' he continued. 'When are you getting married?'

'We haven't arranged it yet,' I said.

'OK,' said Jack, 'we'll fix you up in digs for now and then you can have a club house when you get married.'

I duly reported back to Barbara that evening and we decided that the best thing to do was to arrange our marriage as soon as possible and start our new life in Wolverhampton. We found the earliest we could arrange it for was 7 February 1965. In the meantime, Andy Beattie wanted me to find some temporary digs of my own so that I would not have to travel back and forth to Manchester every day. By this time I had got to know the lads in the squad a bit better and asked around if anybody knew of any digs available. It just goes to show how much the game has changed these days. Imagine today's players asking their teammates if they knew of any digs available until they found a house to live in. Of course, in the 1960s a player's welfare, it seemed, was not the responsibility of the club. He was there to train and play.

Harrow Street in Whitmore Reans was to become my first residence in Wolverhampton. Fred Kemp and Freddie Goodwin had rooms in a terraced house run by a middle-aged lady in Harrow Street and it just happened that there was a spare bed in Fred Kemp's room.

After training I drove to Manchester, packed my clothes and other things that I might need and returned to my new address. I pulled up outside and proceeded to carry my luggage up to my room. The lady of the house came upstairs and knocked on my door.

'You can't leave your car there,' she said, as I opened the door.

'Why not?' I inquired.

'There may not be any wheels on it when you wake up in the morning,' she replied. 'Park it on the forecourt of the shop opposite. It'll be much safer there.'

It was hardly the best welcome in the world. It amused me greatly to discover that Molineux and Maine Road, the stadium I had just left behind, had one thing in common – the local residents looked very similar! It was a quiet life at Harrow Street after the hustle and bustle of a big city like Manchester, but it was comfortable and the meals were good. Fred Kemp and I never did find out why there was always a nice cream cake in the fridge for Freddie Goodwin after his Friday meal. There was always an air of expectancy after tea on Friday, waiting to see if Wolves were mentioned on Simon Smith's sport spot on ATV Midlands. There was no local radio in those days and, except for newspaper reports, it was incredible to think that the whole Midlands soccer scene was rounded up by a five-minute report from Simon Smith.

Freddie Goodwin was a model professional and rarely ventured out in the evenings, but we did manage a few games of tenpin bowling at the Birmingham New Road bowl with some of the other lads. Fred Kemp was a little more outgoing and some evenings we ventured up to the Molineux Hotel for a pint and a game of snooker. The Molineux Hotel was quite a popular place with the lads. Apart from the fact we had our pre-match meals there, it was a handy place to go after training for a sandwich or bar snack and had the added attractions of snooker and darts. One particular lunchtime I saw George Miller – he was the pencil-slim left-footed dynamo from Dunfermline – sat in a corner scribbling away on scraps of paper. I sidled over with my sandwich and sat down.

'Writing home?' I inquired nosily.

'No,' replied George, 'just writing my bets out.'

I was a bit of a gambler myself in those days, but I could not understand why he had so many bits of paper. George soon explained why. He had covered horses in every race of the two meetings that day with sixpenny doubles and trebles. I could not believe it. I had met some gamblers in my time but had never come across any that believed they could pick winners from every race.

'Do you have a bet?' he asked.

'Yes,' I replied, 'but not on every race.'

'Come on,' he said. 'I'll show you where the betting shop is.'

We walked over the road and, if my geography is correct, I would say that the betting shop was just about where Kwik-Fit is now – at the top of Stafford Street. George placed his bets and, just to try to prove a point that his was not the way to gamble, I promptly put two pounds on the first favourite, which finished fourth. By 5 o'clock that afternoon

I had not backed a winner but George had £11 to draw from his sixpenny doubles and trebles. Out of the blue many years later I had a phone call from George and guess what? His sixpenny doubles and trebles must have paid off over the years, because he had got his own betting shop in Dunfermline.

Knowing that I liked a gamble, George introduced me to a regular card school that was held daily in a room above a café somewhere in the vicinity of the library. I cannot remember the exact location because the streets have changed so much in Wolverhampton since then, but I do know that the bus stop outside the café was a change-over point for drivers and conductors changing their shifts. One or two of these used to grab a cup of tea and proceed upstairs to join in the action. It was not heavy gambling, just three-card brag for minimal stakes, which was a pleasant way to spend an afternoon. More often than not the card school consisted of George, myself, one or two bus drivers, Johnny Kirkham, Terry Wharton and Ted Farmer.

At that time Ted Farmer's career was confined to the treatment table. I knew very little about Ted, but he was held in very high regard by the fans of Wolverhampton after he had burst on to the scene with his goalscoring exploits in 1960–61. My only encounter with Ted, as I have mentioned, was the opening day of the 1962–63 season when he scored four goals against Manchester City. According to the pundits of the day Ted had all the attributes to become a prolific goalscorer but, sadly, due to the injuries he had sustained, his career was to finish after a mere 60-odd games for Wolves. I have met Ted many times since and was only too pleased to provide a buffet – at the at the Old Wulfrunians' Club where I was then steward – for the teams who appeared in his testimonial game in the late 1980s. It's a pity we never got the chance to play in the same side.

Barbara and I got married on 7 February 1965 at Stretford, Manchester, not far from Old Trafford. Next morning we travelled down to Molineux to meet Jack Howley, who had fixed up some new digs for us. Jack was too busy to show us the exact location so we had to find our own way to Mrs Harman's in Trysull Road, just a couple of hundred yards from the Merry Hill pub. This was to be our temporary home until we could find a club house. It was bitterly cold as we went up the path and rang the bell. No answer, so we rang again, and again and again! After five minutes we went back and sat in the car because it was so cold. We could not understand it because Jack Howley had told us that Mrs Harman was expecting us. Ten minutes later we tried again. We were just about to walk away when the door opened and Mrs Harman appeared.

'Have you been ringing long?' she asked.

'No,' I replied, not wanting to appear rude.

'I was in the back garden, bringing the washing in,' she said. 'Come on in, you must be cold.'

She was right. We were absolutely freezing by this time. It was not much warmer as she showed us into the lounge. There was a welcoming fire in the grate but I could not see any sign of any other form of heating. After a cup of tea, Mrs Harman showed us up to our rooms. As we walked in, Barbara turned round and looked at me. I knew exactly what she was thinking – we had been married for only 24 hours and finished up in a room with no heating and single beds! We had not the heart to tell Mrs Harman that night but we all had a good laugh the next day when we explained to her that we had only just got married. She was a lovely lady but she was deaf in one ear so you had to stand on her good side in order to have a conversation with her. She looked after us and fed us well during our stay with her while we were waiting for our club house.

Wolves did have some club houses at the time but the new policy was that if you could find a house for sale in a certain price range then Wolves would buy that house and you could live there at a nominal rent. Jimmy Melia had recently left Wolves and had vacated a club house opposite the old entrance to Aldersley Stadium. So Barbara and I went along to look at it. It was a very modern house, built among older properties. It stood out, in fact it still does to this day, so we decided to look nearer the motorway end of Wolverhampton to make it easier to travel home to visit our respective parents. The estate behind the Vine public house at Fordhouses seemed the ideal place – five minutes from the ground one way and with easy access to the motorway the other way.

No. 40 Cottage Lane was up for sale and was in the right price range. So for something over £2,000, Wolves bought the house and Barbara and I had a home to move into for the princely sum of 25 shillings a week. However, before we could move in we had to furnish the place with carpets, curtains and the rest. On one occasion we had been over to the house to fit some carpets upstairs and it proved fortunate, because on our return to Mrs Harman's that evening we discovered that we had forgotten our key and no amount of banging on the door or ringing the bell could wake Mrs Harman. So we had to return to Cottage Lane and sleep on the carpets that we had just fitted. Mrs Harman laughed the next day when we told her of our plight and explained that if she slept on her good ear then nothing short of earthquake could wake her.

Not long after that we moved in and that seemed to be the start of the invasion of Fordhouses by Wolves players. Here's my own list of those who lived on that estate at one time or another: Ray Crawford, Bobby Woodruff, Dave Burnside, Hugh McIlmoyle, Dave Woodfield, Dave Maclaren, Peter Knowles, John Oldfield, Mike Bailey, Ernie Hunt, Danny Hegan, Steve Kindon, Frank Munro and Peter Withe. Phil Parkes also moved there and, at the time of writing, still lives there. Shortly after moving in I asked Peter Broadbent, who was still training at Wolves occasionally, about the social life around the area. He immediately invited Barbara and me to the Oakley Country Club, which he frequented virtually every Saturday night.

'It's not too far from you,' he said, 'just up the Stafford road, through Coven then on to "Brood".'

'Sounds simple enough to find,' I said to Barbara as we set off early one Saturday night. We had no problem finding Coven, but where on earth was this place called Brood? We finally gave up and went in a pub called the Ball, at Coven, for a drink. It was a really gloomy pub but I must say the beer was second to none. I asked the landlady the whereabouts of the Oakley Country Club and it gradually dawned on me that the signs I had seen which read 'Brewood' were the signs I should have been following. To this day I have never been able to fathom why the people of Wolverhampton pronounce Brewood as 'Brood'!

My English lesson over, we set off once again for the Oakley, only to run into more problems. On reaching the club we walked through the entrance and were confronted by a very stern lady sat at a desk.

'Evening,' I said.

'Are you members?' she asked, very firmly.

'No, but...' I began before being interrupted.

'Well, you can't come in then. It's members only.'

'We're meeting Peter Broadbent here,' I told her.

'He's not in.' was the blunt reply.

We had no alternative but to walk back to the car park, which is on the other side of the road to the club. Just as we were about to get into the car our luck changed. Peter and his wife Shirley had just pulled up and called us over. I told him of our encounter with the lady at the door.

'Don't worry about Betty,' Peter said, 'her bark's worse than her bite', and with that we all walked in without Betty saying another word. Betty, it turned out, was the sister of Frank Gibbs, the owner of the place, and over the years I got to know them both very well, spending many happy nights at the Oakley.

Down We Go

Life at Molineux was a bit strange in 1965 with a caretaker manager in charge and the club, which just a few years before had been the best in the land, now on the slide both on the field and off.

I felt very sorry for trainer Joe Gardiner, who had been left in charge of the huge squad of players and did not have the best facilities, and who had to produce regular training schedules. Keeping the players happy was a job in itself. I think Joe knew that sooner or later a new manager would come in and he would be relieved of his duties. Joe Gardiner was a Wolves man through and through. In all my years at Molineux I never heard a wrong word said about him. He had joined them in 1932, that's two years BC — Before Cullis. The club was his life and he was respected by both players and staff. Some Wolves record books state that Joe eventually joined Cullis at Birmingham City, but this is not true. It was Bill Shorthouse who followed Cullis to Blues. Joe never left Molineux and would never have wanted to. Typically, the last time I saw Joe he was in his seventies but still managing to organise some young special needs lads in the gymnasium above the old Wolves social club in Waterloo Road. They were having a whale of a time, kicking the footballs into the goals painted on the wall. Yes, football, and Wolverhampton Wanderers, was in his blood. Good old Joe!

Wolves were a famous club steeped in history with a host of famous names and famous games. From an administrative point of view things were fine, but the further you went down the corridor at Molineux, the worse the facilities became. The place was falling apart. Even the ground maintenance lads had to use the boiler room as their base. Looking back, it was farcical to think that First Division footballers played five-a-side on the rough car park behind the old North Bank stand and in front of what was then the club shop. This was a large green wooden hut that sold rattles, hats, badges and souvenirs. I doubt if the turnover was more than £60 a week in those days.

Sprints were the order of the day on Friday mornings before match day at every club in the country. Most of the time ours were done on the wooden sleepers at the back of the North Bank stand. The welfare of the players was the last thing to be taken into account. A lady I was to meet not five minutes after my first game was a particular victim of the inadequacies behind the scenes. Entering the dressing room after that first match I grabbed a cup of tea, lit a cigarette and sat staring at the floor, wondering what on earth I had let myself in for. A pair of legs appeared in front of me, sporting wrinkled nylons just like Norah Batty wears in *Last of the Summer Wine*. I looked up to see a bespectacled middle-aged lady. 'Come on, lad, let's have the gear,' she said.

'I won't be long,' I replied, 'I'll just finish my tea and my cigarette and it's all yours.'

'I mean now,' she said, 'I've got a busy week this week and this lot's got to be washed and ironed ready for next Saturday's match.'

She did not move until I gave her every stitch I had been wearing. 'Ta,' she said. Then, turning to the others, she added, 'Come on, you lot, you know the routine.'

However, by then the rest of the lads had already disrobed and were heading for the bath. Half an hour later, as my dad picked me up from Waterloo Road to take me back to Manchester, I saw the same lady leave the ground, pushing an old pram piled high with the socks, slips, shorts and shirts that we had played in that afternoon. That was my first encounter with Mrs Sarah Clamp. She may not have been as famous as her son, Eddie, the half-back who won two First Division Championship medals, an FA Cup-winners' medal and four England caps, but inside Molineux she was a legend. As I got to know her over the years I found her to be a charming lady.

It was a bit much for the powers-that-be at Molineux to expect her to wash and iron all the playing and training gear in her own home. The ground itself only offered drying facilities under the visitors' dressing room. Just imagine how many trips she must have made each week pushing the old pram backwards and forwards between her home and the ground! She lived round by the old Molineux Street stand. The drying facilities consisted of four hot cupboards, the size of four double wardrobes, heated by gas burners underneath. The other drying facilities were four giant wooden racks which were hoisted up to the ceiling on pulleys once they were laden with kit.

I was being paid only £35 so goodness knows how much Mrs Clamp was being paid. I said I found her to be charming, but she also had a tough side. After Peter Broadbent's testimonial match there was a reception at the Molineux Hotel. The place was packed with former players and guests when suddenly a scuffle broke out. It turned out that Eddie Clamp and his wife were involved in the rumpus. In stormed Mrs Clamp and sent Eddie scuttling off like a frightened schoolboy. Eddie may have struck fear into every famous name in football, but Mrs Clamp certainly showed him who was boss that night.

Adjacent to Mrs Clamp's drying room was what was supposed to be the fitness room. It was known as 'the pen' and was 10 metres long and four metres wide, with a few benches, a couple of old medicine balls and an assortment of dumbbells. As an added bonus, you could pop into the drying room and use it as makeshift steam room to lose a few pounds.

Castlecroft, on the edge of town, was potentially a first-class training centre but it had been neglected and, to be fair, in February 1965 the heavy snowfalls had made ground conditions treacherous. After a couple of months at Molineux I had not exactly set the place on fire with my performances on the field but, deep down, I was reasonably satisfied with my form, taking everything into consideration. Relegation was looking a distinct possibility as we sat firmly on the bottom of the table, five points behind Aston Villa, but we gave the fans something to cheer in a depressing season when we embarked on an FA Cup run. In the third round we held Portsmouth 0–0 at Fratton Park and in a thrilling replay emerged 3–2 victors at Molineux after being 2–0 up at half-time. That meant a home tie with Rotherham, a game we were expected to win. However, they held us 2–2, Ron Flowers popping up with a late goal to save our blushes in front of a crowd of nearly 30,000 at Molineux. Andy Beattie made changes for the replay at Millmoor. Out went young winger David Thompson and former England centre-forward Ray Crawford, who had been playing at inside-forward alongside Hughie McIlmoyle. George Miller was moved up to inside-forward. We gave a much better account of ourselves and won 3–0 with goals from three Ws – Terry Wharton, Bobby Woodruff and me, with one of my rare strikes.

In his *Express & Star* match report Wolves correspondent Phil Morgan was kind enough to write that my goal was 'a fitting finish for the left-winger who had his best game yet for the club although a minute or so after the first goal he had been as near being "kicked in the air" as any player I have seen. The blatant offender, right-half Ray Lambert, got away at the cost of a free-kick.'

Beattie's shake-up had worked and it proved the end of the road for Ray Crawford. Soon afterwards he was transferred down the road to West Bromwich Albion.

The draw for the fifth round paired us with local rivals Villa at Villa Park. A crowd of 52,010 saw us force a 1–1 draw to earn a replay at Molineux four days later. By then we knew that the reward for the winners was a sixth-round home tie against mighty Manchester United, but a crowd of 47,000 saw another stalemate at Molineux. It finished goalless despite extra-time. So a second replay was required, this time on neutral territory – the Hawthorns, West Bromwich. Once again Beattie made changes. Johnny Kirkham was dropped and George Miller reverted to half-back and in came Peter Knowles at number 10 to partner me on the left wing. It was a bitterly cold night, with the remnants of recent snow covering most of the pitch. The Wolves fans were soon thawed out by a magnificent hat-trick from Hugh McIlmoyle to set up the dream clash with United.

The visit of Matt Busby's team was a thrilling encounter. We lined up against United with a certain amount of trepidation. United always have been, and always will be, formidable opponents for any team, but at that particular time the odds were stacked against us. Two weeks previously they had beaten us 3–0 at Old Trafford and stood third in the table, three points behind leaders Chelsea, while we were bottom of the table. Every member of the team was, or would become, a full international. If I remember correctly nine of them had already been capped when we met them so you can see it was a daunting task.

Molineux was packed to capacity with a crowd of 53,581 that evening and I doubt if any one of them could have imagined that we would be leading United 2–0 after 15 minutes. We could not believe it ourselves. Hughie McIlmoyle had struck both goals, but it was not to remain that way. In a magnificent entertaining match we finally lost 5–3. My contribution was virtually nil, as I was marked out of the game by United right-back Shay Brennan. Denis Law put United back in the game just before half-time and David Herd, George Best, Pat Crerand and Law again turned the match on its head. Peter Knowles scored our third nine minutes from time.

I was bitterly disappointed, especially after being 2–0 up, but I suppose it was inevitable that a team of United's calibre would come back at us. Hugh McIlmoyle had more reason to be disappointed than most after a Cup campaign of eight games, of which he played in seven, had brought him seven goals. The teams that memorable night:

Wolves: Davies, Thomson, G. Harris, Flowers, Woodfield, Miller, Wharton, Woodruff, McIlmoyle, Knowles, Wagstaffe.

Manchester United: P. Dunne, Brennan, T. Dunne, Crerand, Foulkes, Stiles, Connelly, Charlton, Herd, Law, Best.

Referee: L. Callaghan (Merthyr).

Attendance: 53,581.

By this time Hughie McIlmoyle, his wife Joy and their three children had moved in next door to Barbara and me in Cottage Lane. Obviously, playing football together and living next door to each other, we became quite good friends. Anybody passing Hugh in the street would never have believed he was a centre-forward in the First Division. He was not tall, he was not broad, but he more than made up for it with his tenacity on the field. He was, as most strikers are, a natural goalscorer, good with both feet and possessing a rare gift that very few other footballers could boast – he had the knack of being able to hang in the air a split second longer than his opponents. It was just natural and even he could not tell you how he did it, but it certainly gave him that extra advantage over his opponents.

Unfortunately, Hughie faced more pressure at home than he ever did from any opposing centre-half. His wife was totally unhappy with their move to Wolverhampton and left everybody in no doubt that she was desperate to get back to Carlisle. Hughie seemed to take it all in his stride and occasionally, when she was in a good mood, he would come out for an hour to the Dowty club for a drink and a game of snooker. Like most Scotsmen I have come across, Hughie liked a gamble and was a regular member of the travelling card school on our away trips. Playing cards was a great way to pass the time while travelling and staying in hotels. There was never a shortage of players. Terry Wharton, George Miller, Fred Davies, Dave MacLaren, Johnny Kirkham, Hughie and I were among the regulars.

I saw Hughie recently at a London Wolves celebration dinner down at Charlton's ground, the Valley. Having not met for many years it was good to reminisce. He told me there was a statue of him outside Carlisle's ground. While it was a great honour, he said, with tongue in cheek, 'I'm a little bit worried because they don't normally erect one of these until you're dead!'

Andy Beattie was seen less and less during the run-in to the end of that 1964–65 season and, sure enough, the inevitable happened. We were relegated. My personal form had plummeted and I was dropped in favour of Pat Buckley for the last four games of the season. It became a miserable time for me and I had the whole of the close season to reflect on whether I had made the right move. The whole atmosphere at Molineux had become flat and the club needed somebody or something to give them a kick up the backside.

I was not fully aware of the ins and outs of the Cullis situation, but I could sense the animosity of the Wolverhampton fans towards the board of directors and chairman John Ireland in particular. All this had happened before my time at Wolves and I personally found John to be a reasonable man with a great sense of humour. However, during the coming months I was to find myself on his carpet, so to speak, and almost on my way from Wolverhampton Wanderers. Ronnie Allen, the former Albion and England forward, had joined the club from Crystal Palace in March as senior team coach. He was coming more and more to the fore and slowly beginning to take charge of the training and the tactics. Ronnie had a ready-made skipper in the experienced Ron Flowers. Joe Wilson provided muscle at right-back and Bobby Thomson culture at left-back. David Woodfield was a more than capable centre-half, with George Miller at number six alongside him. With myself and Terry Wharton two out-and-out wingers and three strikers in Knowles, Woodruff and McIlmoyle, we appeared to have the basics of a very good Second Division side. All Ronnie had to do was get the training, the tactics and the team spirit right.

Joe Wilson was a no-nonsense 100 per cent out-and-out tough guy. No airs and graces, his name just about summed him up: plain Joe Wilson. Sharing a room with him, as I did on our 1966 summer trip to Switzerland, was an education. In a newly-built hotel, Ernie Hunt and I found ourselves billeted with Joe in one of the suites that slept three people. The television in the room was itself a novelty in those days, but there was something else we had not yet come across in the 1960s — a fridge full of drink. Joe stood next to the fridge like a sentry on duty.

'Now listen, you two,' he said. 'You don't touch anything in this fridge. It's all accountable, anything missing has to be paid for and if you look at this price list, they're taking the piss. So it's a no-no.'

'OK, Joe,' Ernie and I agreed, reluctantly.

Next morning, bang on 7 o'clock, Joe was up, curtains open, windows open, deep breathing exercises. Ernie and I looked over at each other and turned over in our beds. After five minutes of exercise, Joe declared 'Right, you two, I'm off for a walk.'

'Thank goodness for that,' I quietly mused.

'I'll order the breakfast on the way back,' Joe added and I thought that was very considerate of him, seeing that he had left the windows wide open, sucking in the cold air off the lake outside. On the one hand he was leaving us wide open to the elements, but on the other he was making sure we got a good breakfast. Nice one, Joe!

At 8.30am Joe let himself back into the room. 'Right, lads, room service will be up in 10 minutes with our breakfast.'

Ernie and I were up, washed and changed in no time, eagerly awaiting our breakfast.

'Right, let's have a few minutes deep breathing at the window,' said Joe.

We went along with this, knowing that room service was imminent. Then there was a knock and a cry of 'Room service!' from the other side of the door. Joe opened it and in walked the waiter, carrying a tray. 'Breakfast,' he declared.

'Put it on here,' said Joe, pointing to a small coffee table. The waiter did as he was told and disappeared out of the door. Ernie and I looked at each other, absolutely perplexed. On the tray were three tumblers partly filled with some liquid and half a dozen eggs.

'What's this?' we asked.

'Eggs and sherry,' said Joe gleefully, 'the finest thing out.'

He continued 'Look, here's what you do' and then cracked two eggs in the sherry in one of the glasses. 'Stir it up and down in one like this' he went on, then his head went back and the concoction disappeared in seconds.

'Your turn now, lads,' Joe said and even cracked the eggs for us and stirred them into the sherry in the other glasses as if to make sure we went ahead with it.

Joe was not a guy you argued with so I knew that there was no way out of this situation. Pinching my nose and holding my head back, I swallowed the lot in seconds. It was awful. Ernie did likewise and, looking at Joe, I was sure I could see the flicker of a smile on his face, the sadistic old devil. Needless to say, Joe was not top of our room-sharing list from that day forth.

We played a friendly game with a local Swiss side that day but in Joe's book there was no such thing as a friendly, such was his exuberance and competitiveness for any match situation. A couple of decisions went against him and, losing his rag, he chased after the referee in a fervour, barking like a mad dog. Facing the ref, he barked a little too hard and his top set of false teeth flew out. He had forgotten to take them out in his haste to get out there and compete. The teeth hit the ref on the back of the hand. Fortunately, the official saw the funny side of the situation and even picked up the teeth and handed them back to Joe. The ref was lucky: had they broken the skin when they hit him on the back of the hand he could have finished up with salmonella from the raw eggs Joe had consumed earlier that day! There was also a gentler side to Joe, as there usually is with even the hardest of individuals. He was allowed to bring his accordion with him on away trips. So, on the way back from wherever we played, there was always a sing-along-a-Joe session, with everybody on the team coach joining in.

Dave Woodfield was another player who was always keen to enhance his fitness, as I learned when I first went to live on the Fordhouses estate. Each morning as I went for my daily newspaper I would catch sight of him walking down the road. Naturally, I waved to him as I drove back home to have a scan through my paper, a quick cup of tea, then go off to training. One day, for whatever reason, I had to be at the ground much earlier than usual and as I approached the Stafford Road I saw Dave ahead of me, walking. I pulled up and asked if he wanted a lift anywhere. To my surprise, he said 'No thanks, I walk to the ground every morning.' Even more surprising was the fact that he walked all the way home again after the morning's training session.

Dave was a good, honest, tough, old-fashioned centre-half, the sort of lad you could always depend on, never one to moan and one who took everything in his stride. Some supporters from the 1960s may remember the day Dave got sent off against Manchester City for a foul on one of my old friends, Mike Summerbee, who finished up in row C of the old Molineux Street stand. Of course, Dave meant to hit him hard and let him know that he was there, but I can assure you that there was no way that Dave intended to put Mike in the stand. It was just the impetus of the tackle and the speed that Mike was running at that made the whole incident look horrendous. Mike himself knew that Dave had no intention of causing him serious harm and there was never any acrimony between them after the incident. Indeed, Mike Summerbee gave evidence when Dave was cleared by an FA inquiry of making a dangerous and violent tackle. Mike said afterwards: 'I always said I was knocked off the pitch by a perfectly fair charge. I think the sight of it all as I came up from the stand with my face covered in blood made it look worse than it really was.'

Dave's dismissal at Molineux in August 1965 was the first for a Wolves first-team player on home soil in 29 years.

When Dave left us and went to Watford it was a tremendous gesture from Elton John to offer to do a brief gig at the Civic Hall in aid of Dave's testimonial year. Standing idly chatting with Dave, a few of the lads and the great man himself, I managed to put my foot in it.

'I must pop to the toilet,' said Elton, 'I'm on in two minutes.'

'You're not nervous?' I asked in all innocence.

'Of course I'm f*****g nervous,' he replied. 'When you go out and perform you've got 10 mates with you. When I go out there to perform tonight I've only got my piano for company.'

How right he was. I'd never thought of it that way. In the event, he did not show any nerves at all. His set that night was absolutely brilliant.

Sent Home

Life in the Second Division was not as easy as we thought it was going to be. We lost three of the first four games, but the tide was beginning to turn as Ronnie Allen created a really good atmosphere around the ground and team spirit was on the up. Mind you, one would not have thought so, because we went to Southampton and were thrashed 9–3. Sitting on the bench watching the game that day at the Dell was Ernie Hunt. He was our latest signing, but the deal had not been completed in time for him to play. He must have wondered what he had let himself in for. Yet this result was the kick start we needed, though Andy Beattie had no influence on our revival as he left the club two days later citing 'personal reasons'. With Ernie making his debut, we went on to win the next four games on the trot, every one 3–0. I scored in each of those first three 3–0 wins to complete the best scoring spell of my career – seven goals in nine games. I had never scored so regularly before and I never did again!

It was no good putting an X next to Wolves's game on your treble chance coupon because when we drew our next game, with Huddersfield, it was the first League game we had drawn since 30 March the previous year, a run of 20 games. After beating Crystal Palace we made up for our lack of draws by being held 2–2 in each of three successive games. John Holsgrove arrived and soon slotted in, wearing the number-six shirt. Did you know that John was a very keen guitarist and was a big fan of the Shadows? He got to meet them on numerous occasions and got some tuition from Hank Marvin. After watching and listening to one of the great guitarists of the world, John decided to stick to football and a very capable footballer he turned out to be. John was also the inventor of the 'Castlecroft Ghost'. It was amazing how many of the lads tripped up or fell over with nobody in close proximity or passed the ball to empty spaces during games at our training ground. It sounds hard to believe, but it was really uncanny the number of silly happenings that occurred when we trained there and John always blamed them on the ghost. Nobody for a moment believed in the Castlecroft Ghost, except John, but it was a great get-out to blame the spirit if you dropped a ricket during training. John would later become a member of an exclusive set of Wolves players, which is something I will tell you about in due course.

By the mid-term of the 1965–66 season we were scoring plenty of goals, if nothing else. Everybody in the forward line, including yours truly, contributed, but the main goalscorers were Hughie McIlmoyle and the ever-improving Peter Knowles. By now Ronnie Allen was pulling the strings and was a real motivator with his inventiveness and enthusiasm on and off the training pitch. As I have already mentioned, the gymnasium-cum-weight room situated under the visitors' dressing room at Molineux consisted of a few dumbbells, medicine balls and benches. Ronnie was to utilise every piece of equipment in there. He had a wonderful knack of making everything you did interesting and, for the first time in my football career, I was actually enjoying training. One great thing Ronnie had going for him was the fact that he was still only in his late 30s and was able to practise what he preached. The number of exercises he devised with a set of four benches for footwork, legwork and bodywork was quite amazing. Even better was the fact that he was still fit enough to demonstrate each exercise.

Many a day after training Ronnie would ask Phil Parkes if he wanted to do a bit of extra shot-stopping and me if I fancied crossing a few balls. We would go out on the pitch, Lofty in goal at the North Bank end, me out on the left wing by the players' tunnel and Ronnie in the D on the edge of the penalty area. There was a groundstaff boy in the centre circle with a dozen footballs. The idea was for the young lad to hit a ball out to me on the wing, for me to bring the ball down, one touch forward, then clip it to land waist high in front of Ronnie, who would volley shots at Phil. Lofty loved it, I loved it and, most of all, Ronnie loved it. You could tell by the enjoyment he got from this that he really missed his playing days and the lads nicknamed him 'Hot Shot'. This and his other ballwork sessions were the nearest he could get to his former match situations. Phil and I were so impressed with his ability to volley the balls — especially as they were coming across him — one of the hardest skills in the game. He did not miss the target with many.

The exuberance of Peter Knowles was clearly showing on and off the pitch and I would say that at this particular time he was totally enthralled by football. In fact, he loved it all so much he would cheat during the shooting session, jumping the queue to get in an extra shot or two.

Amazingly, we again went two up against Manchester United in the FA Cup at Molineux, only to lose the match. This time it was in the fifth round and it took us only nine minutes thanks to two Terry Wharton penalties. United roared back and won 4–2. The team were playing quite well, but we were always trailing those top two promotion places and there were no Play-offs in those days. Ronnie bought Mike Bailey for £35,000 from Charlton and, with Graham Hawkins coming in for the injured Dave Woodfield at number five, and Ron Flowers moving over to number six, we made a final push for promotion. Despite losing only two of our last nine games it was all to no avail and we finished in a disappointing sixth place. However, the acquisition of Mike Bailey would prove to be a major factor in our success in the years that followed.

Graham Hawkins, who would many years later manage Wolves, proved to be a good pal and we teamed up again at Blackburn towards the end of my career. Being old pals, we often roomed together when at Rovers and that led to one memorable incident on a pre-season trip to Ireland. We arrived at a hotel in Dundalk on the border of Northern and Southern Ireland, though it was not so much a hotel as a converted castle. Graham got the bags from reception and I followed him up some stone steps to a room in one of the turrets. As he opened the door, he spotted that there was a single bed and a double bed in the room. Throwing his suitcase on to the double bed he said 'That's mine.' I did not mind because Graham was well over 6ft and stockily built. Moments later there was a knock at the door and in walked our centre-half Glen Keeley, who was 6ft 3in tall. 'It's three to a room,' he explained and I could not contain my laughter as I said 'In that case you're in that bed with Graham.'

It was hilarious at bedtime, watching two strapping six-footers grappling for the covers while I was tucked up cosily in my single bed. If ever there was a case of saying 'You've made your bed, now lie in it', it was then. All of this is quite amusing, but a far cry from that last week of the 1965–66 season, which saw me again sharing a room, though this time with just one teammate, Dave MacLaren. We were due to play Ipswich on the last day but I missed the match and such were the circumstances that it was touch and go whether I started the 1966–67 season with Wolverhampton Wanderers.

When playing Ipswich or Norwich we always stayed overnight at the little market town of Bury St Edmunds. Staying away from home the night before a game is one of the most boring times of a footballer's life. Have a walk round the town after the evening meal then spend the next hour or so lounging around the hotel, waiting for the tea and biscuits to arrive at 10.30, then off to bed. This was exactly how it was on that Friday night in Bury St Edmunds.

Normally there would be a cards or dominoes school in somebody's room for an hour or two but for some unknown reason nobody had arranged anything. This left me in a dilemma – I was not used to going to sleep at 10.45pm. Dave MacLaren had his head buried in a golf magazine so there was no chance of any conversation from him. I wandered down the corridor to the room that Ernie Hunt and Dave Woodfield were sharing. Dave, as usual, had brought a knapsack full of food and the three of us sat there chatting and munching chocolate like three schoolkids in a dormitory. Nothing could have been more innocent, but seconds later all hell was let loose. Bang! Bang! Bang! 'Open up' we heard from further down the corridor. 'Get this door open now.'

'That's John Ireland's voice,' I said to Dave and Ernie, 'what the hell's he doing?'

We cautiously opened the door a couple of inches and peered down the corridor to see the chairman and another director, old Jim Marshall, in their dressing gowns and pyjamas, systematically knocking on the players' bedroom doors.

'I wonder what's happened?' said Ernie.

'I haven't a clue,' I replied, 'but one thing's for sure, I'm for the high jump now for not being in bed and they must know that I'm not in my room because it's at the end of the corridor that they're coming from. I'll hide under the bed, just say you haven't seen me.'

Sure enough, a couple of minutes later, bang, bang. 'Open up!' shouted John Ireland. Ernie opened the door and got back into bed. John Ireland walked over and stood at the end of the bed with Jim Marshall behind him. I was now in the most farcical situation I had ever been in. A professional footballer under the bed with the chairman's slippers three inches from my nose.

'What's the problem, Mr Chairman?' asked Ernie.

'A serious incident has taken place,' replied John Ireland, 'and one of the players is missing from his room. Do you know where he is?'

'Who's missing?' asked Dave, 'and what's happened?'

'Wagstaffe's missing,' growled Jim Marshall, 'and never you mind what's happened. Have you seen him?'

'Earlier,' said Dave, which was not a lie.

'Right, come on John, we'll find the sneaky rat.' And with that the pair of them disappeared down the corridor to bang on somebody else's door.

I rolled out from under the bed and the three of us burst into uncontrolled laughter at the bizarre situation. We all wondered what this 'serious incident' could be, but both Dave and Ernie knew it could not involve me because I had been in their room talking to them.

'Look, lads, I'd better get back to my room and see what's happened,' I said. 'Good night and see you in the morning.'

Little did I know that I would not be seeing them in the morning.

I wandered along the corridor and was just about to enter my room when Messrs Ireland and Marshall came around the corner. 'Ah, we've caught the sneaky rat,' shouted Jim Marshall, as though some master criminal was about to be arrested.

'That's twice he's called me a sneaky rat,' I thought, and I could feel myself getting angry.

'What's the problem?' I snapped.

'You've been missing from your room,' replied John Ireland.

'Firstly,' I said angrily, pointing at Jim Marshall, 'I am not a sneaky rat and, secondly, where the hell do you think I've been in my underpants. I can't have been out of the hotel, can I?' I shouted.

Jim Marshall cowered behind John Ireland and quietly said to him, 'I warned you about these big money signings, John, they're always trouble. He'll have to go.'

'Big money,' I thought. 'I only cost £30,000.'

'Perhaps you're right, Jim,' he replied.

At this I am afraid I lost my temper and told them to 'F**k off' and slammed the bedroom door behind me. Dave MacLaren was chuckling at the whole affair as I jumped into bed.

'What's this serious incident about, Dave?' I asked.

'Search me,' said Dave, 'but no doubt we'll find out in the morning.'

We went back to bed still giggling at the 'big money' statement as we drifted off to sleep. At 8.15 next morning I picked up the phone next to the bed. 'Room service, please,' I said, then yelled across the room 'Dave, what do you want for breakfast?'

'Just order me the same as you,' he mumbled, still half asleep.

'Ah, room service, sausage, egg, bacon, toast and tea twice, please,' I requested.

There was no need to get dressed as the usual procedure was breakfast in bed then back to sleep for a couple of hours. I lay there reading Dave's golf magazine, looking forward to the breakfast that room service would soon deliver to our room. Fifteen to 20 minutes later there was a knock on the door and I shouted 'Come in,' as room service usually had a pass key. Nothing happened so I shouted 'Come in' a bit louder. There was another knock on the door so I had to get out of bed and open it.

'Oh' I exclaimed. It was Ronnie Allen, not the breakfast I was expecting.

'Dave, I need to talk to you,' said Ronnie. 'Late last night the chairman came down to my room and told me I have to send you home this morning.'

'What? Just because I wasn't in my bed for 10.45?' I asked.

'No,' said Ronnie, 'there's more to it than that.'

Then Ronnie proceeded to unravel the mystery of the night before. Apparently, somebody on the second floor had thrown a container of water over some passers-by, a middle-aged couple. Angry at what had happened, as one would be, the couple went into the hotel and complained to the manager. He apologised to the couple and promised to deal with the culprit. He knew full well that it had to be one of the players because we were the only people occupying the second floor. So he decided to throw the ball into John Ireland's court and let him deal with the problem.

The chairman, directors and Ronnie Allen had rooms on the first floor and, unfortunately for me, when John Ireland and Jim Marshall went to investigate the incident my room was the first one that they came to. The fact that I was missing from my room led them to believe that I had to be the guilty party. They then set out to find me and, of course, you know the rest of the story. I protested my innocence to Ronnie and begged him to verify my story with Dave Woodfield and Ernie Hunt.

'No, I can't do that,' he said sympathetically. 'They want you off the premises before all the lads get up.'

He gave me £20 for my expenses and waited for me to get dressed and gather my things. As we were leaving the room my breakfast arrived, but Ronnie ushered me past and down to the reception where we planned my route home. My trip back was to consist of a taxi and three train journeys. Being sent home was a serious thing, but the only thing I could think of on my way to the station was Dave MacLaren tucking into two breakfasts and thinking to myself 'He'll never be able to come off his line today with all that lot inside him.'

I arrived back at Wolverhampton station and walked down to the ground just in time for a cup of tea. It was half-time at the Central League game. I watched the second half, collected my car and drove home. To round off a disastrous day, Barbara had not got me a meal ready because, of course, she did not expect me home until late that evening and amid all the drama I had forgotten to ring home and inform her of my predicament. I knew that I was totally innocent of any serious misconduct and later found out that Peter Knowles was the real culprit. Peter was prone to doing silly things on a whim, but I did not bear him any malice. The people I was really annoyed with were John Ireland and Jim Marshall for jumping to conclusions without investigating the matter thoroughly. After hearing the comments of John Ireland and Jim Marshall that night I was convinced that I would not be starting the following season at Wolverhampton Wanderers. I was not sure that I wanted to, anyway.

For the record, Wolves lost the game at Ipswich 5–2, with Ray Crawford, by then back on his old stamping ground, scoring twice. I wonder if Dave MacLaren's bumper breakfast had anything to do with the result? Paddy Buckley had to travel from Wolverhampton to take my place, but there was no clue to what had happened in Phil Morgan's *Express & Star* report. It merely said that 'Buckley had been preferred to Wagstaffe at the last minute.' I doubt if such an incident would escape the press these days.

Every day of the close season I expected a letter from Wolves to tell me that I would be on the transfer list. Finally, an official Wolverhampton Wanderers envelope appeared behind my door and I opened it with trepidation.

'Dear David,' it read, 'you are hereby summoned to appear at the next meeting of the board of directors,' followed by the time and date of the meeting.

'Board meeting,' I repeated to myself. 'Players are never asked to attend board meetings.'

I must admit that I had some sleepless nights wondering about the likely outcome of my appearance in front of the board. Would I lose my temper and tell them all to 'F**k off,' or should I simply accept the situation and tell them I would like to play for someone else? The day arrived and as I walked through the main entrance I was met by Jack Howley who was waiting to take me into the boardroom.

'Relax,' he said,' there's nothing to worry about.'

This did make me feel a little easier but I was still apprehensive as to what I was about to face. He knocked on the door and as we walked in he showed me to an empty chair at the opposite end of the boardroom table to the chairman. John Ireland was seated, looking down at some papers in front of him, and the rest of the directors silently flanked the table. He rose from his chair without even looking at me, the papers still in his hand. Still looking down at the papers he began 'A serious incident occurred at the hotel during our stay at Bury St Edmunds. No action will be taken about this incident, it will never be mentioned again; indeed, it is forgotten. Thank you, gentlemen.'

He sat down, apparently still looking at the papers in his hand, and never even glanced my way. Jack Howley held the door open and showed me out. As we walked along the corridor he whispered 'That's the nearest thing to an apology anyone will ever get from a board meeting.'

The incident, was, indeed, never mentioned again. It turned out that during the close season they had found out that the origin of the incident was some horseplay from a young impish Peter Knowles, and from that day on John Ireland set out to be my friend. Not only did he become a friend, he also became a fan of mine.

My Monkee Mate and the American Adventure

For the 1966–67 season, Ronnie Allen had made his intentions quite clear. It was promotion or bust. Ronnie, who had been officially made team manager in July 1966, had a good look at the opposition from the previous season and was confident that with the squad he had got, plus a few additions to the mix, we had a real chance. Team spirit was sky high and it was a laugh a minute in the dressing room before and after training. I don't know where it came from but a miniature cricket set appeared in the dressing room. The stumps were about 15in (37.5cm) high and the bat was about the same. There was a small rubber ball about the size of a squash ball. We made up our own game, the idea being that every time whoever was batting put bat to ball it was counted as a run. Sounds easy, but with a pitch only five metres long and at least 15 fielders crowding round the bat you were lucky to last more than half a dozen balls.

Ronnie joined in this ritual every morning and was the ace spin bowler, bowling both leg and off breaks with that small rubber ball. Great fun was had by all. Peter Knowles, being a Yorkshireman, was not too bad at cricket, but he would get bored just playing a defensive game and sometimes have a lash at the ball, making us all dive for cover as it ricocheted round the room off the walls. On at least a couple of occasions Peter managed to smash the ball straight through the frosted windows. Jack Dowen would come dashing into the dressing room, having heard the sound of breaking glass. 'Oh no!' he would shout disappointedly, knowing that he would have to spend the morning sitting there waiting for the glaziers to come and repair the window.

Jack was another smashing bloke from the Molineux past. He teamed up with Ronnie Allen, helping him in all sorts of capacities, leaving Ronnie to get on with the football side of things. As you can imagine, anyone who set foot in that dressing room was wide open to a certain amount of mickey-taking, and Jack was no exception. He would take it all in good spirit and was a very well-respected person among the lads. Jack did not swear but it was hilarious to hear him in his rare moments of frustration refer to things as 'flopping' this and 'flopping' that. That was the nearest he came to swearing. I'm told that, in that respect, he was the same as Stan Cullis. Every Sunday morning around 11 o'clock Jack would be seen waiting at the bus stop opposite the Waterloo Road stand. After a visit to church Jack would pop into the ground to make sure everything was OK, then catch the bus up to Marsh Lane where he lived.

We did not exactly get off to a dream start to the new season, losing our first two games, against Birmingham and Ipswich. I actually made it to Ipswich this time and got a game! Inspired by the team spirit and determination of our new captain, Mike Bailey, 10 goals from Ernie Hunt and nine from Hughie Mac, we lost only one of our next 15 games. The illustrious career of one of Wolves's all-time greats was coming to an end by this time. After 15 years and 500 games for Wolves, Ron Flowers had decided to slow down a little and move to Northampton Town. What a contrast to 12 months earlier when he had been a member of Sir Alf Ramsey's World Cup-winning squad. One of Ron's biggest assets, apart from being a great player that is, was that he was the calmest, most unruffled player I had ever played with. Nothing ever got to him. Off the pitch, despite all his achievements, he was a very quiet and unassuming person and a very approachable one too. Ron does not know this, but a few games before he left he did me a great favour. Playing Norwich City at Carrow Road, Ron had just played a one-two with Terry Wharton to get himself to the byline. Looking up, he spotted me unmarked on the six-yard line. With pinpoint accuracy he chipped the ball back straight on to my head. I could not miss. The pace of the ball made it more or less rebound off my head into the net. In almost 12 years at Molineux that was the only headed goal I ever scored. Thanks, Ron!

It was by now an exciting atmosphere among the players and fans alike with the team doing so well. Behind the scenes at Molineux it was also an exciting time with this little bit of success making the training seem less arduous. As I have already mentioned, Ronnie Allen's training sessions were second to none and he tried to make them as interesting as he could, but, as every player knows, there was always a hard day in the week of training which usually consisted of a very tough running session. It was not everybody's cup of tea and certainly not mine. I would run all day with a ball at my feet, but when it came to the cross-country runs or running to a stopwatch, I was mentally and physically defeated.

To counteract the hard day, Ronnie would, whenever possible, try to incorporate a golf day, much to the delight of the majority of players, who were avid golfers. Ronnie himself was a very capable golfer, playing off a handicap of four. His favourite trick was to place a new Dunlop 65 ball, still in its wrapper, on his tee peg. He would hit the ball, the wrapper flying into the air and his Dunlop 65 travelling safely down the middle of the fairway. I was playing alongside him one day at Enville in a four-ball when he played one amazing hole. One of the early holes at Enville was in those days a par five, some 530 yards. Ronnie hit a super drive down the middle of the fairway and, on reaching his ball, found that he had a completely blind second shot to the green. Taking a three wood, he hit his second over the brow of the hill towards the green. As we neared the green there was no sign of Ronnie's ball. After a couple of minutes' searching, somebody decided to look in the hole. There it was, Ronnie's Dunlop 65, safely in the hole for an eagle two.

Ronnie's other passion was horse racing. He had a share in a racehorse with his singing pal Frankie Vaughan. He loved to go to meetings and one day, while we were in Toronto, Canada, he went to the racecourse and came back with a fistful of dollars — 500 of them, in fact — which he had won that afternoon. He was in his element when we were staying in Los Angeles. There was an incredible 55-day meeting at Hollywood Park races. We all paid a visit at some time but Ronnie, being an enthusiast, was a very frequent visitor and was looked after by our sponsors in a private box. Ronnie loved the big time and it does not get any bigger than Hollywood, where he looked the part too.

Getting back to the 1966–67 season, by halfway through all the signings that Ronnie had made in the past 12 months or so, namely Ernie Hunt, Mike Bailey, John Holsgrove, Dave Burnside and Bob Hatton, were making their contribution to our push for promotion. After three-quarters of the season we needed one final push for that top-two finish and promotion to the First Division. In hindsight, it was probably a good thing that we had bowed out of the FA Cup and the League Cup in the early stages, leaving us to concentrate on the most important thing, the League. With a quarter of the season to go, Ronnie played his master card. He signed the charismatic Derek Dougan from Leicester City for £50,000 and the fairytale began. His first game was down in Plymouth, where we won 1–0. His second game was surely scripted by the writer of *Roy of the Rovers*. At Molineux the Doog treated 31,000 fans to a scintillating display, scoring a hat-trick and becoming an instant cult figure in the process. He went on to finish the season with a creditable nine goals in 11 games.

Losing only two of our last 11 games we finished second, regaining a place in the First Division. I played all 42 games of the campaign, scoring six goals — one with my head, don't forget — after probably the toughest season of my career in terms of the mental and physical strain.

After celebrating our success in getting back to the top flight, Ronnie Allen announced that we had been invited to play in a special North American Soccer League, consisting of a dozen teams from different countries trying to promote soccer in the United States. Our sponsor, a man that you may never have heard of, was someone destined to become one of the biggest names of all in American sport — Jack Kent Cooke. Type his name in your computer search engine and read the chronology of his life. You will be amazed at the things he achieved.

After an 11-hour flight we finally reached Los Angeles and the Sheraton West Hotel, where we were to be based for the next nine weeks. That evening at the Coliseum Stadium a friendly match between Manchester United and Chelsea was to be played and naturally we all went along to watch. At the half-time interval we were individually introduced to the crowd as the team who were to represent them in the forthcoming competition, the Los Angeles Wolves. The manager was introduced first, then the players and then, a nice touch, 'Mr Jack Dowen, the equipment manager.' Jack took some stick about that one, as you can imagine, but as usual took it in his stride.

Back in our seats ready to watch the second half, a large bodyguard type of gentleman came along and asked which of us was Mr Wagstaffe.

'That's me,' said I.

'OK,' he replied. 'Mr Jones would like to see you. Follow me.'

At first I thought it was a wind-up and the lads had set me up. I sat there for a moment thinking they could have come up with a more original name than 'Mr Jones'.

'Come on,' the man insisted, 'follow me. He's only up the steps near the back row of seats.' I did as he bade me but still thought the lads were playing some kind of joke. As I neared the last few rows of seats, I saw him. This 'Mr Jones' was none other than Davy Jones of the Monkees pop group fame. We used to kick a ball about together in the back streets of Manchester when we were kids. The last time we had seen each other was when we were 16 years of age. I was at the bus stop with my suitcase waiting for the trolley bus to take me down to London Road station in Manchester. A few moments later, Davy appeared from around the corner, also with his suitcase, and joined me in the square.

'Where are you off to, Davy?' I asked.

'London,' he replied. 'And you?'

'London,' I said.

Davy explained to me that he was going to London to audition for a part in *Oliver* the musical. I was on my way to Lancaster Gate to meet up with the England Youth team for a tournament in Austria. We travelled to London together, wished each other well and went our separate ways. Little did we know, all those years ago, kicking a tennis ball about down the back of an entry, that he would turn out to be a famous pop star and TV personality and I would be a professional footballer. Nor did we dream when we parted in London some seven years earlier that the next time we would meet up would be in Los Angeles.

Davy had spotted me when we were introduced on the field at half-time and sent one of the security men to fetch me. We had a quick chat and made arrangements to meet up the following day. The Monkees at this time were at the top of their profession and were famous throughout the world, not only for their music but also for their half-hour television shows.

'See you tomorrow, Davy,' I shouted as I wandered back down to my seat among the lads to watch the second half of the United versus Chelsea game.

'Did you find Mr Jones?' asked one of the lads sarcastically.

'Oh yeah,' I said, rather casually.

'Was his first name Tom?' said somebody else, and they all laughed.

'It wasn't, actually, it was the other Mr Jones who sings with the Monkees pop group – Davy Jones,' I replied, matter of fact.

'Oh, yeah,' shouted somebody, and 'Dream on, Waggy,' echoed another, and they all had a good chuckle.

'We'll see,' I said to them all.

On the coach back to the hotel after the game I had a word with Ronnie Allen about the agenda for the next day.

'We'll stretch our legs and have a five-a-side to get rid of the stiffness from that long flight. Then the rest of the day's your own,' he said.

Ronnie had not been sat with the lads to watch the game so was unaware of my meeting with Davy Jones. I told him about it and said that Davy was arranging for the whole of our tour party to visit the Monkees on set at Columbia Studios, Hollywood, to watch them film one of their TV episodes and for us all to be ready at 2 o'clock outside the hotel. Back at the hotel, Ronnie gathered all the lads together.

'OK, lads,' he said, 'light training in the morning at 10am in the park opposite, then everyone outside the main entrance for the hotel at 2pm for a trip to the film studios which Waggy has organised for us all.'

Next morning we trained in the park very aptly named Lafayette Park – Lafayette was the number-one night spot in Wolverhampton in those days – and I was constantly quizzed by the other players about this so-called trip to the studios. All I would say to them was that my friend from last night, Mr Jones, had arranged it. When 2pm came we were all patiently waiting outside the hotel; 2.15 came and still nothing; 2.30 and the sceptics were getting restless, thinking that I had set them all up for taking the mickey out of me the night before. I was starting to panic but I need not have worried. A few minutes later two huge chauffeur-driven limousines pulled up alongside, the drivers asking for Mr Wagstaffe. We were transported to Columbia Studios, waved through security and straight on to the set where the Monkees were preparing to start filming.

It was hard to believe really. Here we were on one of the sets of the giant studios in Hollywood, California, the most famous city in the world for filmmaking. Not only that, we were being entertained by one of the most famous quartets in the world, namely Davy Jones, Peter Tork, Micky Dolenz and Mike Nesmith. You can imagine the excitement, possibly bewilderment, among the lads. The majority of us had never even been to the United States before, let alone Hollywood, the glitziest, most glamorous place on the planet. What a contrast. Three days ago we were boarding the bus on Waterloo Road and now we were in the California sunshine. We watched them film an episode for TV and were then given a tour round the studios. It was a brilliant start to our American tour and put everyone concerned in a good mood.

He did not say as much, but I suppose it was a treat for Davy, hearing all the different accents from back home, especially mine and Wharty's Lancashire twang. You did not get many of them in LA. Davy was a frequent visitor to the hotel poolside, where we played table tennis, and when he was not driving me to different places he gave me the use of a beautiful yellow GTO Pontiac convertible to drive myself and some of the lads around. Davy was adored by many, many thousands of females and was a rich and famous young man, but I suspected that deep down, living thousands of miles from home, albeit in a wonderful place to live, there must have been times when he missed his home city of Manchester. Sitting having a quiet drink one evening, he suddenly announced that he was going to phone his pal, an English chef, at a top restaurant on the famous Sunset Strip.

'He's going to make us something special,' he said, 'for later on.'

A few drinks and a couple of hours later we arrived at the restaurant for our meal. Guess what the chef had made for us? Lancashire hotpot. I must say we got some peculiar looks from the rest of the clientele when the waiter served it up. On another occasion, after a night out playing pool, we went back to his recording studios where the finishing touches were being put to the Monkees' latest record, *Daydream Believer.* To this day, every time I hear the line 'Cheer up, sleepy Jean' my mind goes back to that evening in 1967 at the recording studios.

A few days before they were to leave on their Australian tour, Davy and his good friend Charlie Rocket came to see me down at the hotel poolside, where I was hanging about in the sun with Ernie Hunt, Terry Wharton and Mike Bailey. Mike had joined us after touring with the England party in the Expo 67 tournament in Montreal.

'Come on,' said Davy. 'Let's all go down to Lenny's Boot Parlour. I'll treat you to some clothes.'

Lenny's is actually a boutique situated next to the film studios. We all piled in the car and motored down to the boutique. Naturally, with such a generous offer from Davy we did not go overboard and picked our clothes sensibly. The bill that Davy paid was 600 dollars, which was around £400 in those days, a lot of money in the 1960s. This was a lovely leaving gesture from Davy and a couple of days later he was off to Australia with the rest of the Monkees and their entourage, leaving us in the California sunshine.

The Sheraton West Hotel was an ideal location for us to stay, being about a 30 minute drive from our home ground, the Coliseum. Opposite the hotel was Lafayette Park, which had plenty of grassed areas for us to train and play five-a-side, and the hotel poolside became the regular meeting place for all the party. It became the place where our own little quartet was formed. The 'Tea Set', as they were dubbed by the rest of us, consisted of Derek Dougan, John Holsgrove, Bobby Thomson and Les Wilson. This foursome, when sat at the poolside or round the table, were never seen without a pot of tea in front of them. Even after the tour, whenever we played in Britain, Europe or the rest of the world, that pot of tea for four was always the first thing to be ordered.

Because of our irregular schedule it had already been decided that we would not be eating at the hotel and consequently given an allowance to buy our own meals at eating places of our choice. When local, most of the lads opted to eat at Tiny Naylor's, part of a large consortium of eateries well-known in the United States. Being situated within a couple of hundred yards from the hotel it was handy for us all and was open from early morning until dusk. Peter Knowles used to join us until he got wind of a better place to eat. Surrounding the pool there were several chalets where the most affluent patrons of the hotel used to stay and the majority of them would eat out on the adjoining patios. Peter, probably the most regular sunbather in the party, spent most of his leisure time at the side of the pool and would see everything that was going on. With every meal ordered, a huge salad accompanied it simply because salad ingredients grew plentifully in the sunshine of California and the cost was very, very minimal. More often than not, this huge salad was pushed aside and left untouched. Peter, like any Yorkshireman would, worked out that he could get a free meal every day from these fresh, untouched salads. It was very enterprising, so much so that he was able to save most of his food allowance money. After nine weeks away he returned to buy himself a brand new Triumph Spitfire with the cash he had saved up.

Our first away game of the tour turned out to be another jaw-dropping experience. There is a saying in America that 'everything is done bigger in Texas' and in the case of the venue we were to play at, they do not come any bigger. The Houston Astrodome was the world's first domed all-purpose air-conditioned sports stadium. It is an awesome complex, covering 260 acres of land. The top of the dome was 208ft high, which would have allowed for an 18-storey building to be constructed inside. There was parking outside for 30,000 cars. The interior floor area of four acres was covered by a material exclusively designed for the Astrodome by the Chemstrand Corporation. It was composed of nylon and other fibres about half an inch thick, having much the texture of a stiff hairbrush. They called it 'Astroturf'. Many variations of Astroturf are used today on all-weather sports developments and it is still called Astroturf, but I can assure you that the name originated from its use in the Astrodome.

The rest of the attributes of the Houston Astrodome are too numerous to mention, but it was obvious why the Americans nicknamed it 'The Eighth Wonder of the World'. None of us had played on a surface like Astroturf before and I doubt if our opponents, Bangu, a Brazilian team from Rio de Janeiro, had either. It was difficult to judge the pace of the ball coming off the playing surface. There was no zip like you would expect from grass. It proved a dour game and finished 1–1. The highlight of the evening came at half-time. Dave Burnside had a reputation as a bit of a ball-juggler but I had never really seen what he could do. What I witnessed really impressed me. As we left the field for the interval, Dave stayed behind in the centre circle with the ball. Watching on closed-circuit TV in the dressing room, we could see Dave had the crowd in raptures with his skills, juggling the football. That ball never touched the ground in the whole of the half-time break, and as we walked back on to the pitch for the second half Dave was given a standing ovation. That visit to the Astrodome was something I, and probably all the lads, will never forget. For the record we trailed 1–0 until late in the match when Dave Woodfield came up for a corner and headed in our equaliser.

It was so relaxing, knowing that the sun would shine every day. Training would be a breeze because the matches were so close together and the meeting place at the poolside was conducive to creating a great spirit among the squad. This is what a prominent journalist Ted Fitkin wrote about us: 'You'll like the Wolves. They're young, alive, alert and as refreshing as an ocean breeze and they have a tremendous team spirit.' Sports 'telecaster' Chick Hearn said, after travelling with us to an away game, 'I've travelled with a lot of pro teams, pro football, pro basketball and baseball, and I've never seen or heard anything like these lads.' Very nice words indeed from people on the fringe who obviously picked up the vibes from our squad.

The lads were loving it, the only thing missing was the pints of beer which we were used to back home. It was alright for the 'Tea Set', who could buy their pot of tea wherever we went, but the drinkers among us had to make do with bottles of beer. After one of the evening matches at the Coliseum, Ernie Hunt and I decided not to go back with the others on the coach but to have a mooch around near the stadium to find a bar with some decent draught beer. After 15 minutes of meandering we really did not know where we were and, unknown to us, we had wandered into the notorious Watts district, a predominantly black area of Los Angeles. It was not long before we realised we were being closely followed by a sedan full of black people. Eventually the sedan pulled alongside us and a man asked us what we were doing.

'We're just looking for a bar,' said Ernie.

After looking us over, the car full of people drove off. Suddenly it became a very uncomfortable situation and I said to Ernie 'I don't like this. I'm going to phone a taxi.'

There was a phone booth on the next corner with plenty of taxi numbers advertised in it so I picked one out and phoned. The lady on the other end of the telephone seemed quite concerned when I told her where we were. The address was in the booth above the handset.

'Stay where you are,' she said, 'there will be somebody along as soon as possible.'

We stood outside the phone booth and watched the sedan slowly drive by again. Suddenly, we heard the sound of a police siren and within seconds a police car screamed to a halt opposite us.

Speaking through a loudspeaker, a voice said 'Face the wall and spread yourselves.'

By this time I was petrified and could not understand what was happening. Ernie and I faced the wall and did as we were told. All this time there was a powerful searchlight shining on us from the police car. Then a policeman approached.

'Keep perfectly still,' the cop ordered and proceeded to search us for weapons. 'OK, turn around and get in the car,' he shouted. We quickly did as we were told, sensing that we were in a dangerous situation.

'You're obviously the English guys that called a cab from the corner of this block,' said one of the officers.

'That's right,' I replied.

'What the hell are you doing in this area?' he asked.

'We were just ambling about looking for a bar,' replied Ernie.

The officer gasped. 'Nobody ambles about and certainly nobody wanders into this area. It's the most dangerous area in Los Angeles,' he said with conviction, as if he was telling us off. 'If that taxi receptionist hadn't had the presence of mind to call us when she heard your English accent there's no telling what would have happened to you. This is Watts and no cab driver would have come to pick you up.'

Ernie and I looked at each other, still not fully understanding the seriousness of the situation. It wasn't until some years later, watching a TV programme about this particular area, that I realised how very lucky we had been.

'Right, let's get out of here,' said the officer driving. 'You wanted a cab to the Sheraton West Hotel according to the receptionist. Is that where you're staying?'

'Yes.' I replied.

'OK,' he said. 'On this occasion this is your cab to the Sheraton West Hotel,' and he proceeded to drive us 20 miles to the front door. I shall always be grateful to the taxi receptionist who informed the police and, of course, to the two officers who escorted us back to the safety of the hotel. Needless to say, we never ventured off the beaten track again.

Ronnie Allen was happy to go off during the day to the race meetings or for a game of golf and leave us with Jack Dowen, who would organise a game of five-a-side or a few loosening exercises in Lafayette Park. No serious training was needed because the games came thick and fast. Incidentally, Ronnie was invited to play in the Sportscaster golf tournament, in which he won a prize. The lads could not believe it when he showed us the prize he had won. Somebody was taking the mickey — in a state where the sun shone almost continuously he had won an electric blanket.

John Ireland was really feeling the heat by now. Not one for wearing shorts or clothing suitable for warmer climes, the chairman walked around, sweating profusely, in his normal attire. He had no official duties to perform so it was a wonderful opportunity for him to relax. I do not think that we ever saw him without his camera around his neck, either, just like a typical tourist. It is strange really, having travelled all over the world with John Ireland and his camera, that none of the lads ever saw the final product — a picture! He would wait for the sun to go down and then head for the bar, where we always finished the evening off with a rendition of his favourite song, *Sweet Molly Malone.*

One afternoon a week the hotel management kindly gave the use of the pool over to the local orphanage. There would be a party of about two dozen six or seven-year-olds and it was great for us, lounging around sunbathing, to see how much pleasure these unfortunate kids got from splashing about in the very pool that we all took so much for granted. On one occasion a sudden cry from one of the carers put everyone on edge. There was obviously something seriously wrong. 'Get out of the pool,' he shouted loudly. As the youngsters quickly scrambled out he calmly waded in the shallow end and as the waters calmed we could see a tiny figure lying on the bottom of the pool. Another of the carers ran off to phone the emergency services. The man in the water, without a hint of panic, gently lifted the little bundle off the bottom and carefully carried him, draped across his arms, to the poolside. He laid the lifeless figure down and proceeded to administer life-saving aid. After what seemed like an age there was still no sign of life, and the other carer came back to the poolside, informing everybody that emergency services were on their way. The man who had carried the little figure from the pool calmly persevered with the life-saving procedure.

Suddenly, when all seemed lost, the tiny toes on one of the little lad's feet began twitching — only slightly but the signs of life were there. Everyone of us at the poolside was willing this young boy back to life. As the siren from the approaching ambulance came nearer and nearer the more parts of the lad's body seemed to respond until suddenly he was coughing and his eyes opened. There was a spontaneous round of applause from every single one of us. Moments later the ambulance arrived and the lad was taken to hospital. The following week the carer informed us that the boy had made a complete recovery with no ill-effects but, unfortunately, he was too nervous to visit the pool and we never saw the little fellow again.

We were doing well at the football and had not lost a game halfway through the tournament. Our sponsor Jack Kent Cooke was well pleased with the way things were going and even invited us all for a barbecue and a badminton tournament at his beautiful Hollywood mansion. Our next home match was to be against Shamrock Rovers and Mr

Cooke arranged for a film star to kick-off the game. Who better than Maureen O'Hara? Born in Ranelagh, County Dublin, she brought along 14 of the O'Hara clan with her that night to support Rovers. Only they were not the O'Haras, they were the FitzSimonses, as O'Hara was her stage name. With honours even at the end of the game, a 1–1 draw, everybody went home satisfied. I had one of my good days and Ronnie Allen, in his report home to the *Express & Star*, said 'Dave Wagstaffe had a marvellous game. The crowd simply loved him and it was when he was making one of his tricky runs through the defence that he was brought down and we got a penalty from which Terry Wharton levelled the scores.'

Living in a place like Los Angeles, home to the stars, you never knew which well-known face you were going to get a glimpse of next. One evening, as the team arrived at the players' entrance to the Coliseum, I glanced at the crowd milling around the general area waiting to go into the stadium and I spotted a famous face, not one that the Americans would readily recognise but a famous one to us. He was just ambling about, relaxed, hands in his pockets, taking in the scene in general. I nudged Ernie Hunt, who was just next to me. 'Look who that is, Ernie,' I said. 'He's a long way from home.'

'It's Tommy Steele,' exclaimed Ernie. 'He looks lost.'

After getting off the bus we approached Tommy, not that we knew him personally, but we knew of him.

'Hello, Tommy,' I said, 'what are you doing here?'

It was a stupid question. He had obviously come to see the game. That was what he was doing there!

'Where do I buy a ticket?' he asked.

'Hang on a sec,' I said, just as Ronnie Allen was walking past. 'Boss, is it OK if Tommy comes in with us?'

Recognising Tommy immediately, Ronnie replied 'Of course it is.'

Tommy walked to the dressing rooms with all the lads as though he was one of the players. He even sat on the bench with the subs and watched the game from there. Famous in Britain but not so well known in the States at that time, Tommy was over there making a film of the famous musical *Finian's Rainbow*. He was starring with another British star, Petula Clark, and the great Fred Astaire. Tommy enjoyed the game so much that he was there waiting for us for the next home fixture.

On another occasion, after a light training session over at Lafayette Park, some of us wandered over the road and into the hotel reception. There were five smartly-dressed gentlemen there, leaflets in their hands ready to hand out to anybody passing through that area. I immediately recognised the face of the middle man of the five but I could not put a name to him. I had seen him in many cowboy films. I need not have worried about coming up with his name as a few seconds later he announced it.

'Good morning, boys,' he said. 'My name is Ronald Reagan, and I am canvassing for support to be voted governor of California. Can I count on your support?'

'You probably could if we lived here,' said somebody, 'but we're from England.'

Even though we were no help to his quest, he took time out to have a chat with us and wished us all the best for the rest of our tournament. Likewise, we wished him all the best in his bid to become governor of California. Not only did he achieve his goal, he went on to become the most powerful man in the world, the president of the United States of America.

We lost our first game in nine against ADO (The Hague) and the 1–0 defeat was especially painful for me. ADO were a tough side and I had to go to hospital with a cracked rib. Pat Buckley was substituted for me and he too had to go hospital, with a damaged ankle. We also had Ernie Hunt and Derek Dougan sent off. Ernie had retaliated when upended by another rough tackle, but all the Doog had done was put his hand on the referee's shoulder to ask why we had not been given a penalty when Terry Wharton looked to have been upended.

Obviously, I missed the return with ADO in Los Angeles a couple of days later, when we gained revenge with a 2–0 win. It was after this that John Ireland left for home, having not planned to stay for the whole trip, and when he got back he commented on the poor standard of refereeing in the US. He told the *Express & Star's* Phil Morgan 'The whole object of the exercise in inviting foreign teams to the country was to demonstrate how the game can, and should, be played. We all know it is a fine game when properly played but the public are not given the chance to see it, nor the players the chance to demonstrate it. What they could do with is a panel of English referees if they are going to try again. And they need not fear they would operate in favour of the English players. On the contrary, I think they would bend over backwards in the other direction.'

The chairman added 'I am happy to say our boys did their best and for that reason the time and effort have not been wasted. They played some extremely efficient football when they were allowed to but the referees, who seemed to have their own interpretation of the laws, let the games get out of control and they degenerated in consequence.'

With wins against Cagliari of Italy and Dundee United, we were assured of a place in the Final. Unfortunately, we had to replay the game we had played on 20 June against Aberdeen. Representing Washington, Aberdeen had lodged a protest with the US commissioner Dick Walsh, contending that Wolves had violated the substitution rule by using three players. Ronnie Allen was really annoyed by the accusation.

'The referee certainly didn't object or inform us that we were violating the rules,' said Ronnie.

Losing 3–0 to Aberdeen in the replayed game meant that the Final would be between ourselves and Aberdeen at the Coliseum, Los Angeles. It had been an enjoyable and never-to-be-forgotten trip and by the time we were to play the Final we would have been away from home for nine weeks. In this time we had played 14 games, averaging a game every four days, travelling thousands and thousands of miles in the process. Some of the away games were a six-hour flight back. It was a gruelling routine but players love to play and that made up for everything. On our travels we played in Cleveland, Dallas, Toronto, Canada, Houston, Washington and San Francisco.

On 14 July we played the Final against Aberdeen. I remember looking at the stadium clock as the teams walked out and it was 20 minutes to 8 o'clock The kick-off was scheduled for 8 o'clock, leaving 20 minutes for the introduction of the teams and all the razzmatazz that the Americans love before a game.

The match itself was an absolute classic. Fast attacking football from both sides with goals going in at either end made it a game that would have graced any stadium. I have a video of this game and I cannot believe the pace at which it was played – as fast as any of the present Premier League games of today. The Final was 4–4 at the end of normal time, thanks to a late equaliser from the penalty spot by a promising young Aberdeen player by the name of Frank Munro.

Overtime, the equivalent of extra-time, was called for. Derek Dougan put us 5–4 up and we should have clinched it but Terry Wharton, usually so deadly from the spot, had a penalty saved by Clark in the Scottish side's goal. Then, in the very last minute of overtime, Aberdeen were awarded a penalty and again Munro found the net. So we had to play 'sudden death' – the first team to score would be declared the winner. We had to do this because all the plane tickets had been booked for the next day so a replay was out of the question. After 10 minutes of sudden death Bobby Thomson raced down the wing and his centre was turned into his own net by Aberdeen defender Shewan to make it 6–5 and Los Angeles Wolves were winners of the NASL.

We were all absolutely shattered after such a long and exhilarating game. So much so that Peter Knowles emphasised the point when he crawled on his knees to accept his winners' medal. Our sponsor Jack Kent Cooke, thoroughly delighted by the game, made a speech afterwards. I cannot remember his exact words but he certainly made the point that never in the history of Hollywood had there been a scriptwriter that could have written a script like this. The crowd had stayed on to the very end and cheered us off the pitch. As we left the arena I looked up at the clock. It was 20 minutes to 12. We had been on the field for four hours.

Wolves: Parkes, Taylor, Thomson, Holsgrove, Woodfield, Burnside, Wharton, Hunt, Dougan, Knowles, Wagstaffe.

Aberdeen: Clarke, Whyte, Shewan, Munro, McMillan, Petersen, Storrie, Smith, Johnston, Buchan, Wilson.

Attendance: 17,824.

Scoring: 1–0 Knowles, 1–1 Smith, 1–2 Munro, 2–2 Burnside, 3–2 Burnside, 4–2 Burnside, 4–3 Storrie, 4–4 Munro (pen), 5–4 Dougan, 5–5 Munro (pen), 6–5 Shewan (own-goal).

I had had a very good tournament and was given a wonderful write-up in the *Los Angeles Times.* This was no mean feat. It was quite an honour to be given a personal write-up in the sports pages of this famous newspaper. At a buffet reception after the Final, Jack Kent Cooke called me over and gave me the outline of a plan that he had in mind. He wanted me to come back to the US and put my name to all the soccer gear that was going to be marketed. These were the days before the big sporting companies had got their grips on the industry. He explained to me that I would be to football what Fred Perry was to tennis and promised me that within two years I would be a household name in American sport and a wealthy man in the process. I did give the proposition plenty of thought when I got back home to England. I decided not to pursue the matter and opted for a normal family life in Wolverhampton.

My Moreton Misery

Before we knew it, the 1967–68 season was upon us and we were back in the big time again, the First Division. We were fully confident that we could do well back in the top flight. We had played some great stuff in America and the team spirit was second to none, so we were all looking forward to taking on the big boys again. After a reasonable start we lost four games in a row to bring us down to earth, but we remained undeterred and the dressing room was still a fun place to be.

Every morning before training there was a ritual. 'Titch' Harding, a well-known ex-referee, used to bring the mail down from the office to the dressing room. Obviously, the Doog got more fan mail than the rest of us and Titch would take the bundle to Derek first. Titch, less than 5ft tall and Derek, 6ft 3in, would then go through an imaginary tossing-up procedure, Titch pretending to spin a coin and Derek shouting 'heads' or 'tails'. Whichever Derek shouted, Titch would then look up to the tall centre-forward and say 'Correct'.

'We'll kick that way,' Derek would say.

'OK,' Titch would answer, 'have a good game, gentlemen,' and then he would disappear out of the dressing room and back to the office.

It was only a harmless bit of fun but Titch used to look forward to the little ceremony every morning. He sorely missed his refereeing days and although he was an official of the Birmingham FA it was not the same as being out on the field. That little bit of camaraderie among the lads every day was the nearest he was going to get to a real live situation. A lovely old fella.

It was around this time that I suffered a severe ankle injury and was sidelined for a few weeks. After a really sustained period of treatment I was almost ready for action. One frosty Friday morning, just before Ronnie and the team left for an away fixture, he called me into the office.

'How's the ankle feel?' he asked.

'Feels good,' I replied.

'Do you fancy a run-out in the reserves?' he continued.

'Fine by me,' I nodded.

'Right,' he said. 'If it's like this tomorrow, hard and frosty, don't even think about it.'

'OK,' I said, 'weather permitting, I'll give it a try.'

He said he would leave instructions with the reserve team trainer that I was only to play if conditions were right. So that was how we left it. He went off with the first team and I went off home to Fordhouses.

Sitting watching the telly on my own that night – Barbara and the kids had gone off to Manchester – I spent most of the evening peering out of the window, checking the weather with a view to my chances of having a game the next day. As the evening went on, the frost got thicker and thicker and freezing fog came down.

'That's it,' I thought, when the time got to 10.30pm, 'there's no way I'll be playing tomorrow.'

The nearby Moreton Country Club had a late licence so I wandered round there. After a skinful of Tartan Bitter I staggered back home in the freezing fog at around 2am. I awoke next morning at 11.30 and opened the curtains to a very bright sun dazzling me. My head was absolutely banging and I felt awful. I had a massive hangover. My next thought was to go and get the morning newspaper from the shops around the corner. I opened the door and, surprise, surprise, all the frost had gone. I walked over to the lawn and tested it. It was soft. I was going to have to go and play with this dreadful hangover.

I do not know how I got through the game but I did. I just went through the motions. I did not look bad because, after all, I was just trying my ankle out. My ankle felt good but there again that could have been the amount of alcohol in my blood giving it a nice feeling! Joking apart, I came through the test and the next morning there were no ill-effects from the injured ankle, nor from the head!

On Monday morning Ronnie called me into his office and asked me how the ankle had stood up to the game. I told him that everything was fine and in my opinion the injury had fully recovered.

'That's great,' he said. 'Have a good week's training and I'll put you back in the team next Saturday.'

'OK, thanks boss,' I replied and went to walk out the door of his office.

'Oh, one last thing,' he shouted, 'you won't be going to the Moreton next Friday night before the game, will you?'

I shut the door behind me, pretending I had not heard, and scuttled off down the corridor. 'How on earth did he know about that?' I puzzled. I made a successful comeback the following Saturday and I can assure you that I was not in the Moreton Club the night before.

Ronnie Allen was quite a good wheeler-dealer in the transfer market and when Everton offered £80,000 for Ernie Hunt he decided to accept, making a profit of £40,000. It was surprising as he did not have a ready-made replacement. Even more surprising was the sale of Terry Wharton to Bolton for £60,000 a few weeks later. Two experienced, valued members of the squad had gone without anybody being brought in. I was to learn later that Ronnie did have a player in mind to replace Terry but the deal did not go ahead because of a bizarre incident, which I will tell you about in due course.

I did, however, manage to send Terry off in a blaze of glory, as it were. Just before training I was off to the toilets to have my usual cigarette.

'Have you got a match, Terry?' I asked.

'No, but there's a lighter in my jacket pocket on my peg,' he replied.

Instead of taking the lighter with me, I took it from his jacket, lit my cigarette, put it back and went off to the toilets. As I came back after my cigarette I could hear roars of laughter coming from the dressing room and detected a strange smell. As I walked in, Terry was in the middle of the room, jumping on his jacket with flames and clouds of smoke coming from it – no, it was not a blazer!

Apparently, the little top on his lighter that puts out the flame was faulty and did not close completely, leaving a small flame flickering when I put it back in his pocket. Eventually it set fire to his jacket and there was Terry stamping on it trying to put the fire out. He did not mind that much because he was just about to make a few bob with his move to Bolton. I am sure he would have been able to afford much more than a new suit.

However, back to the bizarre incident that influenced a transfer deal. The previous season we had played Bolton Wanderers at Molineux and Peter Knowles was having a good game and was in one of his most impish moods. At one stage he had the cheek to sit on the ball, inviting the opposition to come and take it from him. One of the Bolton side took exception to this mickey-taking and launched a nasty attack on Peter. This incident was not to be forgotten by a certain member of the Molineux board of directors.

Ronnie Allen had initially set up a player plus cash deal to give him a ready-made replacement for Terry Wharton. The board member I mentioned was chairman John Ireland and, as soon as he found out that the deal involved the player who had taken a swing at Peter, he blocked it. Consequently, Ronnie had to do a straight cash deal, leaving him with no replacement. What an opportunity was missed! That player was none other than Francis Lee, who went on to win a clutch of medals with Manchester City and Derby and played for England many times, including in the 1970 World Cup Finals.

Having to change tack, Ronnie introduced two youngsters, John Farrington and Alun Evans, into the team. John had already had a couple of games the season before, but this was the First Division. I am all for giving youngsters a chance, but two at the same time was a bit extreme. Alun had already been in the side for six games before John joined him and I must say that neither of them disgraced himself. In fact, they performed as well as anybody in the side at that time. Ronnie wanted more experience in the squad, however, so he signed Mike Kenning and Frank Munro, the latter being a player he had admired for his performances against us for Aberdeen in the States. Mike Kenning was an out-and-out winger who slotted into the spot that Terry had vacated. What I could not understand was that apart from a few games in the number-four shirt when Mike Bailey was injured, Frank Munro was limited to a measly seven games from January to the end of the season. He was a very talented player who could have slotted into many different positions.

The experienced Frank Wignall was drafted in from Nottingham Forest to partner the Doog up front for the run-in to the end of the season. He did the job he was signed for, scoring nine times in 12 League games. Another player bought at that time was Derek Parkin, signed in February 1968 from Huddersfield Town for £80,000. He would become known as 'Squeak' to the lads.

We finished in 17th place that season. It did not really look good on paper but, bearing in mind we had just spent two seasons in the Second Division, I think it was a creditable performance. Apparently the board did not agree and rumours were rife that things had to improve next season. The spirit of the squad was not broken. The 'Tea Set' had their tea and the rest of us had our beer, mostly down at the Moreton Country Club at that time. The lads pulled together and it really was a friendly group. This was mostly down to Ronnie, who knew when to mix with the lads and when not to. I never saw him blow his top and he always treated people with respect. I must say that the lads did not like the rumours. Ronnie was good for us and we were good for Ronnie.

As the 1968–69 season got going, Ronnie, sadly, made two mistakes early on. For some reason he tried to replace Phil Parkes with Alan Boswell. Phil made the odd mistake, as we all did, but he was a very competent goalkeeper in whom all the lads had confidence. He was very popular member of the squad. Ronnie's other error would come back at him with a vengeance. He sold Alun Evans to Liverpool for £100,000, making him, at the time, the highest-priced teenager in the land. It looked good business on paper, selling for £100,000 a teenager who had played only 22 first-class games. Bill Shankly must have seen something special to pay so much for one with so little experience.

We had not started the season very well, winning only two of the first 10 games, but the worst was yet to come. On 28 September 1968 Wolves were thrashed 6–0 by Liverpool at Molineux. Two of the six came from Alun Evans, the player Ronnie had sold to them just over two weeks before. The goalkeeper he had just bought with a view to replacing Phil Parkes dropped a couple of clangers, resulting in more goals for Liverpool. The writing was on the wall for Ronnie. The board were disgruntled and a home defeat of this magnitude did not auger well. Mind you, it was over seven weeks later that he left Molineux, with no fuss and with great dignity. The Liverpool defeat was on 28 September and Ronnie's departure was on 20 November. From the day he was officially upgraded to full-time manager at the end of July 1966, he had steered the club towards success. In just over two seasons as manager he had won promotion to the First Division, helped us to the NASL title and cemented a place for a further season in the First Division. Most importantly, with his astute buying, he left some wonderful players behind who would be the backbone of the club for years to come. Just look at the list and judge for yourself:

John Holsgrove. Ronnie's first buy, from his old club Crystal Palace, was a real stalwart who did a first-class job, quietly and efficiently. Played 200 games.

Mike Bailey. A £40,000 buy from Charlton Athletic; he was a magnificent player and a great captain that they have never been able to replace, even to this day. Played 432 games.

Derek Parkin. There was not a better full-back in the country. He played a mammoth 609 games, a club record and one which I doubt will ever be beaten. An absolute model of consistency and not only a credit to the club, but also to the game of football.

Frank Munro. Signed for £60,000, he was the most skilful centre-half in the Football League and a great header of the ball and brilliant reader of a game. Played 365 games.

Derek Dougan. The £50,000 buy from Leicester City set out his stall with a hat-trick in his first home game and never looked back. A wonderful goalscorer and crowd-pleaser, he was a nomad who stopped wandering when he reached Molineux. Played 307 games.

Kenny Hibbitt. He was the bargain of the lot – £5,000 from Bradford Park Avenue. I never saw him have a bad game. He probably had the most consistent form of anyone in the team during his time with Wolves. Played 552 games.

These players went on to amass over 2,500 first-class appearances between them for Wolves and five of the six would complete a period of at least 10 years at Molineux. In my opinion, the board of directors were a bit short-sighted to dispense with the services of Ronnie Allen at that early stage in his career at Molineux. We had lost only once in a spell of six League games when Ronnie departed and, apart from those players that he bought, he also left behind Bobby Thomson, Phil Parkes, Gerry Taylor, Les Wilson, Dave Woodfield, Peter Knowles and myself, all experienced players, and the up-and-coming John McAlle.

I, for one, was sorry to see Ronnie go. I had enjoyed playing football for him, the emphasis being on 'playing football'. He even had the knack of making me enjoy training. Given time, I am sure that Ronnie would have brought a great deal of success to Molineux. Bill McGarry was a very lucky man to inherit such a talented squad of players.

McGarry Madness

After being introduced to Bill McGarry, I immediately knew that he was going to be a very difficult person to get along with, and so did many of the other players. His domineering and obnoxious attitude was obvious, and from the moment he walked through that dressing room door he left us in no doubt that everything would be done his way. From day one, when he laid down his commandments, he made it absolutely clear that if he caught any of his players with another woman he would expose them in the press and make sure their wives were informed. Even eight years later he tried to influence the very last chapter in my life at Molineux. I had just finished a loan spell at Blackburn Rovers and was sat with Jim Smith, their boss, negotiating terms with a view to signing permanently for Rovers. The phone rang and Jim answered. Cupping his hand over the mouthpiece he whispered to me 'It's McGarry' and immediately switched on the intercom so that I could hear the conversation.

'Has he signed yet?' asked McGarry.

'Not yet,' replied Jim.

'Right,' McGarry went on with increasing volume, 'you tell him from me that if he doesn't sign today he can come back and rot in my f*****g third team.'

'OK,' said Jim, 'I'll pass the message on.'

Jim put the phone down and looked at me in amazement.

'That's the kind of attitude I've had to put up with from day one,' I said.

Don't get me wrong, Jim Smith could be hard, very hard in certain circumstances, but he was always fair and, unlike McGarry, never afraid to admit when he was wrong.

The statement from McGarry made me so angry. He knew that Blackburn were financially struggling, but still insisted they pay £6,000 for my services after 11 years at Molineux. On the one hand he was desperate to see the back of me, but on the other he could not resist making the negotiations as awkward as possible. He did not realise how lucky he was, sitting in his plush office at Molineux, while Jim's office was the converted bedroom of a terraced house opposite Blackburn's ground, the downstairs living room being the secretary's office.

Had it not been for the fact that I had sold my house in Wolverhampton and fixed up alternative schooling for the children, I would certainly have gone back and played in the third team, just for the hell of it.

Bill McGarry's arrival at Molineux was a big culture shock for the players after Ronnie Allen's relaxed style of management. Our first away trip with him – to Hull – turned out to be quite an experience. Normal procedure for lengthy away trips was: travel on Friday, arriving at whichever venue around 4.30pm to 5.30pm, evening meal about 6pm, tea and biscuits at 10.30pm and off to bed. It was probably the same routine used by all football clubs in those days. On this particular trip, after arriving at about 5pm, we washed, changed and sat down for the evening meal at 6pm. As normal, we sat around one long table, while McGarry and his staff, travelling directors and Sid, the coach driver, occupied a separate table.

Once everyone was seated, the waiter appeared to take our orders.

'Can I take your order, sir?' he said to big John Holsgrove.

'Right,' said John. 'I'll have a prawn cocktail for a starter, please.'

But he did not get any further. McGarry, whose table was within earshot, was on his feet in a flash.

'Prawn cocktail?' he bellowed. 'F*****g prawn cocktail. What do you think this is? F*****g Butlins?'

We all sat there absolutely amazed, looking down like chastised school kids. McGarry walked over and stood at the end of the table.

'I'll tell you what you can f*****g eat,' he growled. 'Soup to start, steak or chicken for the main course and fresh fruit salad for dessert.'

So we all finished our soup, and soon after the steaks and chicken arrived with the veg and the chips in silver terrines, placed in the middle of the table for us to help ourselves. When they are served in this way, there never seems to be enough to go round, and with some rather large hungry lads in the team the terrines were empty in seconds. The waiter had spotted this and, doing his job, he went back into the kitchen to return with a mountain of chips on a silver platter. He put them down in front of John Holsgrove, who had only managed to rescue three or four chips from the original helpings, but McGarry had spotted the arrival of the extras and rushed straight over.

'More f*****g chips,' he roared at John. 'Is this a f*****g eating contest? You'll make do with what you've already been given. Waiter, throw these f*****g chips in the bin.'

A crestfallen John looked at McGarry just like Oliver Twist.

The menu of soup, steak or chicken and fruit salad stood wherever we went in the country, or in the world, for all of McGarry's days as manager.

One good bit of news that came with the arrival of McGarry and his coach Sammy Chung was that they were both very keen golfers. Indeed, McGarry was an excellent golfer, with a five handicap, and a ruthless opponent. He and Sammy played as a pair and more often than not Mike Bailey and myself were their opponents. None of the other lads felt comfortable playing in the company of the manager. The stakes were not the Crown Jewels, but a new golf ball. If they won, we gave them a new golf ball each. If we won, likewise. However, you would have thought we were actually playing for the Crown

Jewels. McGarry would stand on the first tee and announce 'Strict rules of golf, no gimmes, everything goes down.'

Being a seasoned golfer and a fierce competitor, he knew that those fiddling little 12 to 15in putts would put pressure on any golfer. If you are a golfer, you will know exactly what I mean. When we embarked on our trips to the seaside, which normally preceded our FA Cup games, we were lucky enough to play on the best courses, like Royal Birkdale or Royal Lytham, when staying on the Lancashire coast.

In the week leading up to the 1973–74 League Cup Final against Manchester City at Wembley, we were making our preparations at Worthing on the south coast. On Tuesday evening Bill McGarry announced 'No training tomorrow. We'll have a nice game of golf in the morning and a massage in the afternoon.' This suited us, and we all retired in anticipation of a relaxing day to come.

Wednesday morning, 27 February, was a cold, crisp frosty morning, but by the time we reached the golf course the sun had broken through and most of the frosty areas were beginning to disappear. The stakes were two brand new golf balls. The rules? Strict rules of golf, no gimmes, everything goes down.

After a fierce battle for 16 holes, McGarry and Chung were one up. Mike and I managed to win the 17th, and so we went to the 18th tee all square. It was me to tee off first and, damn, I topped my drive. Fortunately, the ground was quite firm after the overnight frost and my ball ran on about 150–160 yards down the fairway. Mike teed off next and hit a solid drive left of centre with his bit of draw. McGarry was next to go, hitting a superb drive straight down the middle. Then Sammy made one of his usual moonraking drives. We all proceeded down the fairway to where my ball had come to rest, some 50 or 60 yards behind the other three drives. I had no clue what iron to use, having never played the course before, so I settled on my favourite, a six. I made good contact, but as soon as I saw the ball in flight I knew that it was going to be woefully short of the green – at least 35 yards. As the ball came down it got a fortuitous bounce off one of the few frosty patches left on the course. It leapt high in the air, landed on the fringe of the green, rolled at pace across it, hit the bottom of the pin and disappeared down the hole.

Well, you should have seen Bill McGarry's face. I had topped my drive, underhit my second shot and finished with an eagle two. This meant that he or Sammy had to hole their second shots to halve the match. Needless to say, neither of them did, and consequently Mike and I won the match. McGarry fished in his bag for our spoils of victory – two brand new golf balls. He threw them across the green to me with a damning look.

We sat in silence on the team bus, waiting for the other players to complete their round. Once the other lads had boarded the coach, McGarry stood up and announced

'We'll go back to the hotel and train at 2 o'clock, sharp.' This was obviously sour grapes as the previous evening he had told us we would have a massage in the afternoon.

When 2 o'clock came and the lads were all changed and waiting to start training, Sammy and McGarry strolled over with two nets of balls. McGarry placed a net of balls in front of me and told the Doog and John Richards to do some cross-over runs up front.

'You hit the balls up the channels for them,' McGarry said to me.

As I said, it was a cold day and, unusually, we did not do a warm-up session first. I was hitting 40 or 50-yard balls up the channels to Derek and John when, suddenly, ping, I had pulled a muscle in my thigh. Toby Andersen, our physio, took me back to the hotel and iced the injury straight away. Three days from a Wembley Cup Final and I had pulled a muscle. I was totally distraught, not knowing whether I would make it to Wembley, every footballer's dream.

The next day, Thursday, I had some treatment and did some light jogging but feared the worst. On Friday morning I had some kind of fitness test and decided to tell the physio and the manager that I would be OK. I wasn't really, but I wasn't going to miss Wembley for anything. I should never have gone out there and I played the game in agony, but I would not have missed it for the world. With 10 minutes to go I could not stand any more and signalled to come off, having gone down by the touchline. John Richards was also in trouble and wanted to come off, but because I had gone down I was taken off and John stayed on. John scored the winning goal and we won the Cup.

Some 18 months later, the plan worked again! I was recalled from my loan spell at Blackburn to line up against Charlton in an FA Cup tie. John Richards, for some unknown reason, was on the substitutes' bench that day. After about 20 minutes I suffered a hamstring injury and was replaced by John, who went on to score a hat-trick and help Wolves win the tie.

Winning the League Cup at Wembley was probably the best day in my footballing career, but also one of the most disappointing, as I had to play the game in dreadful pain. I wanted so much to put on a great performance against my former club, Manchester City, and there was no finer stage than Wembley to do that. I did not perform anywhere near as well as I knew I could, but the main thing was that we won the game. Before the match we were the obvious underdogs with a forward line of Summerbee, Lee, Marsh, Bell and Law lining up against us. What would they be worth in today's transfer market? Each one was an international and each one was experienced in playing at Wembley in front of a full house. However, a great performance from our defence and an even greater performance from goalkeeper Gary Pierce frustrated City's five-star line up and kept them at bay. McGarry showed more emotion in vigorously congratulating Gary on the pitch after the final whistle than we had ever seen from him in all his days at Molineux.

It was not to last. Half an hour later, in a jubilant Wembley dressing room, McGarry was back to his usual self. The lads had requested that we be allowed to keep our Wembley tracksuits, specially made for the occasion (yellow bottoms and black tops embossed with three Wolves and 'Wembley '74'), as a souvenir of our League Cup triumph.

'No,' was McGarry's reply. 'You can keep the shirts but the rest of the kit goes back to Molineux.'

I do not know what would have happened if he had not allowed us to keep our shirts because Frank Munro had already swapped his with Denis Law immediately after the game. Would Bill McGarry have approached the great Denis Law and asked 'Can we have our shirt back please?'

The Characters

Manchester City originally signed the great Denis Law from Huddersfield in March 1960 for a then British record fee of £55,000. He was a magical player, fast, skilful and elusive, playing in the old style inside-right position while at City. It was soon after Denis's arrival that I got some good news. I was chosen for the England Youth team and made my debut against East Germany at Portsmouth. We drew 1–1 and the team also included Blackpool's Gordon West in goal while the two half-backs, which was the norm in those days, were Terry Venables from Chelsea and Martin Peters of West Ham. I won four more Youth caps that season, including three in the international Youth tournament played in Austria.

As a 17-year-old, I made the breakthrough into the City reserve team and one September morning in 1960 was about to embark on a training session with the second team lads when I was told to report to the manager's office. I wracked my brains, wondering what I could have done wrong because, normally, you were only called up those marble stairs when in trouble or when something important was about to happen.

I knocked on Leslie McDowall's door with trepidation. 'Come in,' he shouted from behind his desk. I nervously entered as it was only the second time I had been in this office.

'I thought I should let you know,' the manager started, 'before I pin the team sheet up for tonight's match against Sheffield Wednesday, I'm playing you at outside-left. Get yourself home now, have a rest and report back here at Maine Road at 6.30.'

I danced back down those steps like Fred Astaire. Me, outside-left. I was to play in the same forward line as the best player in the land. Two bus rides later I was back home telling my dad all about it. Unfortunately, my dad was on the two-till-ten shift that afternoon and was not going to be able to see my debut.

My big night came and went and I gave a reasonable account of myself as we drew 1–1 with Wednesday in front of 35,000 people. On the bus going home I managed to get the last vacant seat upstairs, next to a man with overalls on and his haversack slung over his shoulders.

'Have you been to the match?' he inquired.

'Er, yes,' I replied.

'How did that young lad play who was making his debut?' he asked.

'Not bad. He had a reasonable game,' I said.

'That's good,' said the man, 'I'm on my way to take over from his dad on the ten-till-six shift. He will be pleased when I tell him.'

What a coincidence, eh?

I managed to stay in the first team and played quite a few games with the great Denis until he signed for Torino in 1961. The deal included a game against Torino and Denis was due to play for us in the first half and them in the second, but a torrential thunderstorm turned the pitch into a quagmire, making any further play impossible. I have a treasured memento from that evening, a solid gold commemorative medal with the Torino logo on one side and an inscription describing the occasion on the other side – A.L. Manchester City FC, Torino 7, VI, 1961.

In the return game with Wednesday I scored my first Football League goal, but we lost 3–1. Clive Colbridge was my rival for the number-11 shirt at that time. He was the latest player trying to fill the huge gap left by Roy Clarke. The Welsh international had been a fixture on the City left wing for 10 successive seasons up to 1957. I made 22 appearances in that first season and scored a couple more goals, my first at Maine Road being against great rivals United. Unfortunately we lost 3–1. Injury meant I missed the FA Cup game at Luton when Denis Law wrote his name into football's list of bizarre records by scoring seven times in a Cup tie yet finishing on the losing side. We were 6–1 up at Kenilworth Road and Denis had scored all our goals, but the pouring rain had made the pitch unplayable so the referee abandoned the game. When it was played again we lost 2–1, with Denis our scorer. Yet because the first match was abandoned those first six goals the Scotsman scored do not count officially.

Having staked my claim, I became first choice outside-left in 1961–62, playing in all 42 League matches, Clive Colbridge moving on to Wrexham. I was first choice number-11 for the next two seasons, but another promising youngster soon emerged on the scene – Neil Young. The man who would score City's winner in the 1969 FA Cup Final was being given his chance on the left so I had been switched to the right wing when I got the telephone call that led to my move to Molineux.

However, let me jump 10 years ahead once more to the day we got the better of Denis and Co. at Wembley. After the game we made our way to be reunited with our wives at the Hilton Hotel and on the coach I sat next to our skipper Mike Bailey during our ride across London. He was absolutely full of it, but, as the journey progressed, he became more and more deflated. By the time we got to the Hilton Mike had completely lost it.

All the fervour, trauma and excitement of the occasion had taken its toll on our captain. It had all got to him. I had travelled the world with Mike and had never seen him like this before. We had won the Cup, he had run around Wembley with the trophy but even the most hardy of individuals has to come back down to earth.

'Wag, I'm absolutely shattered,' he said. 'Any chance you could help me with my bags up to the room?'

I helped Mike up to his room where his wife Barbara was waiting and I said 'Barb, an hour's kip and he'll be right as rain.'

Sure enough, an hour and a half later, after a relaxing lie down, Mike was back to his usual self at our celebration dinner.

After the banquet several of us and our wives decided to pay a visit to the Bunny Club just over the road from the Hilton Hotel. Why not? We had just won the Cup and were celebrating. Having secured a table and ordered a round of drinks we were all set for the night when in walked Francis Lee, who, spotting us seated round this table, walked over and promptly called the waiter.

'Two bottles of champagne over here,' he requested.

'No, Franny,' we protested, 'we've won the Cup, you have a drink on us.'

'No,' he insisted, 'there's not a very good atmosphere at our dinner so that's why I've come down here for a drink.'

Minutes later a waitress dressed in the bunny girl regalia carried over a tray with two bottles of champagne and a dozen glasses. The lighting was dim and as she passed me she tripped and the whole lot hit me on the back of the head. The bouncers came running over, thinking there was a fight, but as they realised what had happened they picked me up and dusted me off, so to speak. I got an apology from the waitress after she emerged from under the table where she had been shining her torch, looking for the tips that had also been on the tray. So, easing the pain from my leg injury with a nice few drinks, I now had to contend with a massive lump on the back of my head. What the hell, we had just won the League Cup, hadn't we? Not forgetting the generous gesture from Francis Lee in buying us the champagne.

I never did fully recover from the injury I nursed in the League Cup Final, and I beleive it was fighting that injury which led to my demise, physically and mentally, at Molineux.

When Bill McGarry joined Wolves in November 1968 he inherited a squad of very talented players such as Phil Parkes, Derek Dougan, Peter Knowles, Frank Munro, Derek Parkin, Kenny Hibbitt, John McAlle, John Richards and Mike Bailey, to name but a few. This was a squad that any manager in that era would have loved to take over. The trouble was, not everybody liked being ruled with an iron fist and there were certain individuals, myself included, in that group of players who liked to be treated like human beings. A manager is only as good as his team and has to understand the moods and personalities of each of his players to get the best out of them.

I agree with my old pal Frank Munro, who maintains that if McGarry had given us our head and let us play it as we saw it, so to speak, we would have served up even more attractive football and perhaps won more silverware. The way we were told to play did not allow the real talent to shine through. The players were suppressed in everything they did. Everything was black and white and nobody dared deviate from the norm.

Each player had a pair of trainers, a pair of training boots and, most importantly, a pair of match boots. Everybody had to wear Adidas by order of the manager. I cannot see what difference it made whatever make you wore as long as you produced the goods. Charlie George played in his red boots and Alan Hinton played in his white boots – two very talented players but they would not have been allowed to play in them at Molineux. To get a new pair was like having a means test. The pair you wanted replacing were inspected and whenever possible were sent off to the cobblers to be repaired. If they were considered beyond repair then, and only then, did you get a new pair.

Considering that these were the most important tools of your trade it would have been good to have had a choice. On one occasion before a game the Gola rep was on the Molineux car park with a whole range of boots in his car. He offered us a new pair of boots each if we would play in them that day on TV. We explained to him that we were only allowed to wear Adidas, but when he offered to pay 20 quid to anyone who wore the Gola boots several of us snatched his hand off. To be fair, we knew we would not get away with it, so to keep our promise to the rep we painted three stripes on either side of the boots with Jack Dowen's whitener to enable us to play in them without McGarry knowing. It did not do the rep any good, though, because with the three white stripes on the side it looked as though we were playing in Adidas boots anyway.

Undoubtedly, Mike Bailey was McGarry's favourite from the word go. Mike was our no-nonsense, tough-tackling captain, who would have graced any team. I am sure that in Mike McGarry saw himself in years gone by. Apparently, McGarry was a very similar player to Mike, tough in the tackle and a commanding figure on the pitch. I never heard him admonish or criticise Mike in any situation.

Most of the time on our travels around the world I would share a room with Mike. Bill McGarry was a frequent visitor to our room to pass on the spending money for Mike to distribute among the players. When I say spending money, it was money given to the club by whoever had sponsored the tour for players' expenses. This money was always in the denomination of whichever country we happened to be in – lire, American dollars, pesetas or whatever. What I could never understand was the fact that it was always me who had to divide up the money between the squad. It was quite a simple operation really – 18 players, five days' money easily divided out, or maybe 16 players and six days' money, or whatever the case might be.

The first player that Bill McGarry signed was Hugh Curran from Norwich City. He had had plenty of opportunity to watch this player, Norwich being in fairly close proximity to his old club, Ipswich. We were four months into the Bill McGarry reign when he signed Hughie. Was McGarry looking ahead and beginning to believe the whispers that Peter Knowles's intention was to give the game up to pursue his Jehovah's Witness religion? If he was, then it was a shrewd move to sign Hughie.

There was no doubting that Peter was a brilliant, talented footballer and there was also no doubting that he was in love with the game of football. I know, because I trained with him, travelled with him and played in the same team as him. He never treated the game seriously. It was fun to him and he was lucky – he had the talent to treat it as fun. He wanted to be the tops, he wanted to be noticed. That was why he did all those things on the pitch, like sitting on the ball, swinging on the cross bar and, on one occasion, kicking the ball out of the ground. He did not realise that he need not have done all these things, because the talent that he possessed got him noticed anyway and he did not even have to work at it.

By then McGarry had been in charge for three-quarters of a season, and for all his rules and regulations we did not seem to be making much progress. In fact, from 11 January 1969 until the end of the season on 21 April, we managed to win only three from a total of 18 League games and we finished in 16th place. I could not understand why the talented Frank Munro had not been found a regular place in the team, but all that was forgotten as we were off on tour again to the United States. The biggest reason for all the tours we made was because for three months there was virtually no money coming in to the football clubs and money from tour sponsors went some way to help pay the players' wages in the summer.

This time we were based in the city of Kansas in the mid-west of the US. Walter Bixby was our sponsor, or at least the insurance company of which he was chairman was the sponsor. There was a gruelling schedule ahead, eight games in 29 days and thousands of miles of travel across America. All this after just finishing a season in the First Division, reputedly the hardest League in football. The tour did not get off to a very good start. The hotel that we had been booked into was absolutely awful. It was like one of those sleazy hotels you see in some American films. Bill McGarry went off to see Walter Bixby, and that evening we moved into a much larger and much more comfortable hotel. Things did not change when we were on tour and because we had a game the next afternoon we had to go to bed at 10.30 like good boys to be ready for the match the next day.

'There's no room service so it's breakfast at 8.30 in the restaurant,' said Sammy Chung as we trooped off to bed.

Next morning we were in for a big shock as we went down to the restaurant for breakfast. The restaurant was packed with at least 200 women, at least half of them in rollers or curlers and devoid of make-up. There was very little room left for us to eat. McGarry was not very pleased that his footballers had to mingle with all these females to find room to have their breakfast. It was difficult to understand what was going on but we were soon to find out. An official-looking lady came over and apologised for the fact that they had virtually commandeered the restaurant.

'Today's a big day for these young ladies,' she explained. 'They are all competing in the Miss United States contest and this afternoon are the mid-west divisional heats, the winner going forward to the grand final of the Miss United States of America.'

Seeing this lot in their basics you would not have believed that they were going to compete in such a grand nationwide event, in fact Hilda Ogden would not have felt out of place. You would not have given any of them a second glance.

Having disrupted our breakfast arrangements, the lady felt obliged to recompense us and offered to accommodate the whole party with tickets for the afternoon's event. Obviously we could not take up her offer as we had a game to play. Later we were able to watch the competition on the television and you would not have believed the difference. They all looked like film stars. I would not have recognised any of them from the breakfast room. It just shows what a difference a set of curlers and some make-up can make.

As we lined up just before the kick-off to our first game, the first bar of the national anthem came through the sound system. Peter Knowles was off like a shot on to the bench. He sat there and refused to stand for the anthem. Apparently, this was to do with the religion he was involved with and a sure sign that he was deeply into their beliefs.

During the game, just after half-time, our opposition were on the attack and I just happened to be on the side of the pitch where the bench was, on which Bill McGarry was sitting.

'Get back and fill that space,' he barked.

This was not exactly a vital First Division game and I wondered why I should be running back, filling space.

'F**k off, give us a break,' I barked back.

'I'll give you a f*****g break,' he roared, 'come on off.'

He shouted to the referee and I was immediately replaced.

'Get back to the dressing room, and get changed,' McGarry ordered as I left the field.

I did as I was told and it was three days before he spoke to me again!

We did have some relaxation, though. As our sponsor and to some extent our host, Walter Bixby decided to throw a barbecue for us all at one stage during our stay. We had all seen his house, which was a huge mansion, so we expected it to be held there. When the coach picked us up we were surprised to go on a 40-minute drive, after which we arrived at a fantastic lake surrounded by all types of wonderful trees with log cabins peering out over the lake. Most of the cabins had a small jetty with a boat, or maybe two, moored alongside. Apparently, even in those days, to be a member of this exclusive lakeside community was 100,000 dollars. Goodness knows how much our cabin, and everything that went with it, cost, but I suppose Walter or his company could afford it. There was a wonderful barbecue area in front of the cabin and in the basement was a bar with free beer.

'Help yourselves,' said Walter.

Also in the basement was a games room, which had a table tennis table in the middle of it. We knew that Bill McGarry was a county standard squash player, but we had not bargained for his prowess at the table tennis table. Not one out of at least nine of us who played him managed to beat him. In fact, he gave us all a hiding and, unwittingly, this worked to our advantage. Winning all these games against the lads left him like a dog with two tails and in a good mood. He did not seem to mind how many halves of lager we pulled for ourselves and did not growl at anybody all afternoon. A good time was had by everyone.

Our first game representing Kansas City in the North American Soccer League was at Baltimore, who were being represented by West Ham. We had Derek Clarke, one of the famous footballing family from Short Heath, Willenhall, at centre-forward, as Derek Dougan was with the Northern Ireland team. Peter Knowles gave us the lead with a a real 'daisy-cutter' from 25 yards, but after Trevor Brooking had levelled in the second half the Hammers got the benefit of the referee's judgment. Peter Bennett put in a header which we felt Phil Parkes had pushed out for a corner, but the ref ruled that the ball had crossed the line. The Londoners went 3–1 up with a goal from an 18-year-old from Bermuda. That youngster was Clyde Best, who proved a real handful for us that day and went on to make quite a name for himself at Upton Park. We grabbed a late consolation thanks to Mike Bailey.

Two days later Mike was on target again as we got into our stride in our first 'home' game with a 4–2 win over Dundee United, who were representing Dallas. Peter Knowles collected two more and Les Wilson also weighed in with one.

We won our next game in Kansas, too, with a sweet revenge victory against West Ham 4–2. The strange feature of the game was that John McAlle, who never scored a goal in over 400 League games for us, hit a hat-trick. However, it was a most unusual one as John scored two goals to put us ahead and then managed an own-goal to make it 2–1 at half-time. There was no stopping John, though, as it was his passes that laid on further goals for Mike Bailey and Hugh Curran before Trevor Brooking hit a consolation for the Hammers.

Next to lose to us in Kansas were Kilmarnock, who were based at St Louis. We had Frank Munro wearing the number-nine shirt in this one and we thought it was going to be a stroll when we went 2–0 up thanks to two strikes from Hugh Curran. However, Killie got one back through Eddie Morrison before the break and Tommy McLean levelled with just over 20 minutes left. We did not let them stay level for long and a couple of minutes later John Farrington was on the spot to head the ball home when the 'keeper punched it out. So we won 3–2 and were in just the mood for our game against our local rivals Aston Villa in Atlanta, Georgia.

McGarry had this thing about the sun sapping your energy and was always quick to point this out. When we went to Atlanta we stayed in the same hotel Villa were using as their base. On arrival we could see all the Villa lads lounging around the pool, supping cans of beer and generally relaxing.

'Don't even think about it,' said McGarry. 'If I catch any of you players down by the pool drinking beer, you'll be on the first plane home.'

It was farcical really. Some of their lads were mates of some of our lads but they were not even allowed down by the pool to pass the time of day with them. The match was not until the next day and although there was a trophy at stake it was meant to be a friendly tournament. Derek Dougan had flown out to join us and, typical Doog, made an immediate impact with the winner in our 2–1 success. Villa, who had Peter Broadbent at inside-right, had equalised through Brian Godfrey after Peter Knowles had given us the lead from the penalty spot. McGarry decided to give me a rest in the second half and sent on young Paul Walker as substitute. Hugh Curran also got a rest as Dave Woodfield took over in what was a real Cup-tie atmosphere. There was no doubt Villa boss Tommy Docherty really wanted to put one over us, but we were in no mood to surrender Midland pride.

We made it five wins in a row when we gave Kilmarnock the St Louis blues to the tune of 3–0, with me getting one of my rare goals, or so I believe. The Doog had headed us in front from one of Mike Bailey's trademark long throws and I thought it was me who made it 2–0. I say 'thought' as my lobbed centre seemed to go over the Killie 'keeper straight into the net. The Doog was worrying him though, and reckoned he got a touch. McGarry sided with me and his telephoned report back to the *Express & Star* said it was my goal. Mike Bailey laid on the third for Hugh Curran.

We had virtually made sure of winning the competition but a win over Villa in Kansas would make it certain. However, there was no incident-free build-up to the game, which will probably not come as a surprise. I have mentioned earlier about the trip to play Aston Villa in Atlanta when they were all lounging by the swimming pool. For the return match we had to be in bed by 10.30 again the night before. Next morning the heavens opened and, unfortunately, the game had to be postponed until the next day. Disaster! This meant we would have to be in bed for 10.30 again.

That evening, sitting in the hotel lounge, waiting for our tea and biscuits again before we went to bed, Hugh Curran, who had joined our drinking school, noticed that it was pouring down outside. 'That's it,' he said to the lads, 'I'm not staying in again. It's going to be off tomorrow with this rain.'

Several of us agreed with him on both counts. Hughie, Frank Munro and I decided to sneak down the back stairs to the swimming pool area and out through the back gate. Down we went to the back gate. So far so good but then, problems, it was locked. Seconds later the floodlights of the security guard picked us out. We came clean and told him that we were sneaking off for a drink.

'That's fine,' he said, 'give me five bucks each and I'll let you out, then between one and one-thirty I'll look out for you to let you back in.'

That was fine by us and we did the deal. Off we went and had a good few drinks and I mean a good few drinks. Hughie was absolutely smashed and we had to keep him quiet as we got back to the swimming pool gate so he would not wake anybody up. The security guard, true to his word, was waiting for us and let us in the back gate. Having had a few, we gave him an extra few bucks and went off to bed.

We awoke to a beautiful morning of sunshine. Sammy Chung came round the rooms and told us the match was rescheduled for that afternoon and it was definitely on. Later on we had a team meeting and McGarry made a statement.

'Last night some of you players went out drinking. If I find out the identities of the players involved they will be on the next plane home.'

We found out later that he had also given the security guard a few dollars to let him know if any of the lads went out the back door. The security guard did not know names and could only give our descriptions to McGarry. The manager added that he would be scrutinising all performances during that particular game. In other words, anyone who did not do the business would be suspected of being one of the culprits.

As it turned out, we were well on top from the start and I laid on our first two goals as we cruised home 5–0. The Doog headed home my corner for the first and things were really going our way. Hughie was playing with a terrible hangover and I did not help it when I drove the ball across at head height just in front of him. Instinctively he powered a header into the net and was obviously pleased to score, but grimaced at me as if to say 'That hurt!' He was grimacing again halfway through the second half when he powered in another header, this time to a Mike Bailey centre. Peter Knowles and Dave Woodfield added two more and, although Paul Walker took over from me, I had not done too badly. Frank and Hughie had also played well.

I think that, deep down, McGarry knew that we were the three culprits, being the drinkers in the team, when he made the threat about sending people home. With the title safely won, it did not matter too much that Dundee United got revenge over us in the final game. Derek Dougan put us ahead in the first half, only for the Scots to battle back to lead 3–1 before the Doog scored his second. The scoring system meant a team were awarded six points for a win with an extra point for each goal up to three. So we won the title with 57 points, ahead of West Ham 52, Dundee United 31, Villa 28 and Kilmarnock 26.

Knowles's Farewell

On the trip to the United States, and even before that, we all had lengthy discussions with Peter Knowles about his religious beliefs and tried to talk him out of his conviction that he could not be a Jehovah's Witness and still play football. However, as is the norm with people who have firm beliefs, your opinions do not count. They seem to have an answer for every question you throw at them and it becomes a frustrating conversation. I suppose we could all accept that Peter had found something that he truly believed in, but we did not think that he would abandon football completely to concentrate on his newly-found religion. I could understand him being excited at finding something new and something that really interested him, because for all the time that I had known him he had been a bit of a wayward lad and did not seem to have any direction in life.

As our US tour came to a close, Peter hinted once again that his retirement from the game was in the not-too-distant future. The team had won six out of eight tour games and had travelled thousands of miles across the States. We said goodbye to our sponsor Walter Bixby and to our favourite bar, the Red Onion, and headed back to Wolverhampton.

In July, prior to the 1969–70 season, Bill McGarry signed Jim McCalliog from Sheffield Wednesday. Seeing him in pre-season training, it was obvious that he was a very fit young man with an astute football brain. I was looking forward to playing with him on his debut against Stoke on the first day of the season. Unfortunately, I did not last very long. After a completely innocent collision with Alex Elder, the Potters' Northern Ireland international full-back, we both fell over and Alex landed on my outstretched leg, damaging the ligaments in my knee. By the time I had recovered from the injury, seven games later, I was to play in one of the most significant games in the history of Wolverhampton Wanderers – Peter Knowles's last.

The match was on 6 September 1969 against Nottingham Forest at Molineux. Peter walked out of the stadium only ever to return for the Jehovah's Witnesses conventions in future years. His training kit was still laid out for him on Monday morning in the hope that maybe it was all a big publicity stunt, but as time went by we realised it was all for real. To the general public, this young man had everything – talent, good looks, fame, adoring fans and a bright future in football. It was something that most youngsters could only dream of, but to Peter the moment he turned his back on football was the moment he had everything that he wanted. Whenever I saw Peter in years to come and asked him how he was, I always got the same reply. 'Every day's a wonderful day. I haven't a worry in the world.' How many of us can say that?

Soon after that, Bill McGarry went shopping in Yorkshire again, this time signing Bernard Shaw and Mike O'Grady. I don't think that he particularly liked me or my lifestyle and I think that he bought Mike to replace me. After all, he had been playing as an orthodox left-winger for Leeds. Much to my surprise, I kept my place and Mike took over Peter Knowles's number-eight shirt. It was McGarry's first full season in charge and it was an in-and-out campaign with us just about holding our own. We finished in 13th place, with the Anglo-Italian tournament to come. Three or four games from the end of the season I had been troubled with a foot injury, so our physio took me down to see Mr Freeman at his rooms near West Park in Wolverhampton. After an X-ray next door from Mr Booth, I was told that the problem was a small piece of bone that had chipped off and was aggravating me under my foot.

'There's a choice of action,' said Mr Freeman. 'I can open up the skin under your foot and remove the piece of bone, which will take some time to heal up before you will be able to walk or run on the affected part. Alternatively, we could put you in plaster for at least a couple of weeks and possibly the floating piece of bone will attach itself and the problem will be solved.'

He opted for the second solution and put me in plaster up to the knee. After a couple of weeks or so I had the plaster off and tested the foot out by walking up and down Mr Freeman's room.

'How's that?' he asked.

'Can't feel a thing.' I replied.

'OK, job done,' he said. 'Off you go and take it easy,' he added, as I walked out of his room.

My legs were not very big to start with, but after the plaster had been removed the muscle had wasted away even during that short period. I arrived back at the ground with Toby Andersen just as the lads were about to have a general warm-up session ready for the match that evening against Fiorentina in the Anglo-Italian Cup. Bill McGarry and Toby then had a little hush-hush conference for about 30 seconds and then Bill McGarry walked over to me.

'How does it feel?' he asked.

'Very good, boss,' I replied.

'How very nice of him to be concerned about my welfare,' I thought. Normally when you were injured he just ignored you because you were no good to him.

'Why don't you get changed and have a little jog about with the lads? Do you good,' he went on.

'How thoughtful,' I said to myself, wondering why I was getting such attentiveness. I did as he suggested and had a leisurely jog around, then did a few half-hearted sprints and, overall, was very pleased that he had suggested that I get out there in the fresh air with the rest of the players. Having done nothing but body exercises since my last game, against Liverpool almost a month before, it was good to stretch my legs, albeit very minimally. I was relaxing in the bath after my little warm-up session when Sammy Chung appeared in the bathroom.

'Waggy,' he shouted, 'soon as you're changed the gaffer wants to see you.'

Puzzled, I walked up the corridor and knocked on McGarry's door.

'Sit down,' he said as I entered his office. 'Toby informs me that Mr Freeman is happy that your injury has healed up,' he continued. 'You yourself have told me that the injury was very good. Do you agree?'

'Yes, boss,' I said.

'In that case, then, you're playing tonight,' he replied.

'But I haven't trained for a month,' I protested.

'You've just confirmed to me that your injury has healed,' he said sternly, 'so you're playing tonight. See you at 6.30pm.'

I was flabbergasted. Anyone who plays sport knows that if you have not done anything for some time the first thing you will struggle with is your breathing. Anyhow, I did play the game. I did struggle with my breathing and I was slow off the mark, but I scored a goal and we won the game 2–1. A little bit of Bill McGarry psychology, would you say?

A week later we had a home game with Lazio in the same tournament. Lazio were known for their hardmen tactics and, true to form, there were some very hefty tackles in the first half. Walking into the tunnel at the interval, their right-back decided to take a swing at me. It spread to the rest of the team and for at least one minute there was an almighty punch-up. The officials eventually sorted it out and we managed to win the game 1–0, but at a price. We were promised, or should I say, threatened, with trouble in the return leg in Italy.

While in Italy we stayed at the small seaside resort of Vearagics on the east coast. Messing about on the beach one afternoon, a stray shot landed next to a young lady who was sunbathing, making her sit up with a start. As I went to retrieve the ball I apologised as a matter of courtesy, thinking she would not understand me anyway.

'That's OK,' she replied in perfect English, 'I was dozing and it made me jump a little. What are you lads doing here? Are you on holiday?'

I explained to her why we were there and that we were going to play the local team. She expressed an interest in going to see the game and asked where she could get a ticket. I had not a clue but right on cue 'Uncle John', the chairman, was passing by, taking photographs with the camera that permanently hung around his neck.

I shouted 'This young lady would like to come and see the game. Will there be any complimentary tickets?'

'I don't think so,' he said to the young lady.

'That's a pity,' she replied in a perfectly normal English accent.

'I don't suppose you speak Italian?' John Ireland asked.

'I do,' she replied. 'I also speak four other languages fluently. I take coach loads of tourists round the town of Pisa.'

'You're just the person I need,' said the chairman.

He explained to her that there would be a small reception after the game and he would have to reply to the speeches of the mayor and other dignitaries. She could be his guest in the directors' box for the game and his interpreter afterwards. So the deal was done and they arranged to meet outside the hotel at the time the team bus would be taking the party to the football ground. True to her word, she was there as we left the hotel to board the bus. She was standing by the door of the coach conversing in Italian with the driver, who was sitting in his driving seat.

McGarry gave her a cursory glance as we all filed on to the bus, probably thinking she was the bus driver's girlfriend. As usual, John Ireland was last and he ushered the girl on to the bus, when McGarry, sitting in his normal front seat, roared 'Who the f*****g hell's this?'

The young lady stared at him, leaned over, looked him straight in the face and said in a loud voice 'I'm the f*****g interpreter, how do you do?'

McGarry never expected that!

His face was like thunder as John Ireland explained that he had forgotten to tell him that his interpreter would be travelling with us. She did very well after the game, interpreting the speeches, otherwise the lads would not have had a clue what people were talking about. You can imagine the ribbing we gave the chairman later about him having his own personal interpreter – out of earshot of McGarry, of course.

We travelled to Florence and got a good result, beating Fiorentina 3–1. Next stop was Lazio, where I was to experience something very unusual on the pitch. As the teams went out for the kick-in the Lazio right-back came and stood with me for the whole five minutes, repeating 'Murder, murder' and spitting at me. I could not believe it. Nothing like this had happened to me in all my days in football. Right up to the moment we were due to kick-off he was like my shadow, constantly spitting at me. I was expecting a rough game, but this was something new to me. He was like a man possessed. This went on for most of the game, plus he kept standing on my fingers every time I was on the floor, pretending he was helping me up. Fortunately, that was as bad as it got and we came away from there virtually unscathed, although we lost the match 1–0, unlike the Arsenal team, who some years later after a match with Lazio came out of a restaurant to be confronted by the majority of the Lazio team spoiling for a fight.

So that was it, the end of the first complete season under the McGarry rules and regulations and I can tell you that not many of us liked them. He had left John Holsgrove behind when he was late for the team bus leaving for an away game and, on another occasion, he did the same to one of the directors.

Personally, I was very lucky not to be left behind at Heathrow prior to one of our pre-season trips abroad. Sitting in one of the lounges a couple of hours before take-off, I was idly thumbing through my passport when I was horrified to discover that it had expired a week earlier. I approached Bill McGarry with trepidation, not knowing what his reaction was going to be. I knew that he was not going to be very pleased about it, to say the least, but was he going to bawl and shout and embarrass me? There was no easy way out for me. So, taking the bull by the horns, I bravely marched over to where he was sitting, reading his newspaper.

'Boss, I've got a problem,' I said. 'My passport is out of date.'

He raised his eyebrows and looked up at me. 'You what?' he hissed. 'You have got a problem – a major one because if you miss this trip I will fine you two weeks' wages.' With that he threw the ball back into my court and carried on reading his paper.

Panic set in. I could not afford to lose two weeks' wages and so I needed to find a solution, and quickly. I approached an officer at passport control to see if there was any way that I could be allowed through with an out-of-date passport, but was sympathetically told 'No chance.' However, he did give me a glimmer of hope.

'During my career in passport control,' he said, 'I have obviously come across this problem before and there might be a solution. Just depends if the right person is on duty. Come with me to the taxi rank.'

Puzzled, I followed him outside.

'You're in luck,' he said, pointing to a group of taxi drivers standing chatting. 'Charlie's there and he knows the routine.' With that he beckoned him over.

'This young man's plane takes off in approximately 90 minutes and his passport is out of date. Do you think you could get him back here in time for his plane with an up-to-date passport?'

'I'll do my best,' replied Charlie and with that he ushered me into his cab and we were off, weaving in and out of the traffic. At first I could not even contemplate where we were going but Charlie explained to me as we made our way towards Hounslow. First stop was Woolworth's. 'Get in that photo booth and get four pictures,' ordered Charlie as he sat outside with the engine ticking over. I did as I was told and as soon as I got the pictures we were off again, weaving in and out of the traffic. Next stop was Hounslow

Labour Exchange, where Charlie told me which desk to go to, with strict instructions to tell them that my plane was waiting on the tarmac ready to leave within the hour. Ten minutes later I was the proud owner of a 12-month passport and on my way back to Heathrow in Charlie's cab.

He got me there with minutes to spare to board the plane and the £20 he charged me for his services saved me a fine of two weeks' wages. Of course, the whole situation could not have happened these days, because neither 12-month passports nor labour exchanges exist any more. Obviously, I was the last to board the plane and as I walked up the aisle Bill McGarry, who had already taken his seat, was aghast to see me. I nodded smugly as I passed him on my way to the rear of the plane to take my seat. He never did ask me how I managed it all!

On the positive side, one thing McGarry did do right was to give a young man his first four games in the First Division of the Football League. That young man went on to become a Wolves legend, none other than John Richards. John came with us to Italy and was a scorer in the win over Fiorentina, along with Hugh Curran and Derek Dougan. Before we left for those two games in Italy, McGarry had signed a new four-year contract and also clinched the signature of Danny Hegan from Ipswich. Before the 1970–71 season began he also signed Bobby Gould, and McGarry could not have signed two more contrasting players.

With Bobby, it was definitely a case of what you saw was what you got. A typical old-fashioned centre-forward with a limited amount of ball skills, he certainly made up for it with his outstanding enthusiasm and goalscoring ability. If McGarry wanted players with positive attitudes he need not have looked any further than Bobby, a player I admired for his approach to the game. A good lad to have in your team, Bobby was also one who joined in the dressing room banter.

Whereas Danny Hegan…well, what can I say? I must admit that I had never heard of him before McGarry showed an interest in buying him and, consequently, knew nothing of his background or personality. Getting changed for training shortly after he joined us, Danny asked me if I would give him a lift when training was over to pick his car up from Wednesbury. I could not help but notice that even though it was only 10am he was reeking of booze. As I agreed to take him after training I did not bother going into the ins and outs of why his car had been left in Wednesbury. I did not know him that well and, anyhow, it was none of my business.

I found out a lot more about Danny on our trip to Wednesbury and realised that we had a lot in common. Like me, he hated training, unless it was with a ball, he hated having to play strictly to orders and, surprise surprise, we both liked a drink. Mind you, I was to find out in time that I did not like it quite as much as he did. Nowhere near, in fact.

We reached the car, which stood out like a sore thumb. It was parked half on and half off the pavement on double yellow lines in the narrowest part of the main road and he was lucky not to have had a ticket put on it.

Obviously I got to know Danny a lot better in the following weeks and months and, putting his football ability to one side for a moment, I could not understand why Bill McGarry had signed him. He was everything that the manager detested – a bad timekeeper, bad trainer and a drinker. Surely McGarry knew all that because he had managed him before, at Ipswich, or did he believe that he could tame the tiger? Please, do not get me wrong, I had nothing at all against Danny. In fact, I got on great with him, but it was the McGarry angle that I could not work out.

It immediately became obvious to us all that Danny had a wonderful talent. His vision, his ball skills and his all-round ability were second to none, but where did McGarry intend to play him? With the signing of Bobby Gould he now had three experienced strikers – Dougan, Curran and Gould. I was at number 11 and I do not think that Danny would have relished playing there, and Jimmy McCalliog, who along with Derek Parkin had finished with all 42 League games under his belt, was the man with the number-seven shirt.

For the opening game of the 1970–71 season, McGarry opted to leave out one of the strikers, Hugh Curran, and play Danny in the number-eight shirt. We lost the game, 3–2 at Newcastle, so he played all three strikers in the second game, with Jimmy Mac and Mike Bailey in midfield and myself out wide. We lost again, this time 4–2 at home to Derby, so McGarry then brought back Danny and played Dougan and Curran up front. This time we went down 3–0 at Tottenham.

After half a dozen games of juggling around, he gave a baptism to another young man who would eventually be one of the all-time Wolves greats – Kenny Hibbitt – and left out Danny. He also brought in Frank Munro at number five and John McAlle at number six. The majority of the team would become a familiar line up: Parkes; Parkin, Shaw; Bailey, Munro, McAlle; Hibbitt, McCalliog, Dougan, Curran, Wagstaffe. Danny was to start in only six games that season. It was a shame, really, all that talent and there was not a natural place for him. Jimmy Mac was playing well, and from the moment Ken Hibbitt got into the side he was a natural for that wide right midfield spot, becoming a scorer as well as a provider.

We won six games on the trot and, as you can imagine, spirits were high, or at least until McGarry showed his face. The dressing room was our sanctuary where we could have fun and take the mickey out of each other and Danny Hegan was a welcome addition with his own brand of humour. Just to make things clear, when I mention the dressing room I am referring to the mornings when we were changing before training sessions. There was no such fun on match days when McGarry was there.

Actually, having been a professional for almost 20 years, I can tell you that there is always a slight air of tension in every pre-match dressing room. Every player has his own little routine to go through and if any of them tell you that they were never nervous, do not believe them. I suppose it is like a performer waiting in the wings to go on stage. It is alright when you get out there but the build-up is the worst part.

I was probably the worst one for pre-match tension and had my own little agenda at Saturday home games. After reporting to the dressing room at around 2pm to let Sammy Chung know I was there I would wander down the corridor and go and have a look at the condition of the pitch just in case a change of studs was required. My next stop would be the tea room, where Alma and the other tea ladies would be preparing the board room spread. I would have half a cup of tea and a cigarette. Just after half past two I would meander back to the dressing room ready for Bill McGarry to come in with his last-minute orders. Off with my clothes at 2.45 and into the toilet for a glance through the programme and a last-minute cigarette. By seven minutes to three I would have all my kit on and be ready for the bell to ring at five minutes to three. That was my routine for the whole of my career at Molineux.

Players like Derek Parkin and Gerry Taylor, to name but two, were stripped just after two o'clock, having a rub down or doing stretching exercises. Everybody had their own routine, anything that would put you in the right frame of mind and relax you before you went out on to the pitch.

Most fans think you just go out on to the pitch and play the game but, believe you me, there is a lot more to it than that, before and after the match. In a normal occupation if you make a mistake you can put it right the next day. If we dropped a clanger it could be up to a week before you could try to make amends, plus 30,000 or more people watched you drop that clanger. I know that you are probably thinking 'You got well-paid for it.' I have already mentioned what I was earning when I signed in 1964. Well, just after Ronnie Allen left in 1969, I was earning £60 a week, so it was not that fantastic. There were win and draw bonuses and also a crowd bonus, but it still was not a fortune when you considered the fact that you would be finished by more or less your mid-30s.

Bill McGarry soon put a stop to the crowd bonuses. I must admit that I did not like it, but I could see his point of view. We could earn a £30 crowd bonus when playing one of the top attractions then lose the match 3–0. His point was that you should earn your bonus. We were midway through the season and doing alright, so much so that Bill McGarry seemed in a milder mood. For Frank Munro and myself, letters from the taxman put us in a sombre frame of mind. Apparently, the taxman thought that we were not paying enough rent for our houses, so it constituted a benefit in kind. We were being landed with a demand for money from time gone by. We both decided that the best thing to do was to buy our own properties and move out of the club houses. By coincidence, we both chose to view a new development in the Compton area of Wolverhampton.

The next thing was to see secretary Phil Shaw and see what the chances were of getting a mortgage off the club. The house Barbara and myself wanted was a brand new Hathaway cottage in Forton Close, Compton, at the princely sum of £6,200. With the thumbs-up from Phil Shaw we moved in as soon as possible, even before the road was surfaced and while many of the other houses were only partly built. Frank and Margaret did likewise and moved in four or five doors further up the cul-de-sac.

Taking it in turns to drive each other to training seemed the obvious thing for Frank and me to do. So we did and early on there was a problem when we arrived back from training, having driven there in Frank's car. On the way back Frank realised he had not got a key to his house and that Margaret had gone to town. As we pulled up he noticed that an upstairs window was open.

'Go and get that builder's ladder from over there,' Frank said to me.

As I mentioned, the site was barely finished. The road was not made up, the gardens had not been finished and the numbers had not even been put on the doors. Standing in the mud, I held the ladder while Frank climbed up and pulled the window open wide so he cold step in. He was just about halfway in when he suddenly retreated and hurried down the ladder.

'Quick,' he said, 'dump the ladder, that's not my house.'

Just then Margaret came round the corner and saved the day. She had the key to the house next door, which was Frank's house. Imagine if the police had come round at the moment that Frank was halfway through the window and I was holding the ladder. After the episode with the ladder I used to wind Frank up by saying 'Now, remember when you've been out, your house is the one with the red door.'

He would scowl at me and reply 'At least they've made it easy for you — they've given you the corner house.'

Frank got his own back some time later on when we were driving home after a visit to a casino owned by one of the area's well-known businessmen, Solly Wernick. I was driving one of the black-and-yellow VW Beetles that most of us had hired for a nominal fee. Approaching Forton Close, which was a U-shaped cul-de-sac, Frank and I living at the furthest end, Frank said 'Get some speed up as you enter the cul-de-sac, then switch off the engine as we approach our section, coast round the corner and the wives won't know what time we've arrived home.'

'That's a good idea,' I thought.

So I switched off the engine and coasted swiftly and silently up towards our corner but the car did not turn — one thing that I did not cater for was that the steering lock came on as I tried to turn the corner and, in the confusion, I went straight onto a neighbour's driveway. Having to start the engine again to reverse out of the driveway, I not only woke up the wives but half of our neighbours as well.

Frank was still laughing as he got out of the passenger's seat. 'Now that's very strange,' he said to me.

'What is, Frank?' I asked.

'The same thing happened to me the other night!'

Discipline's the Thing

If you're disciplined off the pitch, you will be disciplined on the pitch — that was one of McGarry's favourite mottos. To a certain extent I would agree with that. You do have to have discipline and principles in your life. This left the creative players with a dilemma at times when playing. Should they stick to McGarry's strict disciplined way of playing, or risk creating something different that could easily go wrong and lead to an explosion of expletives from him in the dressing room afterwards? Many of the younger players were grateful for the discipline McGarry instilled in them when he introduced them into the team, such as John McAlle and, later, Geoff Palmer. It stood them in good stead in later life. Having said that, it seemed to me that they were frightened to death of him.

Most of the apprentices absolutely hated McGarry for the way he treated them. When he was an apprentice, Phil Nicholls recalls a particularly traumatic time in his life when his sister died. He was left in charge of his brothers and sisters while his parents were out making the necessary arrangements after such a tragic event. When McGarry found out Phil had been off for three days he pulled him into his office and gave him a dressing down. Phil explained the situation but all McGarry was concerned about was that he had not phoned in.

'We haven't got a phone,' explained Phil, 'and even if we had I wouldn't have known how to use it.'

'Get back to your duties,' ordered McGarry, 'and next time get somebody to phone in.'

McGarry showed no concern or compassion for Phil and his family and from that day on Phil hated him.

Each morning after training the apprentices had to take it in turns to run a bath for McGarry. This was no ordinary bath, because certain apprentices took it in turns to urinate in it! McGarry's shampoo was placed on the side of the bath for him, but this was no ordinary shampoo. It was topped up with urine every day. It may seem a crude thing to do, but it showed what they really thought of the manager. They were in no way influenced by the professionals. We saw them each day as they went about their daily duties, bringing in the training kit and the like, but no way would they engage in conversation with us about McGarry. Their attitude to him was based purely on their direct dealings with him.

Sitting relaxing one evening in my house in Compton I answered a knock at the door. Standing there when I opened it were two strapping 6ft 2in young chaps, none other than Bob Hazell and George Berry, who would both become very useful central-defenders in the top flight of English football. The sight of these two big lads on your doorstep when you opened your door on a dark evening was enough to frighten anyone but I was lucky. I knew them. Even so, I was a bit taken aback because I was not expecting them.

'Hello, lads,' I said, 'what can I do for you two?'

'We're in trouble,' they said in unison.

'Come on in and tell me all about it,' I said.

George explained to me that they were sharing a flat in the Tettenhall area of Wolverhampton and had had an altercation with the landlord. Not only that, they had threatened him.

'Nothing serious about that,' I thought, 'they haven't physically hurt him.'

'So what's the problem?' I asked.

'He's going to see McGarry in the morning,' said Bob.

Now that was a problem. A visit and a complaint from a landlord would constitute at least a week's wages fine, anything after that was in the lap of the gods.

'What do you want me to do?' I asked.

'Go and see him and talk him out of it,' they replied.

I agreed to go and see what I could do. Surprisingly, the landlord was very cooperative and agreed to forget about the incident. The lads were overjoyed to hear the good news. The point is, these two strapping lads could have eaten Bill McGarry for breakfast, but the bottom line was that they were frightened of him and his ways. Even John Richards, a great player and a very level-headed young man, admitted the same to me when I asked him about his younger days at Molineux under McGarry's regime.

'He frightened the hell out of me,' John replied.

John was a quietish lad, kept out of trouble and was as near to being the model professional as you could get, yet even he did not escape the needless punishments handed out by McGarry. John's parents lived in Warrington, an hour and a half's drive from Wolverhampton, and being a young man living away from home he liked to visit them whenever he got the chance. After one weekend visit he left Warrington at 7am on the Monday to be at Molineux for training at 10pm. This was plenty of time under normal circumstances, but due to an unfortunate accident on the Thelwall Viaduct John was stuck in a tailback of traffic for some time. This was in the days way before mobile phones, remember. Once the traffic was moving again John had the presence of mind to pull in at the first services to inform Molineux of his plight and say that he would be late for training.

In my eyes, John had done nothing wrong. He had visited his mum and dad, left them in good time to get back for training, but due to circumstances beyond his control was delayed. He had let the club know and still did his training even though he was late. However, when John received his wage packet that month he was a week's wages short.

John confronted Phil Shaw, the secretary, only to be told that McGarry had fined him a week's wages for being late on that Monday. Next stop for John was McGarry's office – a daunting place – to see McGarry.

'You knew the circumstances, why have you fined me a week's wages?' was the question.

'You shouldn't have gone visiting your parents at the weekend,' was the answer.

Poor John had to accept McGarry's decision because any appeal would have gone to McGarry himself and he knew the boss would not change his mind.

John's best mate, Kenny Hibbitt, was another one to fall foul of McGarry. Kenny and Jane invited McGarry and his wife, Connie, to their wedding. Being a young man in McGarry's team, perhaps he thought they were obliged to ask them. In hindsight he probably wished he had not. Midway through the reception McGarry looked at his watch and promptly disappeared for a game of golf he had arranged earlier, leaving his wife behind. As you know, both John and Kenny went on to play a major part in our successes on the pitch in years to come, in spite of their treatment by McGarry. In fact, I would say Kenny was the most consistent performer in a Wolves shirt during that time.

Another player to play a magnificent part in our successes and form a formidable partnership with John Richards was the charismatic Derek Dougan. Derek was no stranger to controversy and publicity and was the chairman of the Professional Footballers' Association, the PFA, at that time. All things that McGarry did not like. Swords drawn, they were at arm's length for the rest of their days together at Molineux. McGarry hated it when he had to allow Derek certain days off to attend official PFA commitments. Derek was a very fit man and missing a day's training would not have been any detriment to him at all. However, McGarry just hated anybody missing a day's training. So much so, that when I was called up for jury service he phoned the court to try to get me released from my duties. When he could not cut any ice with the authorities he made me train at Molineux on my own after the courts had finished for the day.

Even a funeral was no excuse for missing training. A young man who was my number-one fan, who wrote songs about me and even wore a number 11 on his back before the days of fans wearing replica shirts, had a tragic accident on his motorbike travelling away to watch his beloved Wolves. Naturally I wanted to attend his funeral, but when I approached McGarry about having the morning off I was given an emphatic 'No'. To him, training was more important than a funeral.

At that time the Doog was a household name, appearing on many radio and television shows, apart from the publicity he received in the newspapers, not only for his expertise on the field but also for his high-profile position at the PFA. McGarry could not do a thing about it, but on one occasion I am sure he tried to turn the lads against Derek.

We were scheduled to play a midweek game in London. Normally, for a midweek match in the capital we travelled down in the afternoon and returned home after the game. Unusually, Sammy Chung informed us that we would be staying overnight after the game. Mystified, we asked Mike Bailey to go and see McGarry to request that we travel back the same night, as it was only a couple of hours' journey. Mike came back and told us the request had been granted. Wow! We were mystified again. Why in the first place did he want us to stay overnight in London and why did he so readily change his mind and accommodate us?

We played the game and travelled back to Wolverhampton, arriving shortly after midnight. McGarry stood up at the front of the coach and said 'See you all in the morning at 9.30, sharp, collars and ties and tell your wives you will be away for the rest of the day.'

We were mystified yet again. The only person who had not travelled back with us was the Doog, who had been given permission to be interviewed on *Woman's Hour*, the BBC radio programme, in his capacity as chairman of the PFA.

Next morning at 9.30 the coach left Wolverhampton, destination unknown. Down the M6 and on to the M1, pulling up at the services. McGarry stood up and made an announcement. 'We're now going back to London where you didn't want to stay last night. We are going back to the television studios to appear on Derek Dougan's *This Is Your Life.*'

Why did he not tell us the previous day that Derek was due to be on the famous TV programme? We would not have let the secret out to Derek and would have been prepared to stay in London for the night. McGarry informed us that we had ruined the plan for the programme. Had we stayed in London, the plan was for us to leave the hotel the next day, drop Derek at the *Woman's Hour* studio and supposedly carry on to Wolverhampton. As we were to leave the hotel Sid, the coach driver, was to pretend to break down and call the AA. Eamonn Andrews was to turn up dressed as an AA man and walk on to the coach with the famous red book under his arm to announce 'Derek Dougan, this is your life.'

Of course this did not happen, but we all went to the studios regardless, appeared on the programme and had a great time. I am sure that McGarry let the whole incident happen in order for the lads to moan about having to make a further trip to London just for the sake of Derek Dougan. Nobody moaned and, as I said, we had a great time. If McGarry had come clean in the first place, a second journey would not have been necessary.

On the subject of the Doog, it was he who was instrumental in bringing a young man all the way from South Africa to try his luck at Molineux — none other than Peter Withe.

When Peter was introduced to us in the dressing room prior to training one day, a few eyebrows were raised among the lads. He wore a dowdy green suit, sported a beard and looked overweight and anything but an athlete. I nudged Frank Munro and whispered 'He's in for a big shock when we start training.' Frank nodded in agreement. How wrong can you be? We were the ones in for a big shock.

Training on Cannock Chase was the worst session of the week. No footballs were ever taken with us and we knew it was a case of run, run, run. Hill climbs, downhill runs, exercises, pressure runs and, to finish off, a three-mile cross-country run back to where the coach was parked, waiting to take us back to Molineux. Peter was an absolute natural, like a mountain goat up the hills, at the front of the pack all through the session and, to cap it all, he finished hundreds of yards in front of his nearest rival on the cross-country run.

I hated these sessions and always finished at the rear of the field. Distance running was not my scene. Peter was a smashing lad, full of endeavour, and what he lacked in skill he certainly made up for in effort. Unfortunately, he only made a dozen starts for Wolves and was released in 1975. McGarry was heard to say to Mike Bailey 'He'll never make a footballer.'

Again Peter was to prove people wrong by having a highly successful career, gaining First Division Championship medals with both Nottingham Forest and Aston Villa as well as a European Cup-winners' medal with Villa and England caps, too. Ironically, had he been allowed to stay at Wolves he would have been the natural successor to Derek, who was just coming to the end of his illustrious career at Wolves.

Our coach driver, Sid Kipping, was one of the nicest chaps you could ever wish to meet. I never saw him without a smile on his face, except, that is, when he felt the wrath of Bill McGarry. He did not look one bit like a coach driver, with his grey flannel suit and gold-rimmed glasses, but this was to be part of the cause of his downfall with the manager.

When staying in hotels, as I have already mentioned, the players all sat together and the manager, travelling directors and Sid would sit at a separate table. Sid, the smartest man at the table, looked more like the chairman than the coach driver, so he always seemed to be attended to first by the waiters. This really irritated McGarry, who could not very well say 'Hey, he's only the coach driver, serve me first'.

Sitting in the front of the coach, McGarry was forever passing snide remarks at Sid about his driving or the route we were taking and things like that but Sid just kept smiling and took it all in his stride. Over the years, however, he did at times get his own back. Whether he meant it or not, I do not know, but I will tell you about a couple of instances involving Sid and you can make up your own mind.

For one of our UEFA Cup trips abroad, Sid drove us down to Heathrow Airport for an early morning flight. I was one of the last ones leaving the coach and as I neared the front I saw McGarry hand Sid a £5 note and say 'Here you are, you fat b*****d, that's your food money for on the way back, not that you need it, the size of you.'

Sid grinned. 'Thank you very much, Mr McGarry,' he said and with that we went to check in for our flight. After arrival, Mike Bailey and I had not been in our hotel room more than five minutes when there was a knock on the door. Mike opened it and in walked McGarry with a face like thunder.

'Have you got a spare shirt?' he asked Mike.

'There's a couple on the bed,' said Mike, who had just begun unpacking. 'Take your pick.'

'Can't understand it,' growled McGarry, 'my suitcase hasn't arrived.' And off he went.

Of course all the lads were highly amused when we heard of McGarry's plight. Meanwhile, a few hours earlier at Heathrow Airport, according to how Sid related the story to me a few days later, Sid realised that it was only 9am and he had all day to get his coach back to Molineux. He had his fiver in his pocket but thought 'There's no way that's being spent on lunch,' as he had brought his sandwiches with him. 'I'll go and lie on that comfy bed at the back of the coach with my newspaper and pick out some horses. That's where the fiver's going.'

After selecting his horses, and having had a good rest, Sid decided it was time to head back to Wolverhampton. Walking down the bus towards the front, he noticed one of the travelling blankets hanging down from the luggage rack. As he attempted to push the blanket back he saw it – the label hanging down from a small suitcase. 'W.M. McGarry' it read, right in front of his nose. Sid was supposed to have put McGarry's case on the trolley carrying the skips. At this point Sid had to sit down because he was feeling rather faint. He knew he was in trouble. He had a very uncomfortable journey back to Wolverhampton, knowing he had a three-day wait to face the consequences.

Meanwhile, back in Portugal, where we were due to face Belenenses, McGarry almost had the courier by the throat. 'Go back to the airport and find out what's happened to my f*****g suitcase,' he fumed.

Three days later, back at Heathrow, Sid was waiting for the plane to arrive and had placed McGarry's case on his usual seat at the front of the coach. We arrived at Heathrow, collected our luggage and wandered through the customs. One customs officer had the misfortune to call McGarry over and inquire 'Do you have anything to declare, sir?'

'I haven't even got a f*****g suitcase,' bawled McGarry and stormed off. And on boarding the coach the first thing he spotted was his suitcase.

'Where the f*****g hell has that come from?' he said to Sid, who was sat behind the steering wheel, looking straight ahead.

'Er,' said Sid nervously, talking through his fingers with his hand over his mouth, 'I forgot to put it on the trolley with the skips when you left for Portugal.'

'You what! You f*****g fat slob,' bawled McGarry. 'You left me for three days in Portugal without a change of clothes? Right, get your foot down, up the motorway and I'll deal with you when we get back home.'

The lads at the back of the coach had to stifle their mirth at the situation. Now I never did find out what Sid's punishment was, and I've often wondered whether Sid planned the whole operation to embarrass McGarry, because the easy way out would have been to dump the suitcase in a dustbin somewhere and nobody would have been any the wiser. Perhaps Sid wanted us all to enjoy the whole episode.

On Wednesday night, 23 January 1974, we played Norwich City at Carrow Road in the first leg of the League Cup semi-final. We drew the match 1–1, a result that any team playing in the first leg of a major semi would have settled for. The players were delighted at the result and, with the return leg scheduled three days later on Saturday 26 January, we were confident that we could get to Wembley. However, McGarry was not happy. He thought we should have won the game. Afterwards we travelled back to our hotel and had a meal. After the meal, McGarry stood up as he normally did.

'Nobody leaves the hotel,' he said. 'If you want a drink you can have one in the hotel bar.'

OK, fair enough, at least he was allowing us to have a drink. We filtered into the bar, and I and a couple of the lads sat at a table with a friend of ours, George Hayes, the owner of a garage in Coven, who had travelled to the game and was staying at the same hotel. Surprisingly, McGarry walked into the bar and commandeered the barman. 'These guys here,' he said, pointing in the direction of the lads, 'get one drink on the bill. Any more and they pay for them themselves.'

As he turned to walk away he spotted George Hayes sat among the lads. He immediately commandeered the barman again. 'That man there,' he said, pointing at George, 'doesn't get a drink on the Wolves bill. He's not in the official party.'

This man had driven hundreds of miles to watch Wolves play, only to be shown up in a hotel bar by the club manager. George was quite a wealthy person who did not need to be bought a drink by anybody and was very hurt by McGarry's attitude towards him.

In complete contrast, in walked the manager of the opposition, John Bond. 'Hello, lads,' he said, 'what will you have to drink?' and he actually paid for them out of his own pocket, including one for our friend George. We all sat there talking football with John Bond until the hotel bar closed. It turned a sour night for George Hayes into a very enjoyable one, being able to talk football with a First Division manager for a couple of hours.

Next morning at 10 we were all on the team bus, driven by our genial driver Sid. Our destination was Droitwich. We were to spend the next couple of days relaxing – a bit of light training and a brine bath at the Royal Worcester Hotel in Droitwich, then travel back to Molineux for our return leg of the semi-final against Norwich on the Saturday afternoon. Sid's next major encounter with McGarry was waiting to happen.

Whenever we visited Droitwich, which was two or three times a season, we would always approach the hotel from the north. This particular time, because we were travelling back from Norwich, the coach had to approach the hotel from the south. The entrance to the car park was flanked by two large red-brick pillars, topped by two large stone balls.

It was relatively easy for a coach driver of Sid's experience to negotiate the huge coach through this gateway when approaching from the north, because he was on the opposite side of the road and could just about get the angle right. This time he was on the nearside and had to swing over the white line so as to get some kind of angle. With the coach being longer than the width of the road, Sid had to perform a number of forward and reverse manoeuvres in order to get the coach through the gateway. After a few of these McGarry, sitting in his usual seat at the front and still annoyed about the previous night's result, was beginning to get irritated.

'What are you trying to do, you big puddin'?' he said to Sid.

'I've got to be careful,' was Sid's reply. 'I don't want to scratch the coach or knock one of those pillars down.'

'Right,' said McGarry, 'open the door and I'll guide you in.'

McGarry proceeded to stand on the step of the coach looking down at the nearside red pillar.

'Come on, come on,' he instructed Sid, who was gently edging the coach forward. 'Keep going, keep going,' encouraged the boss as the coach crept closer.

McGarry must have realised that Sid was going to catch that nearside pillar and shouted 'Whoa, whoa, whoa.'

Sid reacted by braking suddenly and depressing the clutch, which caused the door to automatically close, unfortunately trapping McGarry's head in it.

'Open the door, you fat b*****d!' McGarry screamed.

Sid opened the door to release McGarry from his predicament and McGarry snatched up his briefcase and scurried off into the hotel, leaving Sid to find his own way through the gates. While all this had been happening, everybody had watched in total silence, too scared to interfere, but as McGarry disappeared into the hotel the whole team fell about laughing like those little Martians in the old Cadbury's Smash adverts. I never did get to ask Sid whether that door closed automatically or whether he just had a little something to do with it.

Poor old Sid, he was soon to be in trouble again. Our schedule for Saturday 26 January 1974 was to have our pre-match lunch at the hotel in Droitwich and travel to Molineux for our home leg of the semi-final. Pre-match lunch in those days consisted of steak or chicken with tea and toast, a light meal in view of the fact that kick-off was only three hours away. Having had our lunch, a 20-minute tactical talk with McGarry and vacated our rooms, we were ready for our trip to Molineux.

Normal procedure on these occasions after a pre-match meal in a hotel with a coach trip to follow was to walk the first mile and for the team bus to pick us up 10 minutes later, McGarry's idea being that would 'walk your meal off' and stretch your legs at the same time. Bags on the bus, or so we thought, we ambled off towards the A38 and the M5. Sure enough, seven or eight minutes later our friendly coach driver Sid drew up alongside.

Sid used to have a little trick of spraying some air freshener into the heating vents at the front of the coach, enabling it to circulate through the heating system and create a wonderful smell of freesias throughout the entire coach. As Sid opened the door and we began to board the coach a fantastic aroma wafted from the inside. This was not air freshener, this was a really expensive aroma.

'What's that wonderful smell, Sid?' we all inquired.

Sid did not answer, so somebody else asked 'Come on, what is it, Sid?'

'I'm in trouble again,' said Sid nervously.

We immediately knew something was wrong. Bill McGarry and Sammy Chung were the last to board the coach.

Sid beckoned to Sammy and said 'I'm afraid there's been a slight mishap.'

'What's that then, Sid?' asked Sammy.

'You left your case in front of the bus for me to put on when you went for your walk,' replied Sid. 'I didn't realise it was there until I ran over it!'

Inside the suitcase was a very expensive bottle of perfume that Sammy had bought for his wife. This, unfortunately, had been crushed when Sid had run over the suitcase. This was the wonderful smell that wafted through the coach, coming from Sammy's suitcase, which Sid had tucked down behind his seat. Sammy, being a calm and resolute type of person, accepted the situation and declined to remonstrate with Sid. By the time we got to Molineux we were all smelling delightful, and with a John Richards goal that afternoon clinching our place at Wembley everything really was coming up roses.

At the end of one season we flew to Israel to play a game against their national team. Arriving at the Hotel Sharon in Haifa, on the outskirts of Tel Aviv, we found ourselves in the middle of a security operation. A prominent member of the Israeli defence cabinet was in residence at this particular hotel and consequently there were guards posted at every entrance and exit and at the end of every corridor.

The good thing about this was that you knew that with all those guards around you were safe in your bed at night. Anyway, we played the game after our second day and, with this under our belts and the season behind us, we were looking forward to a few days relaxing in the sunshine, safe in the knowledge that there was to be no more football until next season.

Late the following morning, half a dozen of us were sitting around a table at the pool, idly chatting in between having a quick dip. A gentleman who had been sitting reading a newspaper at the next table inquired 'Morning, lads, you're obviously from England, what are you all doing in Israel?'

After we had explained our situation, he told us that he was a Jewish businessman from London who had some meetings in Tel Aviv. He was not an avid football fan but had obviously heard of Wolverhampton Wanderers.

'Let me buy you all a drink,' he said, 'so I can boast about it when I get back home.'

With that he ordered bottles of beer for himself and the rest of us and told us of the jewellery business he had in London. Then, almost from out of nowhere, Bill McGarry appeared.

'What the f*****g hell's this? Professional footballers drinking at lunchtime. You're a f*****g disgrace. Get those bottles off the table and keep out of the sun.' And off he stormed.

'Who was that?' asked our Jewish friend in amazement.

'That's the manager,' one of us replied.

'I thought he was a sergeant major,' our friend said, 'and the rudest one I've ever seen.'

'Thanks for the beer,' we shouted as we trudged away from the pool, leaving him totally bewildered by the whole episode. Still, he had a good story to tell his friends when he got back to London.

We could not understand it ourselves. We had not even got a training session until six weeks later at pre-season.

Recently, while driving down the road in Tettenhall, I was aware of an elderly gentleman striding towards me at a fair rate of knots on the opposite pavement. As I passed him I got a glimpse of a face that I was sure I recognised from my past. My curiosity getting the better of me, I turned left, left and left again so that I was driving towards him again. So I could get a good look at him I parked the car, crossed over and walked towards him. We were approaching each other and I was certain it was him.

'Dr Horsley,' I said. 'Yes' was the reply. 'Oh, it's er?'

I had to prompt him. 'Waggy,' I said.

'Of course,' he replied.

We had not seen each other for more than 30 years since he was club doctor at Molineux and our own family doctor. I did not dare ask his age but I reckon he must be at least 80, not that he looked it, nor would you think it seeing the way he was striding out down the road.

He was the fastest doctor in Wolverhampton in his prime. He would dash into the ground, trot down the corridor and burst into the treatment room. 'Morning everybody,' he would shout and then would come his favourite saying. 'Are we all full of the springs of joy?' Then it was down to business, see who he had got to see and write the necessary prescriptions, then jog off up the corridor again. I did think of challenging him to a race along the corridor one day but if McGarry had found out and I had lost he might have fined me.

One foul, frosty, foggy morning, I went straight to his surgery before training. He diagnosed bronchitis and advised me to go home and go straight to bed. After returning home I asked Barbara to phone the office and advise them that I would not be at training that day. I had not been in bed a minute when the phone rang.

'You get down here, get your training gear on and make your way to the racecourse. That's where we'll be,' growled McGarry down the phone.

When I arrived at the racecourse I could not see the lads, I could only hear their voices somewhere in the middle.

'Join in on the end,' said McGarry when I finally found them, jogging along in single file.

Never in my whole career did I train in conditions like it. You could barely see 30 yards in the freezing fog conditions and under foot it was treacherous from a thick overnight frost. Everybody's eyebrows were white. Anybody with a moustache had a white one, likewise with anybody who had not shaved for a few days.

McGarry ran us into the ground and I struggled along at the back of the group, a place I normally occupied, but I was really weak at the knees and gasping for any air available. After the running session was over, McGarry made us all jog back to Molineux where he announced 'Day off tomorrow for a game of golf, weather permitting. Those who don't want to play will come here and train.'

I could not get my head round it. Why could he not have left me in bed to give me 24 hours of recovery from my condition, then let me train with the lads who were not going to play golf the following day. I struggled through the rest of the week, taking my antibiotics and, needless to say, performed abysmally the following Saturday.

McGarry never ceased to amaze us. After a morning's workout in one of America's hot and dusty cities we were given a few hours off to do some shopping. The temperature was in the 80s but the good thing was that every store had air conditioning. After a couple of hours, five or six of us decided to make our way back to the hotel and, as you can imagine, after an afternoon of dodging in and out of the blazing afternoon sun we were quite ready for some refreshment. As we arrived back at the hotel we were met with this wonderful surge of cool air as we entered the lobby. We were hot and thirsty and, just like those soldiers in the film *Ice Cold In Alex*, we made our way to the bar for an ice-cold beer. Not surprisingly, the first one never touched the sides – well, they were only halves – so we ordered the same again. Each time we requested another drink we were given a small white receipt, the idea being that we paid at the end of the session. After three or four beers the receipts were lying in the middle of the table around which we were sat.

My God, it must have been hot – lo and behold, who should walk into the bar, pull up two chairs and join the company? None other than Bill McGarry and Sammy Chung.

'Two ice-cold beers and the same again for this lot,' said McGarry to the waiter.

The waiter brought the order over and gave the little white receipt to McGarry.

'This is nice,' I thought, ' having a beer and a bit of a chat with the manager and the coach. Is he mellowing?'

A couple of minutes later it got even nicer. Having finished their drinks these two sweet gentlemen, Bill and Sammy, picked up the receipts from the middle of the table and McGarry declared, 'I'll pay for these lads' and off they went, Sammy reminding us to be up at 9.30 next morning.

'How very generous,' said one of the lads in a very sarcastic voice.

'The f*****g sun's got to him,' said Hughie Curran.

This was totally unexpected and had never been known before. Had we all pre-judged McGarry? Had he turned over a new leaf? He certainly gave us something to talk about round that table as we downed a few more beers. Next morning, standing out on the field waiting for the session to start, we were boasting to the other lads about the 'gaffer' buying us a drink, but the next minute we were given a real kick up the backside. McGarry and Chung arrived on the training pitch and gathered the lads around to tell us what we would be doing that morning.

'Right, Sammy,' said McGarry in a loud voice, 'run the f*****g b*****ks off them. I want every drop of alcohol out of them.' Then he turned around and walked off.

'The sadistic b*****d,' I shouted, when he was out of earshot. 'I'll never accept another drink off him.'

It turned out to be no idle threat. In the whole of my time at Molineux with him he never ever offered me one!

Crazy 'Keepers

Goalkeepers! What a special breed they are! They say you have to be mad to be a goalkeeper. I would not go as far as that but there is certainly something different about them. It is a lonely old job between the sticks — I know, I did it once, only for a few minutes but that was far too long for me.

Back in the First Division, we had begun with a 2–1 win at Fulham, and we could hardly have had more fitting opposition for our first home game back in the top flight, our local rivals West Bromwich Albion, and it was during this match that I got my one and only taste of life as a goalkeeper. It was Wednesday evening, 23 August 1967, and we were leading West Brom 3–2 at Molineux when Phil Parkes came off his line to catch a high ball. Tony Brown jumped with Phil and, just like Maradona did many years later, fisted the ball into the net. Disaster! The referee failed to spot the handball and signalled a goal. Naturally, Phil was incensed and chased the referee down the field, giving him a volley of verbals. The ref took exception to Phil's reaction and pointed to the dressing room. Phil trudged dejectedly towards the touchline, removing his goalkeeping jersey in the process. Being out on the wing I was the last person Phil would pass before he left the pitch. As Phil walked towards me I could see he was absolutely seething. I did not utter a word so as not to upset him further. He stopped in front of me, then, amazingly, gave me a present. Yes, he gave me the jersey and walked off the pitch.

We had no plans in place should the goalkeeper have to leave the field, so I was stuck with the jersey. Slipping the jersey over my number-11 shirt, I knew it was going to come down almost to my knees. The sleeves had to be rolled up innumerable times to reveal my hands. The ref was anxious to get on with the game and ushered me to the goal area. We kicked-off and proceeded to attack the Albion goal and at this point I realised how lonely life in goal can be. My nearest teammates were on the halfway line.

We continued to press and then it happened. A desperate clearance from an Albion defender landed in our half. John Holsgrove, chasing the ball back to his own goal, slipped the ball back to me, as you could in those days. Now what to do? There were almost 52,000 people watching this match and I did not want to look like a clown in front of them. Should I whack the ball back down the field as it rolled to me, or should I pick it up? I decided on the latter option and picked the ball up. I bounced it a couple of times and launched the ball as high and as far as I could. As I watched it coming down in their half the referee put his whistle to his lips and blew for time, thankfully bringing down the curtain on my career as a goalkeeper. Having looked at the game that night from a different position, albeit only for a few minutes, I have the greatest of respect and regard for goalkeepers.

Fred Davies was the regular goalkeeper when I first joined Wolves, having taken over from Malcolm Finlayson and Geoff Sidebottom. He was a very steady 'keeper, nothing flashy but a good shot stopper. Fred was a very keen golfer and it was he who was instrumental in my taking up this frustrating but very enjoyable game. Wolves had an agreement with Oxley golf club in the town, whereby any player wishing to play golf there had to pay one shilling of the 7s 6d green fee and Wolverhampton Wanderers would pay the remainder. This suited all the lads, especially Fred, who was quite a thrifty person. Some years later, in Texas, Fred and I were on the first tee of a local golf course, starting a round with the resident professional and his colleague. Fred unwrapped a shiny new ball and hit it sweetly down the right-hand side of the fairway but, unfortunately, it took a bad bounce and finished 20 yards into the rough.

'Play another ball,' said the pro.

'Oh, I'll find that easily,' said Fred.

'Play another ball,' the pro reiterated.

Being the thrifty chap I told you he was, Fred did not like the idea of having to lose a new ball — they were not cheap — so he announced to the pro that he knew the exact clump of rough that it had landed in.

'You probably would find it,' said the pro, 'but there are rattlers in there and they might find you.'

Fred promptly unwrapped another ball and made sure it landed on the fairway this time.

Another golfing goalie, Dave MacLaren, interrupted Fred's run in the Wolves goal during the 1964–65 season. Dave, nicknamed the 'Cat' by the lads, was a prolific six-handicap golfer, which was not surprising since he had been brought up on the fairways of Gleneagles golf course in his home town of Auchterarder. His father had been employed at the golf course in many different capacities during his working life and in his later years became the starter, sitting in his little green hut by the first tee.

Dave knew that I and Mike Bailey and Phil Parkes were planning a week's golfing trip to Scotland and suggested that we book in at a place he knew in Auchterarder and go and introduce ourselves to his dad. This we did and it turned out to be to our advantage. It did not matter what time of the day we strolled down the path to the first tee, Mr MacLaren, without a flicker of recognition, would announce 'Next on the tee, Mr Bailey's party' and we would go straight to the front of the queue. It did cost us a few whiskies in the local bar each evening, but it was well worth it.

Dave, as many Scotsmen do, liked a gamble and was a member of our travelling card school. This was in the days of old-style trains with a corridor and compartments to seat six people with a table in the middle, just right for a card school. On one particular journey, just before the said school began, Dave had been to the buffet and got himself some refreshments, bringing them back on a tray. As the train chugged along, swaying from side to side, Dave was standing stupidly trying to balance the tray on the edge of his chin in sea lion fashion. Terry Wharton and I, watching Dave's antics, dropping the tray every few seconds, fell for the sting and got completely sucked in.

'I wonder if I could balance this on my chin for one minute,' said Dave.

'No chance,' Terry and I said in unison.

'OK,' said Dave, 'I'll tell you what. If I balance this tray on my chin for one minute on this moving train will you give me 10 bob each? If I don't, I'll give you two half a crown each.

'Done,' said Terry and I.

'Somebody keep the time,' said Dave, 'starting now.'

You would not believe it. He stood there on a moving train balancing that tray on edge, manoeuvring even better than a seal. After one minute Terry and I both had to hand him a 10-bob note. He had obviously done this before and we had been well and truly done. Dave had got his stake for the card school and Terry and I started minus 10 bob each.

Not many Scotsmen I know are into cricket, but when we were trying to raise a team for an end-of-season charity cricket match against Wolverhampton side Wightwick, surprisingly Dave was one of the first to volunteer. It turned out that he fancied himself as a fast bowler. He was not bad, either.

I was fielding in the covers and, unfortunately, when one batsman drove him 3ft to my right and 3ft off the ground I could only dive and parry the ball, dropping the catch. Dave was absolutely furious, came over and gave me a dressing-down, much to the amusement of the watching crowd. I was embarrassed and smoothed the situation by saying 'You saved a shot last week, same height, same width, but you could only push it round the post for a corner. At least I stopped this one, Dave.'

What I could not understand was the fact that I had never seen him that angry on a football pitch. Fortunately, he calmed down after he took a wicket with his next delivery.

After some to-ing and fro-ing between Fred and Dave, Fred regained his place in the early part of the 1966–67 season and Dave moved on, only for Fred to come up against another contender for the goalkeeping spot – a young Phil Parkes. Phil impressed Ronnie Allen on our tour of America and Ronnie rewarded him with the number-one spot. With Fred eventually moving on to Cardiff, Ronnie had to bring in another 'keeper as competition and cover for Phil. Evan Williams, a Scot with a Welsh-sounding name, arrived at Molineux from Third Lanark. There is not a lot I can tell you about Evan because he was not with us very long. I found him a nice, unassuming young guy who got along well with all his teammates. He was laid back but very focused on the football field. Evan played only 13 League games for Wolves but 13 certainly was not unlucky for him as he got a dream move to Celtic. It was the equivalent of an English player being bought by Manchester United. He had a very successful time at Celtic and probably finished up with more medals than any of us. He played for them in the European Cup Final against Feyenoord in 1970.

Talking of medals, when I meet people on holiday or at social events and they discover that years ago I was a footballer they always presume that I have a house full of medals. In the early days there were only two medals up for grabs, one for the League and one for the FA Cup. Later there was the League Cup but, having said that, when we won it in 1974 the prize was a tankard. In fact, amateurs win far more medals than professionals, unless, of course, you play for someone like Celtic or Rangers who over a period win the majority of the major honours in Scotland.

I said that there was something different about goalkeepers and the next contender for Phil Parkes's crown was just that – something different. He was Alan Boswell, 'Bozzy' to all the lads. He was a likeable character but appeared to be obsessed with all things black. From day one, and every day until he left, he was never seen without his black bag. What was inside? His training gear, of course. Black boots, black socks, black shorts, several pairs of black gloves and, of course, a black goalkeeping jersey, plus, even more sinister, a black book. Very interesting.

The only person we knew with a black book was big Jack Charlton. It contained the names of all the opponents who had upset him, so that he could pay them back. Surely, Bozzy had not got a list of scores to settle? We were all dying to know what was in his black book but, having only known him for a few days, it seemed quite impolite to ask him. We did not have to wait very long, though. One morning, as we were getting changed for the day's training session, Mick Kenning shared a funny joke about goalkeepers with all the lads in the dressing room. As all the lads were laughing at the punchline, Bozzy, holding his pen in one hand and his black book in the other, said 'Er, excuse me, Mick, could you repeat that joke?'

'F*****g hell,' said Mick, 'I'm not going in your black book, am I? For telling a joke about goalies.'

'Oh no,' said Bozzy, 'if you repeat the joke slowly I can write it down alongside all the other jokes I keep in my black book.'

As you can imagine, the whole dressing room fell about laughing as we found out that the black book was nothing more than a list of jokes. If he ever told us any of his jokes from the book he had to read them to us because that's why they were in there in the first place – he could not remember them.

During Bozzy's time with us, training or after games, he never once got in the big bath with the lads. He would wait until all the lads had bathed or showered. In fact, after one home game Mike Bailey and I had been home and got changed and were on our way to a presentation at 6.30 when we passed the ground and Bozzy was just coming out of the main entrance, with his black bag of course.

Bozzy was an exceptional shot-stopper on the training ground during shooting sessions and, unfortunately, he was never able to carry the ability to the match situation. He was certainly a goalkeeper with many differences, choosing to warm up before the game on the halfway line instead of between the sticks like any other goalkeeper. I never got to ask him why he did this but I suppose he must have had his reasons.

He played only 10 League games for us, of which we won only two, but I suppose the writing was on the wall, excuse the pun, for him in his second match, the one against Liverpool. Attempting to line up the 'wall', the ball finished in the back of the net before he could organise the defenders in front of him and Liverpool finished 6–0 winners at Molineux that night.

Sir Alf Ramsey always maintained that Martin Peters was 10 years ahead of his time. I maintain that Alan Boswell was also 10 years ahead of his time. In the infamous black bag that I told you about were several pairs of black gloves. Bozzy had been experimenting with different kinds of materials glued to the insides of the fingers to enable him to catch the ball more securely. Most of these materials were top secret (known only to Bozzy) but I do know that one of them was the material of a table tennis bat with the little pimples on it. I do not know whether he used any of the gloves in a match but I do know that it was another 10 years before goalkeepers began using gloves with material on the inside of the fingers. Perhaps Bozzy sold his secret on after leaving Wolves.

Once more Phil Parkes, known as 'Lofty' to everyone, had triumphed over a pretender to his crown and it was to be over a year before he was to be challenged again. Bill McGarry signed John Oldfield from Huddersfield and he made his debut at Burnley in January 1970 when we won 3–1.

John was one of our neighbours on the Fordhouses estate, where many of us lived. Our local at that time was the Moreton Country Club, which is now the Moreton Arms pub on the corner of Springfield Lane. He became another member of our drinking school, which consisted of at least half a dozen of the first-team squad. Because it was a country club we were able to get a late drink, which was very handy after playing a midweek evening game. John had a very strange drinking habit. After ordering a pint he would have a small swig of it. Putting it to one side he would not touch it again for at least 20 minutes. He'd have one more small swig, then the lot would go in one. There was no messing with the next four or five. They went down very sweetly. A typical

Yorkshireman was our John, he loved his beer. He played only 19 League games, finishing on the winning side only three times.

After John's final first-team game, Lofty incredibly played the next 127 consecutive League games, plus 44 consecutive first-team games in various Cup competitions, making a record-breaking 171 consecutive appearances, a fantastic achievement.

It had been a very patient wait for understudy Gary Pierce during Phil's marathon run between the sticks. Gary finally made his debut against Newcastle United at St James' Park in September 1973. Little did he know that the season ahead would be beyond his wildest dreams. In between his next two games, against Everton and Chelsea, he managed to squeeze in a UEFA Cup game against Belenenses. After Chelsea came the return leg against Belenenses then it was on to face the might of Manchester United. So, in the space of 15 days Gary had faced Newcastle, Everton, Chelsea and Manchester United and played in two UEFA Cup games. I doubt that any other first-class goalkeeper had faced such a baptism. Of the six games Wolves won three, drew two and lost one, scoring nine goals and conceding seven – not a bad start to Gary's career at Wolves, but even better was yet to come for him.

Phil came back into the side in late October, but disaster was to strike in late January. During a routine training session down at the Wolverhampton racecourse, Phil dived for a ball, caught his studs in the ground and broke his ankle. Nobody was near him, it nobody's fault, just one of those freak accidents that are inexplicable. Phil was not a player who got many injuries, as you could see from his previous half a dozen seasons, but the sad thing with the accident was that it happened six weeks before the League Cup Final.

Phil was devastated but, as he explained to me, he was told on the day of the fracture that he would not make the League Cup Final. So when that week came around he had had plenty of time to get over the disappointment. Even though he was included in everything the squad did – except training, of course – he must have been so upset when the big day arrived, knowing he was to miss a match that every professional dreams about – a Cup Final at Wembley. Yes, you could ask all your so-called superstars and they would tell you the same thing: Wembley was the place to be. I could not begin to think what was in Phil's mind when he watched us march down the tunnel to emerge in front of almost 100,000 football fans.

When I came off injured in the game against Manchester City, I found myself sitting next to Phil on the bench. He was totally immersed in the game and when John Richards scored the winner he attempted to jump up like the rest of the bench until he realised he had still got a broken ankle. So did I until I realised I had just pulled a muscle. So we settled for giving each other a hug instead.

Gary Pierce had the game of his life, on his birthday of all days, but was always ready to praise Phil for the big part he played in actually getting us to the Final in the first place. He has always been genuinely generous in his regard for Phil's goalkeeping abilities and insists that the winning tankard he received rightfully belonged to Phil. Gary had no airs and graces and enjoyed his nights at the pub for a game of dominoes and a few pints. He still does, so he tells me, although he lives in Bury, his birthplace, now. Last time we spoke I am sure he said he was with wife number four. It seems he is still enjoying that side of life!

As well as the time spent in each other's company, Phil and I, along with the rest of the lads, have travelled all over the world together on Wolves tours. In the early days a naïve Phil liked to tag along with Mike Bailey and myself. He liked to copy things that we did so as to be one of the lads. At that time Phil was strictly a half-of-lager man, but Mike and I set him up on one of our long-haul flights.

Phil was sitting further up on the arm of one of the gangway seats, watching a game of cards between some of the lads. Mike and I ordered a rye and dry each from the stewardess, who then asked the others if anybody cared to order a drink. 'Yes please,' said Phil.

'What would you like, sir?' she inquired.

'Er, I'll have one of those that those two had,' he replied.

Mike and I nudged each other. We knew he would not like it. The stewardess duly brought his drink and, as he was about to take a sip, Mike and I shouted 'Cheers, Phil.'

'Cheers,' he replied and took a good slug of rye and dry and we could see his face change. It was a shock. He did not normally drink anything like that.

'Nice, is it, Phil?' we shouted.

'F*****g great drink, this is,' he lied.

It was creasing him. We watched him sipping it. 'All right, Phil?' we kept shouting. 'Same again?'

'Oh yeah,' he replied.

After several rounds of rye and dry with Phil, Mike and I did a very sneaky thing. We told the stewardess to fill ours just with Canada dry but still give Phil the full monty. Several rounds later and Mike and I were still egging Phil on. Each time he took a sip we would shout some comment like 'Enjoying, that, Phil?' 'Wonderful' he would reply, but we knew damn well that he hated it. Ten minutes later he was fast asleep in one of the empty seats. He stuck to his halves of lager after that. These days he will drink virtually anything!

Here is a bit of useless information for you. What did these Wolves goalkeepers have in common: John Oldfield, Phil Parkes, Gary Pierce and Paul Bradshaw? The answer is that, strangely, none of them could drive a car, lawfully that is. I know Paul Bradshaw was not at Wolves when I played, but he was a teammate at Blackburn and I recommended him to Wolves.

When on tour we were normally driven around in coaches to local destinations, but on a particular visit to Kansas City, which was to be our base, we were provided with a couple of courtesy cars, two huge, beautiful limousines. McGarry ordered that I was to be the driver of one of these limos. He had seen pictures of me driving a limo during a trip to California and I was given strict instructions that 'Neither Curran nor Munro is allowed behind the wheel under any circumstances.'

While these limos were a good idea to enable us to get to the training ground, it was also an added bonus when training was over. The cars were at our disposal 24 hours a day, so afternoons and evenings we were able to save on public transport and taxis during sight-seeing and shopping expeditions. One particular afternoon six of us went for a game of golf at a nearby course. Having played in two three-balls, Phil, Mike Bailey and I finished our game ahead of the other three, who had been delayed on the course for some reason. Sitting in the limo idly waiting for them, Phil announced out of the blue that he would like me to show him how to drive the car.

'I can't, Phil. You heard what McGarry said. I'm the driver,' I replied, trying to fob him off, knowing he had never driven in his life.

'McGarry only mentioned Curran and Munro not driving,' was Phil's reply.

With Mike egging him on, I had to concede and agreed to show him the basics. It was a massive car park, as they usually are in America, with very few cars on it and a three-quarter-mile straight driveway down to the gates.

'OK, Phil,' I said. Sitting him in the driving seat, I pointed out that it was an automatic with no gears to change and explained that once it was in 'drive' he could gently press the accelerator and the car would move along the car park. Mike was in the front seat next to Phil and I was leaning over his shoulder, showing him the different controls. I let him turn the key and start the engine. Then, leaning over, I slipped it into 'drive'.

'OK, Phil,' I said, 'if you gently press the accelerator with your right foot you'll be driving the car.'

Now, the word 'gently' and a 6ft 3in goalkeeper do not exactly go together. His foot went down heavily and the car hurtled forward. Had we been facing any other way we would have finished up on the golf course itself but, luckily, we were facing the end of the long driveway and the car, as though on automatic pilot, headed straight down it. Mike was loving this. 'Go on, Lofty,' he laughed. Phil, with his arms rigidly stuck to the steering wheel, pressed down harder on the accelerator and we hurtled down the driveway.

'Pull the handbrake, Mike,' I shouted, but Mike was enjoying this too much. With Lofty transfixed and me petrified in the back, he was roaring with laughter. Suddenly a car, having turned into the driveway, was heading our way. 'Hit the brake, Phil,' I shouted.

'Which is the brake?' he yelled back.

'The pedal on the left,' I bawled.

I have said that Phil and gently did not go together and as he stamped his foot on the brake we skidded 40 yards before coming to a halt. I leaned over and switched off the ignition, relieved that we were all in one piece. Mike was still laughing. 'I was enjoying that,' he said with tongue in cheek, 'what have we stopped for?'

Anyhow, as far as I know that was the beginning and end of Phil's driving career.

Bill McGarry must have had a premonition when he told me that Hugh Curran and Frank Munro were not to drive the car. That night five or six of us were going to a small country club on the outskirts of town. It was an awful night with torrential rain and thunder and lightning. Hugh Curran was sat in the front with me and I could sense his curiosity looking at the controls all lit up in the limo. As I pulled up for some fuel, Hugh asked me if he could drive the last part of the journey. I was totally against this but all the lads rounded on me. 'Go on, let him have a go,' they pleaded. Against my better judgement I handed him the keys after filling up with fuel. Actually, he drove quite sensibly and we arrived at the country club in one piece. Because it was raining so hard he wanted to park as close to the entrance as he could. There was a gap between the cars, but it entailed having to park with the offside wheels on a grassy bank, which sloped away from us. I was not completely happy with the way the limo was parked but was assured by Hughie and the rest of the gang that 'It'll be all right.'

Returning to the car after a couple of hours in the club turned into a nightmare. The incessant torrential rain, which was still falling, had washed away part of the grass bank and the car had slid 12 foot to the bottom of the bank.

'I'll get it out,' declared Hughie, taking the keys from me. We pushed and shoved as he revved the car to try to move it from its position at the bottom of the bank. By this time we were all soaking wet and covered in mud from the spinning wheels, which sank deeper and deeper into the quagmire as we tried to get it back on the road. Finally, we all had to concede that there was no way that we were going to move that car and by now it was in an awful state.

There was no way we could leave the car overnight because we were training next morning and it was needed to transport half the squad to the training ground. The manager of the country club phoned a breakdown number and before long we were dragged out of the mire, so to speak. It cost us 40 dollars between us but it was well worth it.

Next morning was a beautiful sunny morning and the car looked abysmal. When McGarry saw it he threw one of his tantrums.

'What the f*****g hell's happened to that?' he asked.

'It's OK boss, we helped tow somebody who was stuck in the mud last night. They were very appreciative and have given us the money to get the car cleaned,' I lied.

'Get it done before training,' he barked.

With a sigh of relief I went down to the car wash and had it sorted. After training I was commandeered to take some of the lads shopping in the afternoon. Getting back to the car after the shopping expedition, Frank Munro decided that he would like to drive the car back to the hotel or, at least as near to the hotel so as not to be seen by Bill McGarry. Along the way we came to a queue of vehicles at some traffic lights and Frank committed the cardinal sin when driving on the right-hand side of the road with a left-hand drive — he forgot that the width of the car was on his right-hand side and hit the back corner of a queueing vehicle. Fortunately there was no visible damage to our car, but there was superfluous damage to the bumper of the other vehicle. We had a roadside consultation with the other driver and explained our situation. With the details we had given him from the glove box he was happy to resolve the situation without informing McGarry. The manager never did find out the truth about these incidents. Then again, we did not find out how he could have foreseen the problems of Hughie and Frank driving the car. Clairvoyance?

As I have already mentioned, Phil Parkes and I have been on many trips together, some good, some not so good, but we always seemed to have a laugh or share some weird incident. On one such trip, we arrived at our hotel in Baltimore, US, around 6pm. After a wash and tidy-up most of the lads met in the hotel bar for a few beers. Hotel bars are the most boring and expensive places to have a drink, so eight or nine of us decided to have a wander round the city and find a nice bar elsewhere. We had already been warned that it was not safe to be out on the streets of Baltimore at night. Nevertheless, we felt that because there was a large group of us we would be quite secure and carried on regardless. As it happened, we had barely gone 200 yards when we came across a likely-looking place so we all piled in.

From the outside it looked just like any other bar but once inside we found a rather unusual servery. The bar top itself was built in a semi-circular fashion, about 25 metres long and lined with high stools in typical American style. Behind the bar, as well as the bar staff, was a large lady, who beamed as the lads walked in.

'Welcome, boys,' she shouted, 'take a seat.' Then she bawled 'Make these boys comfortable and fix them a drink.'

She beamed with the anticipation of taking a good few dollars off a group of Brits. We all grabbed a high stool and sat in a line along the bar. There were about another 20 customers in the bar, everyone male and mostly black guys sitting in twos and threes dotted about at the tables behind us. In a normal pub or bar the back of the bar itself would be full of optics, bottles and mirrors, but this was no normal bar, as we were about to find out. At the back of the bar was a curtain, drawn as if to blank things out. Suddenly, the house lights went down and the whole place became quiet, spooky really. The only source of light was a small spotlight picking out the mamma who was standing in the middle of the servery.

'This is what you've all been waiting for,' her voice boomed out. 'Magnificent Marguerita from Mexico.'

With that the curtain at the back of the bar drew open to reveal a small stage flooded by coloured spotlights. Accompanied by some background music, Marguerita appeared. She was the stripper. Sitting next to Phil on the high stools I became aware that somebody had just walked up from behind and proceeded to lean on Phil's shoulders and mine. I knew instinctively it was not one of the lads. Glancing down and sideways I could just about make out a massive pair of hands with the fingers interlocked.

Glancing at right angles, not daring to turn my head any more than half an inch, I could make out the biggest head I had ever seen. He was just like the heavyweight boxing champion Sonny Liston. He was leaning on our shoulders with his head between ours, gazing at the stripper. Not a word was uttered as he watched, transfixed by the stripper. The room was pitch black, full of smoke, boiling hot and I was petrified. This was one of the scariest situations I had ever been in. It was as though we had turned to stone – Phil, myself and 'Sonny Liston' in the middle. For 15 minutes we sat absolutely motionless until the stripper had finished her act.

Show over, he retreated in silence whence he came to a seat at a table. Phil and I looked at each other and both gave a massive sigh of relief. It was a weight off our shoulders, literally! We had not touched the drinks while the man mountain was breathing down our necks so we desperately sank what was in front of us and quickly ordered the same again.

'Right, Phil,' I said. 'Let's go to the toilets.'

'I don't need to,' he replied.

'Oh yes you do,' I almost begged. 'You don't think I'm going in there on my own with all these shady characters about.'

As soon as we got in the toilets I stuffed all my money down my socks, save for 20 dollars with which to pay my bill. Meanwhile, back in the bar, our eyes, used to the dark by now, we could see that the room had filled up considerably, looking more like a

Chicago gangster movie set. Just as the big mamma was introducing Lovely Linda from LA, we moved en bloc to the exit, knowing full well that setting foot outside we would be safe because every one of us could outrun any one of them in there. Needless to say, we did not look for another drinking place once we had headed back to the safety of the hotel bar. A lesson was learned. Listen to the locals!

Before I end my resumé of Lofty Parkes and the other goalkeepers I would like to relate just one more out of the dozens of incidents in which Lofty made us laugh. One of the lovely things about the big man was that you could laugh with him or at him and he would not mind which.

Landing at Jersey airport once, we had only to walk over the road with our suitcases to the hotel in which we were to stay. Very appropriately the hotel was called the Mermaid, the same name as the pub on the Bridgnorth Road in Wolverhampton, where the majority of us used to drink. Sammy Chung dished the keys out and we trudged off to the annexe, an elongated corridor-type building. All our rooms were situated along this corridor and the lads were simultaneously opening the bedroom doors. At the same time a porter was pushing along the wicker basket skips. Phil, who was struggling to open his door, spotted the porter and loudly exclaimed 'Excusay, key no turna in lock.'

Because he had just stepped off an aeroplane Phil assumed he was in a foreign land and that the porter was some kind of Manuel out of Fawlty Towers.

'Aang abaaht, me old china,' replied the porter, 'I'll be back in a mo' and he carried on up the corridor with the skips.

'F*****g hell, he speaks English,' said Phil.

'So he should — we're only in the Channel Islands,' shouted some of the lads as we all roared with laughter.

Embarrassed, Phil realised his mistake and joined in the fun. To take the incident a little further, knowing that the porter had to come back to help Phil with his key, I popped up the corridor to have a word with him.

'Sorry about the big fella,' I said, 'he's our new goalie from Spain, doesn't speak a lot of English. He's having trouble with the key.'

'I'll sort it out,' the porter said.

Now the only words he had heard Phil say were 'Excusay, key no turna in lock' in a silly accent so he had no reason to doubt what I had said about Phil being our new goalkeeper from Spain. Consequently, when the porter came back to Phil, he slipped into a Manuel-type accent.

'What ees the problem, sir?'

Phil, without thinking, slipped back into his foreign accent mode. 'Key not turning,' he said.

'Sometheeng wrong,' muttered 'Manuel'.

'I know that,' bawled Phil, losing his temper and automatically reverting to his Midlands accent. 'It's supposed to open the f*****g door.'

'Ang on,' said the porter, 'you speak English.'

'Just a minute, so do you,' said Phil.

That was the moment that they looked at each other and both realised that they had been well and truly had. The lads quickly closed their doors and roared with laughter behind them.

Phil Parkes was a giant at Molineux in more ways than one. His record of loyal years and 382 first-class appearances speaks for itself. Many years later, when idly chatting with some of my playing contemporaries about football while having a few beers, the subject of Pelé was brought up. Phil surprised us all by telling us that he played with Pelé. Apparently, finishing his career in the NASL over the Atlantic, Phil was voted the number-one 'keeper in the League and was invited to play in Franz Beckenbauer's testimonial match in New York. So Phil had the great experience of playing in the same team as the two world superstars. Dave MacLaren went on to become a big wheel Down Under in the insurance game and ultimately became a millionaire. Evan Williams owned two pubs in Glasgow and, wait for it, I have heard that Bozzy, too, is now a wealthy man. Perhaps he was the inventor of the modern-day goalies' gloves after all.

I cannot let the subject of goalkeepers pass by without relating a chapter in my life at Manchester City. I joined the club in early 1958 straight from school as a groundstaff boy, not too long after their FA Cup Final victory over Birmingham City at Wembley. The Cup Final was a national institution in those days, and more than half the population found a TV set to watch, irrespective of who were playing. The hero of that 1956 game turned out to be the Manchester City goalkeeper, who played much of the second half with a broken neck.

A former German prisoner of war, Bert Trautmann became the first Manchester City superstar. His heroics in the Cup Final made him a household name and he was welcomed like a film star wherever he went. He even had the looks of a film star. Tall, a magnificent athletic build and a shock of blond hair made him stand out. Bert was everybody's hero, but my first encounter with him was a clip around the ear. 'You knock before you come in here,' he growled. It was my second day at Maine Road and I had been seconded to go and collect the training boots from the first-team dressing room. I was obviously set up by the other groundstaff boys, who knew full well that Bert's peg was number one, the first next to the door, and anybody other than his teammates who did not knock would be admonished or, in the case of us groundstaff lads, a clip around the ear would be the outcome.

Within 18 months or so I was in the same team as Bert, and playing and training with him gave me a bird's eye view of just how good a goalkeeper he was. Even though he was 40 years of age, he was still the most agile goalkeeper that I have ever seen. Throughout my playing career and to the present day I have not seen anybody better. Still a comparative youngster in the early sixties, I played in his testimonial game at Maine Road in April 1964. There were said to be 48,000 fans there that night, though some sources reckon there were many thousands more than that. A combined Manchester City and Manchester United team played an international XI. It was a brilliant occasion and we won 5–3. Denis Law scored three goals and yours truly scored two. We also had Bobby Charlton, Bill Foulkes, Derek Kevan and Jimmy Murray in our team, while the international side included Stanley Matthews as well as England captains Ronnie Clayton and Jimmy Armfield.

To this day I have still got Bert's testimonial match programme and a lovely letter from him thanking me for playing in the game. In the letter he talks about still being overwhelmed by the response. However, the response was due to his huge popularity. He also paid us all £20 for playing – a week's wages in those days.

Working on a farm during the close-season as a 16-year-old with Manchester City.

Eighteen years old and in the same team as two true soccer legends – Bert Trautmann and Denis Law. No sponsored boots in those days. George Hannah (next to Denis Law) has his right boot held together with elastoplast.

A proud moment. Wearing the England shirt for a Youth international against Bulgaria.

waggy

DAVE WAGSTAFFE
Wolves

Me in action. Note the use of the right foot! It must have been a friendly crowd as there isn't a barrier between them and the players.

An encounter with George Cohen, one of the World Cup-winning team of 1966.

The complete playing and coaching staff of Wolves in 1971. I know all the faces so well, but of the 51 people in the picture I cannot put a name to one or two of the youngsters.

The Wagstaffes: Barbara, Mandy, Gary, Scott and myself in the garden of our new home at Compton in 1971.

Outside Lenny's Boot Parlour in California. Davey Jones had just treated Ernie Hunt, Terry Wharton, Mike Bailey and myself to some fashions of the day.

OUCH!!

Never mind the ball! Ron (Chopper) Harris gives me a warm welcome at Stamford Bridge. Is that my shinpad disintegrating beneath his right boot?

A magical moment in my career as I parade round Wembley holding the League Cup aloft with skipper Mike Bailey.

True Grit. Our magnificent skipper Mike Bailey. No need for words – the picture says everything about this Wolverhampton warrior.

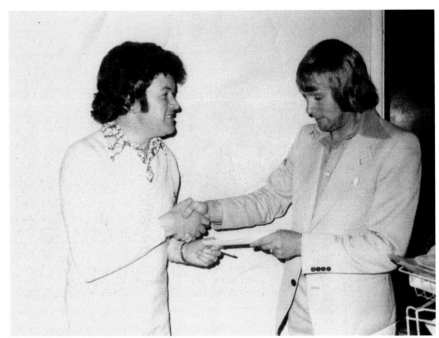

Local night club owner Roger Allen presents me with a cheque – the proceeds from an appreciation night that he kindly arranged at his club.

Back at Molineux with the League Cup.

Some of the players posing with the gold and black 'Beetle', dressed in the gold and black tracksuits that we were not allowed to keep after our Wembley triumph.

Two wonderful reminders of my time at Blackburn Rovers. The Player of the Year trophy, 1976–77, and the plaque recording my 500th League appearance on 5 March 1977.

On the set at Columbia Studios, Hollywood, with the famous Monkees. Note the camera round John Ireland's neck – it's the one we never, ever saw a picture from.

Derek Jeffersen, Phil Parkes, Frank Munro and myself get a few tips from Ray Reardon and Alex Higgins.

A wealth of musical talent (and wealthy too). Roy Wood (Wizzard), Jeff Lynne (ELO), Robert Plant (Led Zeppelin) and Bev Bevan (ELO), among others, enjoy a well-earned drink after playing in my testimonial match.

On the first tee with Mike Bailey, Sammy Chung and Bill McGarry for the infamous game of golf that led to my injury prior to the League Cup Final.

My name up in lights on the 'Stan Cullis' stand. I wish it was still there!

Back at Molineux to manage Waggy's Bar.

Hugh Curran. His favourite party piece was the Norman Wisdom song *Don't Laugh at Me ('cause I'm a Fool)* and we all know the opening line 'I'm not good lookin'. You can say that again Hughie!

Some old faces at Molineux for one of our Former Players' Association get-togethers.

Val and I outside the Valley prior to the 'London Wolves' 40th anniversary dinner.

Jutta Dougan and I meet up again after 30 years.

The class of 1960-something. Enjoying ourselves at a weekend in London generously paid for by the 'London Wolves Supporters' to celebrate their 40th anniversary. What a wonderful nostalgic weekend. From left to right: Hugh McIlmoyle, Ernie Hunt, John Holsgrove, Dave Wagstaffe, Gerry Taylor, Graham Hawkins, Terry Wharton, Fred Davies, Bobby Thomson, Mike Bailey and Frank Munro in the foreground.

One of the buffets prepared by Val and myself for a 'Waggy's Bar' function.

European Adventure

Moving to Compton just happened to coincide with the refurbishment of the Mermaid public house on Bridgnorth Road on the outskirts of Wolverhampton. How good of Mitchells & Butlers to refurbish a pub and enable us to make it our local! It became a very popular venue and was a busy place most nights of the week. I could say that at some time or other every member of the Wolves first-team squad paid a visit to the Mermaid. Frank Munro and I were regular visitors with our friends John Penzer, John Tinsley, Jeremy Martin and George Hayes.

At the time the landlord was a gentleman named Des Kendrick, a very smart man who rarely wore the same suit two days running. His hair was always plastered down with some sort of hair dressing, leading to Danny Hegan nicknaming him 'Dubbin Des'. Danny was convinced that the dressing Des used on his hair was dubbin, the stuff you used to preserve the leather of your football boots. Needless to say, we never let on to Des about Danny's nickname for him.

Many a morning Danny, instead of asking me if I had been down to the Mermaid for a drink the previous night, would ask 'Did you go and see Dubbin Des last night?'

Danny's local was the Vine at Fordhouses or sometimes the Moreton. One Sunday lunchtime he went off for a drink with strict orders from Patsy, his wife, that dinner would be ready at 2pm and he had better be there. You have guessed it! At 2 o'clock he was not there, so Patsy wandered down to the Vine to see if his car was there. No luck, so she decided to walk up to the Moreton and see if he was there. Just before the Moreton stood a large house that had been turned into flats and Patsy spotted Danny's car parked in the driveway to the apartments.

Not knowing which flat Danny was in, Patsy looked through the first window she came to and, as luck would have it, she picked the right one. There was Danny sitting chatting to a young lady. Obviously, Patsy saw red and hammered on the window, yelling at Danny to 'get out of there!' Unfortunately, unknown to Patsy, the situation was not as bad as it looked. Danny had been drinking with a couple in one of the pubs and offered to give them a lift home. He was then invited into their flat for a drink and the precise moment that the young lady's boyfriend went into the kitchen to pour the drinks was the moment that Patsy peered through the window, jumping to the wrong conclusion.

Danny opened the front door, where Patsy was shouting and ringing the bell. Before he had time to explain what was going on, Patsy picked up one of the milk bottles from the step and whacked Danny on the head with it, causing an injury that needed several stitches. Next morning at training he was not very forthcoming about how he had sustained the head wound, but he did not need to tell the lads because the news had already filtered through. Then again, nothing surprised us where Danny was concerned.

We made early exits from the FA and Football League Cups in the 1970–71 season but we were doing well in the League and still had an interest in the Texaco Cup. After a win and a draw against Dundee and a win and a defeat against Morton, our next encounter in the competition was against Derry City in Northern Ireland and this was to prove a very testing trip in more ways than one. Belfast was still a troubled place in 1971 and the evidence of this was all around for us to see, not least in the barbed wire rolls on the ends of some streets and the huge motifs painted on the ends of terraced houses. It was a little bit nervy for those of us who were not used to it, but we were reassured by the Doog, who promised 'Stay by me and you'll be OK.'

The hotel we were staying in was in the centre of Belfast and as usual the night before a game the routine was the same old thing – tea and biscuits at 10.30pm and then off to bed.

Around about 10 o'clock, I was sitting in the hotel lounge chatting with the Doog and John Holsgrove. 'Come on,' said Derek, looking at his watch, 'we've got time for a stroll before the tea and biscuits'. So we wandered off down the street, turning back after about a quarter of a mile. Arriving back at the steps of the hotel, the Doog looked at his watch again and announced that it was only 20 past ten. 'We've got time for a stroll up the other end of the street, if you like,' said Derek.

We thought about it then decided not to and instead went inside to wait for our supper. Suddenly, a few hundred yards up the street, there was a massive explosion as a bomb went off. Not being used to anything like this it really shook me up and unnerved me.

'That's where we were about to walk!' I exclaimed.

Derek was as calm as can be and said 'I told you, stay by me and you'll be OK.'

I did not sleep very well that night, I can tell you. I kept re-living the moment that the bomb went off.

Next day we were to have a couple of hours' journey to Derry City for the game and I was looking forward to the coach trip in order to catch up on some sleep, but it did not turn out anything like I, or anyone else, expected. The coach driver, when he finally picked us up, was in a foul mood, having been held up at some security checkpoints.

'Come on, lads, let's go,' he shouted, as he ushered us on to the coach. 'Traffic's very heavy so we need to be away as soon as possible.'

He was right. It was slow-moving traffic all the way through Belfast out to the road which would take us in a north-westerly direction to Derry. As soon as we met the main road we were stopped by the soldiers at a checkpoint. Two soldiers boarded the coach and did a head count.

'Where's your destination, driver?' one of the soldiers asked.

'Derry,' he replied.

'OK,' said the soldier, 'it's maximum security at the moment and you will be checked every 20 minutes. Do not, I repeat, do not deviate from this main road.'

'Fair enough,' said the driver and we continued, albeit at a fairly slow pace, on our journey.

Sure enough, we were checked again after approximately 20 minutes, another two soldiers boarding the bus and doing a head count before radio-ing to some sort of HQ, then sending us on our way with the same orders not to leave the main road. It was a frustrating journey for the driver, slowly following the convoy of vehicles in front of him which stretched as far as the eye could see, with each one being checked every 20 minutes, just as we were.

After passing the third checkpoint, the driver made an announcement. 'I can't see us making kick-off time at this rate, so about half a mile ahead I know of a short cut down some country lanes and we can come out 10 miles ahead of this slow-moving traffic.'

A few minutes later we turned left down a narrow country lane and he was able to put his foot down. Rounding a bend about a mile down the road there came into view five men dressed in black trousers and black waistcoats, standing in a line across the road, guns at the ready. The whole of the party on the coach fell totally silent as we came slowly to a halt. It was a frightening experience, not knowing what was going to happen, particularly as an Irish pop band had been massacred down a country lane like this. It was a very nerve-wracking moment, seeing these five men stopping the coach from going any further.

'We're in trouble now,' mumbled the driver, not making the scary situation seem any better. Then suddenly, from the hedgerow on the other side of the lane, appeared a sight that brought us all back to reality — half a dozen British soldiers. We were to learn that the men in black belonged to the special constabulary and were on our side but to those of us who did not initially know who they were, it was a heart-stopping moment.

I do not know whether the driver was trying to spread the blame when he mumbled 'We're in trouble now', but it was totally his decision to turn down that country lane and one of the soldiers, I presume it was the one in charge, played absolute hell with him for deviating from the main route. The driver tried to justify the situation by saying that he was struggling for time in order to get the team to the stadium for kick-off. Things then took a turn for the worse.

After carefully checking all the driver's documents it was discovered that he was masquerading as his dad! The coach was registered in his father's name and he was using his father's driving licence. This left us in a farcical situation, stuck down a country lane, surrounded by soldiers and special constables with no legal driver to get us to our destination. His excuse was that his father was ill and the family really needed the money that the hire of the coach would bring in. Whether this was true we would never know, but it seemed to appease the soldier in charge a little. Commonsense prevailed and it was decided that because we were obviously not a security risk the coach could turn around in a clearing and go back to the main road, even though he was an illegal driver. However, this was not before he was given another dressing down and told to report to a certain police station the next day. He eventually got us to the stadium in time and after such a traumatic journey the team did well to win 1–0 in the first leg of the semi-final, thanks to a goal from Bobby Gould. Although I was in the squad, I had picked up a knock and Paul Walker played at outside-left.

It was almost four months later that we played the second leg, winning 4–0 to set up a Final against Hearts. Derek Parkin got one of his rare goals in the Molineux game, with Gould, Hugh Curran and Mike O'Grady also on target.

We finished the season in a very creditable fourth place, something that any of us would have settled for before the season started. Finishing that high in the table entitled us to a place in the UEFA Cup, which was being introduced in place of the Fairs Cup. None of us had played in a European competition so it had been a rewarding season and the lads had worked hard for it. Frank Munro had made the number-five spot his own and had formed a formidable partnership with John McAlle, who had made the number-six shirt his. Add to this the emergence of Kenny Hibbitt at number eight, with John Richards waiting in the wings, and things were looking good for the team. John had made only four starts in the League but had come on 10 times as sub.

The last game of the season was the return leg of the Texaco Cup Final against Hearts at Molineux, after we won the first game 3–1 in Edinburgh, where Hughie Curran scored twice. We lost the return 1–0 but took the trophy 3–2 on aggregate. So all in all, fourth in the League and winners of a Cup, it had been a pretty successful season.

It was round about this time that we said goodbye to big John Holsgrove after 200 first-class games for Wolves. He had gone about his job quietly and efficiently and made a more than adequate contribution to the team. He had lost his place to young John McAlle and was transferred to Sheffield United in June 1971. The original 'Tea Set' were now down to two, but Big John had something else to look forward to. After being on McGarry's rations for the past couple of years he could once again enjoy his prawn cocktail and eat as many chips as he wanted. He did leave one thing behind, though — the Castlecroft ghost!

If I had been puzzled during 1970–71 about why Bill McGarry had signed Danny Hegan and then used him only six times in his starting line up in 53 first-class games, I was even more puzzled by his sale of Bobby Gould to West Brom after just five games of the 1971–72 campaign. He had finished top scorer with 24 goals from just 44 starts in the previous season. Goalscorers are like gold dust and McGarry was blessed with three of the best in the First Division, but the sale of Bobby left the door open for the emergence of young John Richards and if the manager had indeed planned it that way then all credit to him.

Potentially the partnership of John with Derek Dougan looked good, so much so that Hugh Curran was nudged to one side. Hughie had done the job that McGarry had bought him to do – score goals – and was a popular guy with all the lads, both on and off the pitch. He used to like to think of himself as a bit of a singer and whenever we were in a situation where there was some live music going on and a microphone available we used to encourage Hughie to get up and give us a song. It was not that he had a particularly good voice, but more to take the mickey. I must admit he did like the attention, but he did not really want to sing. However, the lads would push him into it and he did not like to refuse in front of an audience. His favourite song was an old Norman Wisdom number entitled *Don't Laugh at Me ('cause I'm a fool)*. Hughie had not exactly got the film star looks of David Beckham, so when he sang the opening line – 'I'm not good looking' – the lads would all stand up and shout 'You can say that again.' After the second line – 'I'm not too smart' – we would respond with 'And you can say that again!' The audience always loved it and Hughie would take it in good part and carry on with the song with the lads joining in in the background.

Yes, Hughie liked the spotlight all right and there was one occasion that we would never let him forget. It was when we found a restaurant in our hotel taken over by the would-be Miss Americas and their chaperones in Kansas City. When one of the organisers found out that we were a soccer team from England she thought it would be a good idea to parade the lads and introduce them individually. Obviously, it was going to have to be one of our party who introduced us because nobody else knew our names. This was where the showman in Hughie came out. 'I'll do it,' he declared to the organiser and suddenly he became a different person. She led him out into the middle of the congregation and he proceeded to introduce himself in an American accent. 'Hi there, everyone,' he said, ' my name's Hugh Ko – ran.' He then proceeded to introduce the rest of us in this wonderful American drawl. We did not let him forget this and whenever the opportunity arose we would introduce him as 'Hugh Ko – ran.'

If it was to be a season of few appearances for Hughie, it would prove to be the longest of my career. It began with one of the busiest schedules I had encountered with six games in the month of August, followed by seven in September. The six in that first month were all League games, but the seven in the second month included a League Cup tie and two UEFA Cup matches. The League Cup tie with my old club Manchester City turned out to be a cracker in front of nearly 30,000 at Maine Road. Unfortunately we lost 4–3, but it was a great game for the spectators. A week later we began our adventure in European football with a first leg home tie against Academica Coimbra. It could not have worked out better, and after a 3–0 win we went to Portugal with great confidence for the second leg two weeks later. It was a rare achievement for a striker to score a hat-trick on foreign soil in European games, but Derek Dougan achieved the feat in our 4–1 defeat of Academica in Portugal. John McAlle scored our other goal.

September was a special month for John. He must have thought this goalscoring lark was run-of-the-mill stuff. He scored three goals in 21 days. On 8 September against Manchester City and on the 15th and 29th against Academica. However, those were the only three goals he scored in 495 appearances for Wolves, apart from a couple on one of our American tours. Goalscoring is not so easy, as John found out, and I should know the feeling as I did not score too many myself and I was a forward.

I did have the good fortune to score a 35-yarder a couple of months later in a 5–1 win over Arsenal, the previous season's double winners. That goal, on a snowy day at Molineux, was voted 'goal of the month' on the BBC programme *Match of the Day*. I scored the following Saturday too – in our 3–2 win over Albion at the Hawthorns – but that proved to be my last goal until the very last match of the season. Going back to John McAlle, he did score a goal in one match equally as good as mine from 35 yards but, incredibly, it was ruled out because Kenny Hibbitt was standing off-side in the extreme outside-right position. 'Scouse', as we called John, was not very pleased, as you can imagine, but he was far more important to us in preventing goals, rather than scoring them.

Our next opponents in Europe were Dutch side Den Haag, again a team we knew very little about. At least in the League games we were given a thorough rundown of our opponents from information gleaned from people specifically sent to report on the tactics and strengths or weaknesses of other teams in the First Division. This, plus our knowledge of certain players whom we had played against and sometimes with during our careers, gave us some idea of what to expect from them. Obviously, somebody was sent to watch them and further information was probably obtained from any other team who had played them. So really we were not as fully prepared as we would have been for one of our League games.

As it was just a short hop from England, our charter plane was one of the smaller turbo-prop craft. At the time, gale-force winds swept the country, and from the moment we took off from East Midlands Airport we were buffeted by the accompanying winds, causing turbulence for the whole of the journey. The pilot performed a minor miracle controlling the plane as we came in to land almost sideways at the airport in The Hague.

I have the greatest regard for these people and the way they always play down any kind of crisis. When asked about the hairy conditions later, the pilot calmly announced 'You had nothing to worry about, lads, I would have put that old crate down in any big field.'

The result of the game was excellent, but if you had read the paper the next day and saw Den Haag 1 Wolves 3 you would have thought what a good performance that was away from home. In a way it was a good performance, but a good defensive performance. We were under the cosh for the majority of the game and from the half a dozen real attacks we made scored our three goals. You get the odd game like that, when the opposition have you on the back foot for most of the time but you come away having sneaked a win. Conversely, it happens the other way round, but I have always believed that over a period of time things even themselves out. With three away goals in the bag we were quietly confident that we would go through to the third round, but the way we were to progress was rather unusual and totally unexpected. I doubt whether any UEFA Cup tie in the past or even in the future would see the away side concede three own-goals. The game unfolded to be completely opposite to the one in The Hague. We were the aggressors on this occasion and pounded the opposition. The mere fact that we put so much pressure on them contributed to the mistakes they made, resulting in three own-goals, from Weiner, Mansveld and van der Burgh. Once again, if you saw the result in the newspaper it would look as though they made it easy for us, gifting three own-goals, but I can assure you it was not easy. On the contrary, it was damned hard work. Derek Dougan was our scorer that night.

To win two away legs in Europe is pretty good going, to win three is something else – but we did just that when the third round took us to East Germany, as it was then, to meet Carl Zeiss, Jena. We had a charter flight from East Midlands and even that turned out to be unusual. It is so much better when the whole plane is taken up by your own party of people and the pilot is able to update you on how things are progressing. We thought he was joking when he warned that nearer to our destination we might be accompanied by a couple of fighter planes but, true enough, as soon as we flew into the East German air space a couple of fighter planes appeared from nowhere. Under normal circumstances you are able to tell when your aeroplane is not far from its destination by the sound of the engines slowing down and the reduction in altitude. This was happening but we were flying round in circles for what seemed ages and there was total silence from the cockpit. The engines were droning and finally we could see the landing strip as we came out of the low grey cloud. The strip was clear but everything else was covered in snow and much to our relief we made a perfect landing.

Later we learned from the pilot that he had been panicking, having been made to fly round in circles at low altitude for such a long period. Eventually he had frantically radioed ground control for permission to land because he was running dangerously low on fuel. Apparently this was not unusual when flying over East Germany. The authorities liked to show you who was in control. It turned out to be the same at the airport, where we were kept hanging about in what was really a large wooden shack with no heating. After what seemed like an age we were taken to passport control, where every passport was scrutinised to the last full stop. The guards stood there in their long green overcoats, cradling their guns and staring straight ahead as though they had been hypnotised. Eventually we left the airport and were taken to our hotel, situated in the town square. Having never been to East Germany before it struck me that everything seemed very dowdy and depressing. Our hotel entrance did not seem very inviting, but once inside, apart from being very old-fashioned, it was very clean. The décor was mostly dark wooden panels and there was not anything remotely bright in sight. Mike Bailey collected our room key from reception and we went off in search of our room along the bare boards of a very long, gloomy corridor. The room itself was very basic, consisting of two old-fashioned but clean wooden beds and our own bath and toilet, but nothing much else. As darkness fell we were both aware of the lack of noise: not just people noise, but traffic noise, just an eerie silence. However, this was 1971 and we were the other side of the Berlin Wall.

As we wandered down for our evening meal, Mike and I joked about how Bill McGarry's pre-order of soup, steak or chicken and fresh fruit salad might have been interpreted. We were soon to find out. When the soup arrived it was clear that we were not going to like it. It was hot water with a bit of flavouring in it. There were chunks of bread in a basket in the middle of the table but, alas, not a bit of butter in sight. I had to make do with dipping my bread in the soup. When the main course came the steak was the size of a normal steak but only about an eighth of an inch thick and the fresh fruit salad turned out to be a basket of apples, oranges and the like. We did not bother about our tea and biscuits routine that night, instead opting for an early night. At about 7 o'clock next morning we were woken by what sounded like a marching army with the crunch, crunch, crunch of boots on the frozen snow lying in the square outside. I looked through the window and saw hundreds of people tramping along on the packed snow, apparently, I was to find out later, off to work. Most manual workers, I discovered, worked until lunch, then after lunch it was compulsory studies until late afternoon.

The Carl Zeiss company were the makers of optical lenses for all kinds of requirements, including microscopes and, if you should visit the trophy and memorabilia display in the foyer of the main entrance to Molineux you will find a microscope that was presented to chairman John Ireland to commemorate the game in Jena. All the players in the Carl Zeiss team were employed at the factory and, in effect, were semi-professional. The game itself was played on a snow-covered pitch surrounded by more than 9,000 standing spectators, 90 per cent of whom were wearing fur hats. It was a strange sight, with no chanting or singing from them as they stood there more or less to attention. I felt sorry for the smattering of Wolves supporters, who must have had an horrendous journey to get to the game. It was freezing cold for them and I can guarantee that there was no chance of a piping-hot Bovril at half-time. The game was won by a John Richards goal, so at least the fans had an away goal to take back to Molineux with them. They must have had an equally horrific trip to get back over the border to normality, and the other players and I take our hats off to them for even attempting such a trip into the unknown.

It was cold, it was dark and it was miserable by the time we arrived at the airport for our journey home. Once again we were the only people there, apart from the obligatory guards, as usual dressed in their long, bottle green overcoats, staring straight ahead as if transfixed. With no heating in the airport it was freezing cold and the long wooden benches we sat on were most uncomfortable. Even our plane looked a forlorn sight, standing alone in the gloomy lights surrounding the tarmac. What should have been a formality for us — having our papers checked — was not, and we were once again hanging about.

John Ireland, sitting with his hand luggage in a corner, looked a lonely figure, huddled up trying to keep warm. Little did we know but he did have some company — a bottle of whisky he was swigging from when nobody was looking. Finally, after lot of unnecessary protocol, we were allowed to go through the doors leading to the tarmac, where the plane was waiting. By this time, the chairman was a wee bit unsteady on his feet. I had a sledge, which I had bought in Jena, over my left shoulder and my hand luggage in my right hand as we left the so-called terminal building, so I could not offer to help John Ireland as he tottered along with his hand luggage. He was on my left as we wandered out into the dark for the short walk to the plane. Twenty or so yards later I became aware that he was no longer by my side. I looked back, expecting him to be lagging behind but, to my horror, I saw him halfway up one of those stairways that enable you to board the plane. Unfortunately, there was no plane at the end of this one — just fresh air and a 40ft drop. It was a free standing one. In the gloom and because he had had a few drinks, he mistakenly thought that it was the way on to the plane. A couple of the lads spotted him and quickly brought him back down to earth — literally. However, the consequences had he reached the top of the stairs were quite unthinkable. Of course, after a good sleep on the plane, by the time he finally arrived in Wolverhampton he could not recall the incident.

I mentioned that I had bought a sledge in Jena. Well, so had Frank Munro. We had spotted them on show outside a shop opposite a hotel, really sturdy and well made ones, just the thing for our kids back home. So we dutifully lugged these things all the way home from behind the Berlin Wall. A couple of weeks later, while walking through Beatties store in Wolverhampton, I saw the exact same sledges on sale for approximately the same price that Frank and I had paid for them. There was a big sign engraved in the wood – 'Made in East Germany.' We need not have bothered!

The return leg with Carl Zeiss saw us full of confidence with our one-goal advantage and we were never under pressure. We beat them comprehensively 3–0 with a goal from Ken Hibbitt and two goals from the Doog. Derek had actually scored eight goals in six games in Europe, an impressive record at that level of football. Had any of the present top stars achieved this in Europe they would have been praised on every sports page in the national papers, but it was very noticeable that Wolves's run in Europe failed to attract much attention from the national media.

By Christmas time we had gained the same number of points as at the same stage the previous season so we knew that a relegation battle was virtually out of the question. As it turned out, there was a controversial climax to the season, but before that we had more UEFA Cup games to deal with. It had been three months since our encounter with Carl Zeiss and our next opponents were a far bigger name than any team that we had faced before. Juventus were then, and still are now, one of the most famous names in Italian football and were going to be our stiffest test to date.

As we boarded the plane for our journey to Turin we were joined by one of the most famous figures in both English and Italian football, none other than the legendary John Charles. As an ex-Juventus player, John was to be our interpreter and, I suppose, goodwill mediator between the clubs. You would not have believed it – from the moment we walked into Turin airport you would have thought that royalty had arrived, such was the reaction when John Charles appeared. It was common knowledge that he was known as 'King John' and it was obvious that they truly regarded him as such. Our hotel was quite a drive from the centre of Turin so there was not quite as much fuss as there would have been in the centre of town with the return of our famous ambassador. Next day we went for a light training session at the Juventus training ground where, much to our surprise, there were at least 3,000 spectators who regularly paid to watch their favourite team train.

Our captain, Mike Bailey, was injured but had travelled with us to give us some moral support. He was a very keen collector of Capo di Monte figures, and where better than Italy to buy a piece to take home with him? John Charles heard about this and offered to come along with Mike and me to interpret for us. As we walked down the main street it was quite amazing how many people gathered around their long lost 'son', chattering away in Italian, patting him on the back and shaking his hand. I do not speak Italian but I am sure he managed to persuade the shopkeeper to reduce the price of the particular figure that 'Manny', as we used to call Mike, wanted to buy.

Mike was concerned, however, about how much duty he would have to pay on this quite valuable piece of Capo. 'Just tell them it was a present from their club to the captain of our club if you're stopped at customs,' I suggested. Mike thought about it for a few moments and then came up with a suggestion of his own. 'If you take it through customs for me and you get stopped, we can say that because I wasn't playing you were captain for the night and they presented it to you.'

'If we get a result tonight, I'll gladly do that for you,' I said.

As it happened we did get a result, a 1–1 draw thanks to a Jim McCalliog goal, and I did carry the figure through customs for Mike and did not get asked if I had anything to declare. Phil Parkes got a souvenir from Fabio Capello, who went on to manage Real Madrid. Gerry Taylor had passed the ball back to Phil and in those days goalkeepers could pick the ball up. As he did so Capello, who was following the ball in, stopped in front of Phil and spat all over his face. Phil did well to hold his temper as he felt it running down his cheeks and even to this day he feels like throwing a brick at the television every time he sees Capello on screen.

It was a great team performance to get a draw away to the mighty Juventus and Danny Hegan, playing his first game in Europe for us, played as well as anybody in the team. Even Bill McGarry got a little excited that night and was sent off from the bench by the referee. McGarry did not get too excited, though. When we got back to the hotel to have a meal he stood up at the table and declared that there was to be no beer. 'A couple of glasses of wine apiece and that's it,' he ordered. It was a good job he was not counting, because there were enough bottles on the tables to have one each, or maybe more. Somebody said 'What's that saying, when in Rome?' Well, we were not in Rome but it was near enough. We were in the same country and the Italians do like their wine, which was our excuse.

Big John Charles, of course, had no reason to adhere to McGarry's orders and made the most of the lavish spread of food and wine laid on by our hosts. So much so, in fact, that at the end of a very late night he needed a little extra help to get up the stairs and into his room. It was two of our biggest lads who helped him, Frank Munro and Phil Parkes, who were staying in the next room to his. Five minutes after leaving him in his room they heard him coughing loudly and, fearing he might be choking, went back into the room only to find that he had lit a cigarette. After settling him down again they left him to sleep peacefully for the few hours left before our flight home.

Before the flight home, Hugh Curran was to find out that Bill McGarry did not want him any more as he informed Hugh that Ian Greaves, the Bolton manager, would be waiting to have talks with him on landing at the airport. In the event, Hugh did not sign for Bolton and opted for Oxford instead, in September 1972, after a very creditable 47 goals in 91 first-class games for Wolves.

Back home we must have been running on the adrenalin from our great result in Italy, winning our next two League games both away from home – 2–1 at Southampton and 2–0 at Crystal Palace. After the Southampton match there was an unexpected call for me from Alf Ramsey. He wanted me to play in the Football League side against the Scottish League at Ayresome Park, Middlesbrough. As I told you earlier, I played six games for the England Youth team in 1960 and three of that side, Gordon West, Terry Venables and Martin Peters, went on to win full caps. I would have loved to have done the same. Many kind people tell me I was good enough to play for my country at the highest level but, unfortunately, old-style wingers like me were not in fashion after Alf Ramsey won the World Cup in 1966. When Ramsey first became England boss, he would employ wingers like Terry Paine, Peter Thompson and John Connelly, but he had ditched them all by the time we beat West Germany 4–2 on that famous day at Wembley. Not for nothing were that team known as the 'Wingless Wonders.'

That lone representative honour saw me help the Football League beat the Scottish League 3–2. Geoff Hurst, the hat-trick hero of the World Cup Final, and Newcastle hot shot Malcolm Macdonald were in the team, but our goals in came from midfield with Tony Currie scoring twice and Mike Doyle getting the other. I was a last-minute replacement and had to make the long drive to Middlesbrough, but I thought I had a decent game. However, I never received another call, confirming that my choice was just a stop-gap. I did at least have the pleasure that night of playing in the same team as the late, great Bobby Moore. The teams were:

Football League: Clemence (Liverpool); Lawler (Liverpool), Nish (Leicester), Doyle (Manchester City), Blockley (Coventry), Moore (West Ham), Hughes (Liverpool), Currie (Sheffield United), Macdonald (Newcastle), Hurst (West Ham), Wagstaffe (Wolves).
Scorers: Currie 2, Doyle.

Scottish League: Hunter (Kilmarnock); Brownlie (Hibernian), Forsythe (Partick Thistle), Jardine (Rangers), Connelly (Celtic), Blackley (Hibernian), McQuade (Partick Thistle), Phillip (Dundee), Stein (Rangers), Hay (Celtic), Ford (Hearts).
Scorers: McQuade, Stein.

My brief outing with the stars of England was soon forgotten and suddenly the return leg with Juventus was upon us, and even though we had home advantage we knew that it was going to be a very tough occasion. Our confidence was boosted by the statement made by John Charles after the first leg in Turin. 'You've won this quarter-final by your performance tonight. They expected to win the game easily and now you'll find that some of them won't fancy playing in the second leg.'

Just over 40,000 turned out at Molineux for that UEFA Cup quarter-final second leg, obviously the majority of them Wolves fans, and they were not disappointed with the result. Helmut Haller, the West German international, who scored in the 1966 World Cup Final, struck with a penalty for Juventus but goals from Derek Dougan and Danny Hegan won the game for us — Danny's being a 30-yard screamer that he reckons Dino Zoff, the great Italian goalkeeper, is still looking for. Danny had been marking Haller that night and thought that the only way the German could have scored a goal was from the penalty spot. Any future mention of that Juventus game would bring an immediate reaction from Danny — he would look in his pocket and cheekily declare 'It's OK lads, Helmut's still in here.'

Two weeks later we had a date with another famous club, Ferencvaros of Hungary, in the dizzy heights of the semi-final of a European competition, and once again we had been drawn away from home in the first leg. Budapest was the venue and, with skipper Mike Bailey still on the injured list, we were led out by Jimmy McCalliog for the Wednesday afternoon kick-off in the Nep Stadium. After 20 minutes John Richards got us off to a flyer with a great shot from the edge of the penalty area, but a penalty and a goal from the talented Florian Albert meant we went in 2–1 down at half-time, even though we had played reasonably well.

It looked as if we were going to go further behind in the second half when they were awarded another penalty. The player who had scored from the spot in the first half, Szoke, stepped forward to take it and, much to our delight, Phil Parkes saved it with his legs. This inspired us to go all out for the equaliser and Frank Munro scored with a powerful header late in the game. It was a great result, and more importantly we had two away goals in the bag which would mean a 0–0 or 1–1 result in the second leg would see us through.

Within an hour we were at the airport, ready to board our charter flight for our journey back to Birmingham. There were no delaying tactics like we had experienced in East Germany so it was up, up and away in no time and we were back home in Wolverhampton by early evening. A little later I was having a pint in the Mermaid when I was approached by a fellow customer.

'You are Dave Wagstaffe?' he quizzed with a puzzled look on his face.

'I am,' I replied.

'There's something wrong here,' he said.

'What do you mean?' I asked.

'Well, either you're not Dave Wagstaffe or the radio commentator made a big mistake,' he continued.

By now I was quite confused. 'Look, start at the beginning and tell me what the problem is,' I said.

'Well,' he began, 'I was listening to the commentary on the match in Budapest this afternoon and the commentator many times mentioned Dave Wagstaffe. It's now 20 minutes past eight and the landlord has just confirmed that you are Dave Wagstaffe so you couldn't possibly have played in Budapest this afternoon. Therefore, the commentator got it wrong.'

'Sit down and I'll explain to you,' I said. 'Most times travel arrangements are a bit hit and miss but on this occasion everything went as sweet as a nut.'

I then explained about the swift journey of the coach to Budapest airport, then straight on to the plane for a trouble-free flight, followed by a traffic-free journey back home to Wolverhampton. 'And here I am enjoying a pint in the Mermaid,' I added. After another pint I think I managed to convince him, but he still gave a perplexed shake of his head as he left the pub.

The second leg was to take place at Molineux two weeks later and we were a little disappointed that there were only 28,262 spectators for the semi-final of a major European competition. Then again, looking back at the fixtures, we had already played six games in the month of April and, although it was not as expensive as the present-day games, it was quite a lump out of anybody's money to watch every game. I was suspended for the game so young Steve Daley made his debut in Europe, and what a debut it was! He scored a goal in the first 30 seconds to put us 3–2 ahead in the tie. I must admit that I would not have scored that goal, because I would not have been as far up the field or as far infield as Steve. He set the tempo and we went further ahead when Frank Munro repeated his heroics of the first leg, heading in the second. When Ferencvaros were awarded a penalty you had to admire the courage of Szoke, who again tried to beat Big Phil but with the same result, Phil saving the kick with his legs once more. We eventually won 2–1 to go through to the Final 4–3 on aggregate.

Would you believe it? Twelve months previously, give or take a few days, we were in the Final of the Texaco Cup and now we were in the Final of the UEFA Cup. What a world of difference! This was a remarkable achievement when you consider none of the lads had played in a European competition before, nor had the management or staff been in charge of a side in a competition of this magnitude. It was all the more remarkable when you realised that John McAlle and Kenny Hibbitt had barely played two seasons of first-class football and John Richards was only just embarking on what would turn out to be a wonderful goalscoring career. Add to this the baptism of Steve Daley, scoring on his debut in Europe, and it was a satisfactory journey, well negotiated.

Then came the big anti-climax – we were to play Tottenham Hotspur! We had been all over Europe, gaining some wonderful results, only to meet an English team in the Final. It just did not seem right and all the lads were disappointed. No disrespect to Tottenham, but it took away the aura, the mystique of playing and travelling into the unknown. On the other hand, they probably felt the same about having to play against us after their own exploits in Europe. I had played 10 times against Spurs in seven years at Wolves so it was not anything special for me, nor for most of the others.

We usually played well against Tottenham, but in the first leg of the Final at Molineux we did not and that was to prove our downfall, losing 2–1. Any other time I would have fancied us to beat Spurs at Molineux, but we could only manage a penalty while Martin Chivers scored twice against us, his first being an absolute rocket of a shot. It was a bitter blow because we did not particularly like the Tottenham team nor any of the other London clubs for that matter. They always seemed to have this air of cockiness about them. It was not only the Wolves team who had this opinion. The rest of the League teams did not take kindly to teams from the capital either.

Wolves: Parkes; Shaw, Taylor; Hegan, Munro, McAlle; McCalliog, Hibbitt, Richards, Dougan, Wagstaffe.

Scorer: McCalliog (pen)

Tottenham: Jennings; Kinnear, Knowles; Mullery, England, Beal; Coates (Pratt), Perryman, Chivers, Peters, Gilzean.

Scorers: Chivers 2

Disheartened, and a goal down from the first leg, five days later we had to face a massively important League game against Leeds United, arguably the best team in the First Division at the time. Due to a fixture pile-up this game and that between Arsenal and Liverpool had to be played two days after Leeds had triumphed 1–0 over Arsenal in the FA Cup Final at Wembley. Traditionally, the Cup Final was the last game of the season and I cannot remember another occasion on which League games were played after the Wembley showpiece. After their Cup win, this match would determine whether or not Leeds did the double – FA Cup and First Division title in the same season. It was an incredibly important game for both the Leeds team and their fans, with a lot of money and prestige at stake. Liverpool could also have won the title as, going into these last two games, the top of the First Division (games and points) was: Derby 42–58, Leeds 41–57, Manchester City (42–57), Liverpool (41–56).

Two days before our game there was a telephone call to a Wolves player intimating that there would be some money for any of the Wolves team willing to just go through the motions, giving Leeds an easy ride to complete the double. After all, it was not going to make any difference to Wolves's status in the League should we lose.

The player in question who received this call did not like the situation and decided to tell Bill McGarry all about it. McGarry was absolutely furious and quickly ordered a team meeting on the morning of the game in the dressing room. I do not know whether he thought the room was bugged because he then marched us all into the centre circle of the empty stadium.

'I've heard what you've heard,' said the manager. 'If any of you don't perform tonight I will personally lead an inquiry as to why you didn't and, furthermore, should any of you be found guilty of not performing to the best of your ability I will make sure that you never kick a ball for this or any other club again.'

This statement really put the pressure on each and every one of us. Suppose you gave away a penalty, suppose you made a bad pass back to the 'keeper, suppose this, suppose that – anything that might lead to them scoring could point the finger at you. There was only one way to show that none of us was involved in anything underhand and that was to win the game.

What a game it was! I have never seen so many people in Molineux. Though 53,379 officially paid to get in, there must have been another 10,000 who did not. There was not a space anywhere. The game was played in a fantastic atmosphere with Frank Munro and Derek Dougan scoring the goals in a 2–1 victory. Billy Bremner scored for Leeds. At Highbury Liverpool were held to a goalless draw by Arsenal, but our win meant that if Liverpool had beaten the Gunners they would have taken the title on goal average. So the glory went to Derby. It does not matter after all these years whether a bribe was offered or not, but one thing is for sure – when you look back to Monday 8 May 1972 and see the score you can be sure that none of the Wolves team accepted one.

Nine days after the trauma and excitement of the Leeds game we had some unfinished business of our own at White Hart Lane – the second leg of the UEFA Cup Final. From the moment the referee started the game and Cyril Knowles came over and stood by me I knew I was not going to see a lot of the ball. He had been designated to man-mark me, which meant that he would be following me all over the pitch. When you are as tightly marked as this your teammates find it hard to supply you with the ball and consequently you are out of the game for long periods.

Neither team dominated the game but when Alan Mullery scored with a header to put them 3–1 in front in the tie, it was a big ask to try to pull the game back. I got a fortuitous rebound 30 yards out in the inside-right position and hit a hopeful left-foot shot at Pat Jennings's goal, the ball hitting the far post before going into the net. It was late in the game but gave us fresh hope and with the introduction of Mike Bailey and Hugh Curran for the last quarter we strived to get the equaliser, alas, to no avail. The final curtain came down on a journey that had taken us from Portugal to East Germany, from Italy to Hungary, only to end in tears in our own capital.

We were disappointed, dismayed, disconcerted and distraught, but in no way were we disgraced. At the final whistle we shook hands with our opponents and headed straight down the tunnel into the dressing room, leaving the Spurs team to be presented with the trophy. This was not sour grapes, it was a reaction to a collective upset at the outcome after such a long campaign.

Tottenham: Jennings; Kinnear, Knowles; Mullery, England, Beal; Coates, Perryman, Chivers, Peters, Gilzean.

Scorer: Mullery.

Wolves: Parkes; Shaw, Taylor; Hegan, Munro, McAlle; McCalliog, Hibbitt (Bailey), Richards, Dougan (Curran), Wagstaffe.

Scorer: Wagstaffe.

It had been a long season, with 57 competitive games played and thousands of miles of travelling, but it was not over yet by a long chalk. There were many more thousands of miles to travel and another 14 games to play. Bill McGarry had fixed up a tour which was to circumnavigate the world and take in a game approximately every two and a half days.

Four days after that exhilarating final game against Tottenham and a 12-hour flight to San Francisco we were to play an exhibition game against Aberdeen, with a further three games to follow against them in different cities. At the hotel the night before the game, Bill McGarry had announced that having brought a large squad of players he would be able to switch the team around so that everyone would get a rest in turn. That was alright in theory but he did not reckon on injuries and he had forgotten that he had left the Doog and Danny Hegan behind on international duty.

The first game, in San Francisco, was billed as an exhibition match and it was played like one – very poorly. We were still recovering from our last game, plus the 12-hour flight across the Atlantic and the time change. McGarry was not very pleased. We lost the game 3–1 with a very lethargic performance. His philosophy was that every game was a challenge and every effort should be made to win it.

The lads relaxed with a few beers in a San Francisco bar that evening and for once it was good to get an early night ready for our plane journey to Seattle the next day. We did not fare any better in Seattle, losing 3–0, and once again Bill McGarry was furious. After such a difficult and successful season we should have been allowed to relax and try to enjoy the arduous tour that was in front of us. A wealthy doctor, who had sponsored the game, put on a lovely buffet and drinks back at his mansion on the outskirts of the city, but the lads were a little hesitant to let themselves enjoy the party because of the mood of our manager. Fortunately he retired early and we were able to let our hair down.

From Seattle we moved on to Canada and the beautiful city of Vancouver. It really was a fantastic place, with wonderful scenery in whichever direction we looked. After a light training session to get rid of the stiffness of the travel and a light lunch, the lads were sitting in the front lounge of the hotel waiting for the coach to arrive to take us to the stadium. We were just chatting idly and generally lounging about when a middle-aged gentleman literally burst through the front doors, full of the joys of spring as it were, seeming as if he had had a drink. He looked around the room and asked out loud 'Why is everybody so gloomy? My name's Brad. I've just won thousands of dollars at the races so let me buy you all a drink and cheer you up.'

We explained that it was very kind of him but we were off to play a soccer game and that we could not possibly accept a drink from him before the match. 'We'll be back later,' we told him and to pacify him we said that if he was still around when we got back we would have a drink with him then.

'I'll do better than that,' he declared, calling over the duty manager. 'Because it's the Queen's birthday holiday weekend and these lads are from England, see to it that when they return from the match there's enough food and drink laid on for them in the suite on the first floor.'

Reaching in his pocket he handed a wad of notes to the duty manager who said 'OK, leave it with me,' and walked off down a corridor. 'And invite some women,' shouted Brad, laughing coarsely and loudly, and with that he walked off towards the lift with the parting shot 'I'll see you lads later.' Just then the coach arrived and off we went to the stadium for our third encounter with Aberdeen. We fared much better this time and won the game 3–0, which put McGarry in a better mood, at least for a while.

We were all responsible for our own kit on this tour, each one of us having a sports bag containing two pairs of boots, a pair of trainers, some training kit and a tracksuit. After the match Sammy Chung, as he did after each match, made sure that every one of us cleaned our boots before putting them away in our bags. We were not used to this but it was a job that had to be done and in actual fact it stood us in very good stead about a week later.

Back at the hotel we dumped the sports bags in our rooms and headed for the bar. Sitting having a drink in the bar, none of us had given much thought to the promises that Brad had made about food and drink when he appeared and said 'Everything is ready for you in the Athlone Suite.' Nobody needed telling twice, so we scampered up the stairs into the suite. There was no sign of our friend Brad but there were quite a few of the hotel guests in there, whom he had obviously invited after we had left to go to play our game.

There was a wonderful buffet laid on and a waiter behind a long table serving iced beers or spirits of your choice. Soon the rest of our party had been ushered in, including Bill McGarry, Sammy and Toby, our physio, and with the influx of some more of the hotel guests and piped music it was quite a good party atmosphere. However, there was one thing missing – our host Brad.

'I wonder where Brad's got to?' I asked Mike Bailey.

'He's probably having a lie down after a few drinks,' replied Mike.

'I'm worried,' I said. 'I know we saw him slip that duty manager a pile of dollars earlier today but there wasn't enough to pay for all this. Suppose he's done a runner? We're going to be left with a big bill at the end of the night.'

As soon as Mike realised he might have to shell out a few dollars he was on the case. 'Let's go and find that manager,' he said, beginning to panic.

'I'll go,' I said. 'Have another drink. I don't like to see you worrying about money,' I added, laughing.

Downstairs at reception I found the manager and explained that we were a little worried as to the whereabouts of Brad and about the bill for the mountain of food and the drinks being consumed upstairs.

'Don't worry,' he said. 'Brad went off in a taxi and said that he'd be back later and, most importantly, he has left more than enough money to cover any costs upstairs. I went back and reported the conversation to Mike, who sighed with relief at knowing that he was not going to have to spend any money.

A short time later, Brad made an appearance accompanied by five females. Heads were turned and, being at the far end of the suite, we could not quite see what was going on because the place had quite a few people in it by then. It was not long before Brad wandered up with his entourage. 'Hi, guys,' he drawled, 'thought I'd bring a bit of female glamour to the proceedings.' McGarry almost choked on his drink because it was obvious that the women accompanying Brad were all prostitutes. McGarry walked over to Brad and said in a stifled voice so that the whole room could not hear 'Get these f*****g women out of here.'

'You're forgetting something,' replied Brad. 'It's my party and I'll invite who I like.'

McGarry quietly put his drink down and left the room. I do not know if he complained to the management or whether some of the other guests objected to being in the company of five prostitutes, but half an hour later Brad was seen handing over another dollop of dollars and the girls left the scene to go back to work! We had a pleasant few beers but not too late a night because next day we had a long flight to Los Angeles.

It was déjà vu in LA. We had been booked into the same hotel, the Sheraton West, which had been our headquarters for the 1967 tournament and my room overlooked the swimming pool where five years earlier that little orphan boy was carried out of the pool and brought back to life at the side of it. The match itself was between the same teams who contested that epic Final in the same stadium, the Coliseum, all those years ago. That Final ended with a 6–5 win to Wolves, but this one was to be an exhibition match. It was played in the afternoon in a temperature high in the 80s and the players more or less strolled through it, with Wolves emerging 4–0 winners. Four exhibition games against Aberdeen and we had only another 10 matches before we went home.

Our next hurdle was a 17-hour flight to New Zealand with a stop in Hawaii to refuel, and guess who was not with us? Bill McGarry. He was the one who had sanctioned such a gruelling tour and he was not going to be there. When we arrived at Los Angeles airport to catch the flight to New Zealand McGarry disappeared to catch a flight to who knows where. However, arriving on a flight from London to join our flight to New Zealand and the rest of our tour in Australia were the Doog and Danny Hegan, fresh from Northern Ireland's 1–0 victory over England at Wembley a few days before. They were both in high spirits, with Danny carrying a small Irish flag when they met us, the emphasis being on spirits after a 12-hour flight from England with the bar open.

The Irish had won 1–0 at Wembley in the Home International Championship, thanks to a goal from Terry Neill. The fact they had lost their opening game 2–0 to Scotland and could only draw the final one 0–0 with Wales at Wrexham was quietly ignored by Messrs Dougan and Hegan. I sat on the back three seats with the two of them and heard a detailed account of how the Wembley goal was scored. Then the bar opened as soon as the plane levelled out, then came another account of the game, then another drink, then the game again and so it went on…all the way to New Zealand. By the end of the journey I knew about every move that was made and every ball that was kicked during that game at Wembley. We had also had plenty to drink by the time we got to New Zealand and just wanted to get to the hotel to get some sleep. Danny and Derek must have felt far worse than me. They had had 12 hours start in the drinking stakes.

On leaving the plane, first stop was the customs shed. A very stern-looking customs officer got all the lads together and lined us up in front of a couple of long trestle tables. 'Right, fellas,' he ordered, 'I want every pair of football boots placed on the tables in front of you.'

'Oh no,' muttered one of the lads, 'he's taking the p**s.'

'Oh no I'm not,' replied the officer.

'Come on, lads, the sooner you get this over with the quicker you'll get to your destination.'

It was not a difficult ask really, because we all had our boots in our sports bags, which we were carrying as hand luggage. Soon there were at least 40 pairs of boots in a long line in front of the customs officer. He picked up every individual boot, turned it over and carefully inspected it.

'Absolutely excellent,' he exclaimed, after getting to the end of the line and inspecting the last pair of boots. 'OK, fellas, thank you very much, you may now continue your journey.'

'Hold on,' said one of the lads, 'are you sure you're not taking the piss? You've looked at all our boots and nothing else. Now you're telling us to go.'

'That's all I needed to see,' replied the officer and explained the reason why. 'The main industry of this country is lamb and should we lose this it would be a national disaster, so every care is taken to make sure that no considerable deposits of rogue soil are introduced into our country. Had I found such amounts on the bottom of your boot they would have been put in the incinerator. Fortunately, they were spotlessly clean so you are all free to leave the airport.'

Just imagine what would have happened had we not cleaned our boots after the last match in Los Angeles. They would have all been burned and with 10 games in front of us we would have had no boots to play in.

We were given a warm reception when we arrived in Christchurch to play our first game in New Zealand. The staff at the hotel were welcoming and friendly and our rooms were clean and comfortable. On 2 June we played a team selected from the South Island, winning 2–0 in a match played in a very sporting spirit. In the evening there was a reception for us in the local social club and we were treated to the full Maori welcome from the locals dressed in their traditional regalia. A couple of days later we were on the move again, to Wellington in the more northerly of the two islands.

Our game against a Wellington Select XI was scheduled for Monday afternoon, 5 June, and it was the Queen's birthday bank holiday weekend. Just like 12 days ago in Canada the Queen's birthday was celebrated by a long weekend. In Canada it was on the nearest Monday to 24 May, whereas in New Zealand it was the first Monday in June. So, for the second time in less than a fortnight, after a resounding 6–0 win over the Select XI, we had to go out that night and celebrate the Queen's birthday with a few drinks. Cheers, Ma'am!

Our third game, against an Auckland side, was a low-key affair and I cannot remember the score, but once again we were warmly welcomed and given a good reception after the game. We were reluctant to leave New Zealand after what seemed such a short stay. The people were so friendly and the atmosphere so laid back and relaxing, but it was time to move on to a much bigger and busier country – Australia.

Going through customs at Melbourne airport, the Doog was asked, as we all were, 'Have you anything to declare?'

'Only a hundredweight of marijuana,' he replied.

The words had hardly got out of his mouth when the officer called a colleague and Doog was marched off to an interview room. They kept him there for a good hour while we were sat on the coach outside waiting to be taken to our hotel. It was petty, really, because it was obvious that Derek was joking, but after getting some stick from the lads for keeping us all waiting he was happy to let the embarrassing incident die a death.

Customs officers can go over the top at times and there was an incident at Heathrow after we arrived back from a friendly game in Greece a few years before. Just before we left for the airport, the officials of the Greek club that we had played presented every one of us with a small cardboard case containing three bottles — two of Greek wine and one of Ouzo. The lads had already bought their duty-free booze on the way out to Greece so these presentation packs put everybody over the limit. It would have been a little ungrateful if we had refused these presents, so each of us carried them as hand luggage and consequently when we all went through customs at Heathrow each person was carrying one of these packs. It was sod's law that one of us would be stopped by a customs officer and it just happened to be full-back Gerry Taylor.

Gerry tried to explain the situation, but the officer did not want to know and insisted that Gerry had to pay duty on the gift from the Greeks.

'Look,' said Gerry, turning round and pointing to the rest of us, 'I'm not telling lies, all the lads have got one.'

'Right,' said the officer, 'in that case if any of those lads are over the limit they will also have to pay extra duty.'

We were all standing there watching this, absolutely gobsmacked. In desperation Gerry said 'OK, I don't want this pack' and promptly put it on the floor and added 'You can keep it.'

Almost as one the rest of us put the cardboard packs down and said 'You can keep ours, too.'

By this time we had attracted a lot of attention and a senior customs officer appeared on the scene. As we were all walking away, leaving the floor space littered with these packs, the senior officer shouted 'You can't leave those there!'

'We have done,' shouted one of the lads, 'you can have them.'

'Just wait a moment,' pleaded the customs officer, who by now was in a very embarrassing predicament. He had a quick tête-à-tête with his colleague and the senior of the officers said 'It's quite obvious that you were presented with these because of the fact that everyone of you has one. So, on this occasion, you may keep the presentation packs and no duty will be charged.'

Common sense should have prevailed at the outset when Gerry proved to the other officer that everybody had been given a pack. I must admit that I was a bit put out when it looked as though we were going to leave all that booze to the customs men but then very relieved when they let us have it back.

Returning to our Australian trip and Melbourne, where we had a date with the Australian national team…our bus drove into the Olympic Stadium before the game and two large wrought-iron gates closed behind it. As I stepped off the bus I heard somebody shouting to me from these gates and walked back to see who it was. I could not pinpoint anybody that I immediately recognised at first, but on nearing the gates I spotted the person shouting – an old classmate from North Manchester Grammar School whom I had not seen since 1957. It was I.D.G. Davies, known to all his classmates as 'Idge'.

I had a chat with him before the game and, of course, a quick drink with him after the match, sharing some laughs about our schooldays. I have never seen him since, but how about this for coincidence? Many years later my old pal and ex-neighbour Frank Munro emigrated to Australia to wind down his career and build a future in a new place, Melbourne in fact. After spending years there he decided to return home and settle in Wolverhampton and guess who bought his house off him when he left? Yes, my old classmate 'Idge' Davies.

Our match in Melbourne was an ill-tempered affair because, as you know, the Aussies have always been great competitors and, not being as skilful as our players, resorted to bullying tactics. They were absolutely tenacious in everything they did and even the hardest members of our team were spared no mercy. Hugh Curran, in particular, was a marked man and, believe you me, when he came off the field he was a 'marked' man in the other sense of the word. As you can imagine, fatigue had set in by now with most of the squad after all the travelling and playing of the past months. In fact, we did not have a fully fit squad by then and some of the lads were having to play nursing injuries. Consequently, we were not playing at 100 per cent but, conversely, they were supposed to be friendly games. In the eyes of an Aussie there was no such thing. We lost the match 2–0 and as a result our pride was dented, more so because of the way we lost. We were kicked off the park.

We were to play them again in Sydney and the lads were determined that it was not going to end in the same result. The Australian team just happened to be on the same flight as us, which could have caused a few problems had Lofty and Frank not been able to keep Hughie in check while they were having a drink on the plane. Hughie was still incensed about the kicking he had got during the 'friendly', and when Hughie had got one or two drinks down him he could get the blinkers on and only see what he wanted to see – the man who kicked him was only eight or nine seats away having a laugh with his mates, which was infuriating Mr Curran.

Lofty and Frank persuaded him to leave anything he wanted to do until the next day when we were to play them in Sydney. Hughie scored in a match we drew 2–2 but managed to control himself until, surprise, surprise, he was kicked again. He could not contain himself and gave the Aussie a smash, knocking him down, for which he was immediately sent off. After the game, John Ireland, who had taken it upon himself to be the man in charge in the absence of Bill McGarry, admonished Hughie in front of the lads – for not hitting the Aussie hard enough!

Back at the hotel we had our meal and were soon out on the town. We had to be, it was the Queen's Birthday long weekend so we had to celebrate that, didn't we? The Queen's Birthday in Australia is celebrated over the second Monday in June. So in the space of a little over three weeks in three different countries we had drunk a toast to Her Majesty. Cheers, again, Ma'am!

They have got some lovely place names in Australia. Wollongong, just outside Sydney, and Toowoomba, just outside Brisbane, to name but two. Try talking about those when you have had a few. My favourite, and I wish I had been able to play there, was Wagga Wagga. I could have written my own headline – 'Waggy a Wagga Wagga winger!' Unfortunately, we flew straight over it on our journey from Melbourne to Sydney, so I only got to see it from 30,000ft. Moving further up the east coast, our next stop was Brisbane. We were not used to delays, but the amount of travelling that we were doing meant that, by the law of averages, somewhere along the line there would be technical hitches. Up to then most of our flights had been alright, give or take 15 minutes. This was the day. We were three hours late, which meant that we did not arrive at our hotel until 10.30pm, and by the time the rooms were sorted out it was 11pm and everybody was really tired.

'OK, lads,' said Sammy Chung before we all retired, 'the restaurant is through that door on the left, just past reception, and breakfast is 8am. You will find that there has been a cold meal left for you in your rooms and there are facilities to make hot drinks. See you in the morning.'

So off we went to our rooms. I say 'rooms' but the hotel was more like a motel with chalets, consisting of a small lounge, a double bedroom and a bathroom, spread around the grounds. Mike and I found our chalet and saw that there had been two seafood salads laid out on the coffee table, plated up with those plastic covers sitting on the top. Seafood was in abundance in Australia, with crayfish, prawns, crab and the like as popular as meat pies in Manchester. Unusually, I was not at all hungry. I was more tired than anything else, having had a few drinks on the plane. 'Carry on, Mike,' I said, 'you can have mine as well if you want. I'm going straight to bed.'

Unknown to us these seafood platters had been delivered to our chalets at 7pm by the waiting staff because, of course, we were due to arrive at the hotel at 7.30. So I went to bed and Mike ate his meal and part of mine before he too went to bed. At 3am I was woken by the sound of Mike being violently sick in the bathroom. Over the years, sharing a room with him all over the world, I had heard Mike being sick before, as he had also heard me – but this was different. Mike was heaving and retching like never before. I was trying to pacify him but he seemed in a world of his own. I got him to back to his bed, but within 15 minutes he was up and was back in the bathroom vomiting again.

I coaxed Mike back to his bed again and sat by him, willing him to go back to sleep, but he was tossing and turning in a very agitated state. By this time I was becoming quite concerned. He was not getting any better and when he started retching again, rolling around the bathroom floor, I felt I had to do something about it. I picked up the phone with the intention of speaking to reception in order to get Sammy Chung or Toby Andersen's room number. There was no answer from reception and I could not phone the emergency services because to get an outside line one had to go via reception. I decided to walk up to the reception area, but when I approached it I could see that it was in complete darkness. I could not have expected anything else as it was by now 4am. There was not a light on anywhere else for that matter so I headed back to the chalet where Mike was still groaning about how ill he felt. I could not think what to do as I did not possess any medical skills to deal with his condition and, with nobody to call on, I was in a real quandary. Again I got him back to bed and gave him glasses of cold water, but he was still in a bad way. I sat by his bed again, looking at my watch, willing the hands to go round so that the rest of the world would wake up.

Soon it was light and I knew that Sammy would be up early, but I still did not know which chalet he was in. If only someone would open reception. Mike had by then settled down somewhat but he still was not right. Eventually I heard a car and returned up the driveway to see if it was anybody who could help and, to my delight, I saw a person walking up the steps and opening up reception. Within minutes they had got in touch with Sammy, who then oversaw the situation, relieving me of the problem, and managed to get a doctor to see Mike. The diagnosis was a severe case of food poisoning, obviously the result of the previous night's seafood platter. The doctor explained that with seafood even an amount as small as one prawn could cause a really bad bout of food poisoning if it had gone off. The doctor prescribed something to make Mike feel better with orders to stay in bed but not for too long because once again we were off on our travels.

Back on the road again, and we were off to Adelaide with our skipper feeling much better. Sitting next to him on the plane I kept telling him that he ought to drink more alcohol to kill all those food bugs. 'I'm trying, I'm trying,' he said, sipping his Bacardi and coke.

Obviously, while on tour we regularly phoned home. To make a call from your room in the hotel you would have to go through the switchboard at reception and on one such occasion, phoning Barbara and the kids to see if they were OK, I encountered a major problem. Contacting reception was no problem and the receptionist did not have to ask my room number because it was lit up on her board. As soon as I asked to make a call to England and gave her my name there was a brief silence.

'Hello?' I said.

'Oh, I'm sorry,' she replied, 'may I get back to you when I have completed the connection?'

She sounded a little taken aback but after several minutes the phone in my room rang.

'I'm sorry I haven't been able to get your call yet,' she said. 'In the meantime could you possibly pop down to reception. The manager has a matter he'd like to discuss with you.'

Puzzled, I went down to reception to see him. 'Come in,' he said, holding open his office door and offering me a seat.

'I'm sorry that we are unable to let you make your call to England,' he began.

'Why not?' I interrupted.

'Well, there's the matter of 48 dollars unpaid phone bills from your stay here last year.'

I was gobsmacked. 'I've never been here before,' I replied. 'In fact, I've never even been in this country before.'

'Here are the photocopies of the phone calls made last year from here to England,' he said.

They did have a Mr Wagstaff at the top of the copies but without an E and I pointed out 'I have an E on the end of my name and besides I've told you that I've never been in this country before.'

'I'm sorry,' he insisted, 'the football team from England stayed here last year and Mr Wagstaff left without paying for his phone calls. How many teams from England have Mr Wagstaff playing for them?'

'Just a moment,' I said, 'do you have the names of the other members of the team that stayed here?'

When he showed me a copy of the register I realised what had happened. Twelve months before the FA had sent a representative touring party to Australia. Among this touring party was a certain Mr Ken Wagstaff, a Mansfield player. Apparently it was not the same hotel manager as the previous year but it was the same receptionist who had cleverly picked up on Wagstaff, knowing that there were unpaid telephone bills in that name. It took a lot of convincing but as the real story unfolded the hotel manager grasped the plot and was finally sure that I did not owe the hotel any money and even offered for the hotel to pay for the telephone call to Barbara because of my inconvenience. Damn! There was nobody in when I at last got to make that free call.

After a couple of minor games against local opposition our tour was grinding to a halt as we reached our last port of call on the south-western tip of Australia – Perth. On our last night before the scheduled flight home we were given a rousing send-off at a local social club. There was food and drink and entertainment laid on and we even provided our own artist, yes, Hugh Ko-ran. He finished off the evening with his by now well-known rendition of *Don't Laugh At Me*.

Next day the plane was packed and, not having designated seats, we were dotted about all over the plane. The jumbo seats of nine in a row were arranged with three by one window, then an aisle, four in the middle, then another aisle and then two by the other window. I was unlucky and could only get the second one in the row of four. It was going to be a long journey and I was sat cramped with three strangers. I was not looking forward to it in the least. Then my luck changed after our first top at Kuala Lumpa. The three sitting with me got off the plane, along with many more people, leaving lots of spaces. I had now a row of four seats to myself and was able to detach a couple of the arms so that I could lie down. Finally, after further refuelling stops at Bahrain and Athens, we arrived at Heathrow 32 hours after leaving Perth.

It had been a long, arduous tour, playing 14 games in 31 days and travelling virtually right around the world, visiting Canada, the US, New Zealand and Australia, not forgetting, by the way, three times joining in birthday bashes for the Queen. In fact it had been a long, long season for us all, taking everything into account. I had played 39 of the 42 League games, two in the FA Cup, one Football League Cup game, 11 UEFA Cup games and one Football League representative game. That was a total of 68 games and thousands and thousands of miles travelled. I think you will agree it had been quite a season.

Mr Chairman

As you know, my first close encounter with John Ireland was the Ipswich affair which, as promised by him at that board meeting, was never mentioned again. After that incident, whenever we were away on tour in different parts of the world he seemed to rely on me to be his link with the players. It was not the normal thing for a player to fraternise with the chairman of the club that he played for, but whenever his fellow directors or the manager were not about he liked to think he was part of the party and more often than not it was me he came to.

I never saw him in a really bad mood. Even when confronted by the players about some extra money before our first trip to the United States he did not hold it against us. Ronnie Allen, off his own back, had told us that we would get £10 a day food money — we would not be eating at our hotel — and something like £20 per game that we won. These were nothing like the figures that had been offered by our sponsors, but when John Ireland found out that it was rumoured that the team would refuse to go, except on these terms, he called a meeting with us and we will all never forget his words.

'You players are holding a gun to my head,' he said but he promised that he would take on board our demands. Whether or not Wolverhampton Wanderers FC paid the shortfall we never knew, but the terms that I have mentioned were the terms on which we went to America.

It was on the tour to America that the players really got to know John Ireland. He had no official duties to perform and had nothing more to do than be a tourist with the obligatory camera round his neck, wandering around mostly on his own. He would always join us in the bar late on at night for a nightcap and, as I mentioned, we would not go to bed without a rendition of his own personal anthem *Molly Malone,* to which we all sang along. It was bedtime after that and he would whisper to me 'Waggy, make sure I get to my room OK.' At the time I was sharing a room with Ernie Hunt and the pair of us would coax him up the steps and to his room. Over the years this became the norm when he had had a few too many and on each occasion that I got him to his room he would make sure that he gave me all his money, be it dollars, lire, schillings or whatever, and ask me to keep it safe until the next day.

America was not really the place for him because he hated the heat and could always be found sitting in the shade sweating profusely, puffing away on his pipe with that damn camera hanging round his neck. We saw him point it at hundreds of different scenes and objects over the years but, as I have already mentioned, none of us ever saw the end product. Come to think of it, strangely enough he never took a picture of any of the lads. Perhaps he did not want any of us asking to see them when we got back home!

Talking of sitting in the shade reminds me of an incident in Texas. During a conversation with Mike Bailey and myself a few days earlier Mr Ireland had mentioned that his doctor had warned him about his drinking habits and had told him to try to leave it until at least 9 o'clock at night before he had his first drink. Trying in our way to sympathise with him we both said we would watch out for him and help him to keep to that. Anyway, one of our generous hosts had arranged a barbecue for us at his ranch in Texas. It was a beautiful sunny afternoon, as was every afternoon in Texas for months on end. The temperature was in the 80s. The steaks were grilling and the beers were on ice. Bottles of every spirit you could think of were lined up on the bar; you could not wish for anything more pleasant on a lazy afternoon. Country and western music was playing in the background and the whole scene looked like something from a Western movie set. The lads were really enjoying this, a big fat Texan steak with a lovely salad and an iced beer to wash it down, plus plenty of other things to eat.

John Ireland had settled for a chair in the shade of a tree about 30 yards away. Even though he had on his straw hat and khaki jacket, he still looked as though he was being baked.

'What will you have to drink?' asked one of the hosts, walking over to him.

'Two glasses of iced water, please,' he replied politely.

'Are you sure that's all you want?' quizzed the host. 'We have a variety of refreshments.'

'Thank you, but that will do me fine,' said John.

'Good for him,' said Mike Bailey as he heard what the chairman had ordered.

Mike's opinion changed a short time later as he noticed something strange going on.

'What's that old devil up to?' he asked.

'What do you mean?' I replied.

'I've been watching him and he keeps fumbling about down the side of that chair,' said Mike.

'Let's go and ask him, then,' I said.

'You go that way and I'll go this way and we'll meet behind the tree he's sitting under,' said Mike, 'and we'll be able to see what he's up to.'

'OK,' I said.

Here we were, in the middle of Texas, like two Apaches circling round trying to ambush a cowboy. In my own mind I already knew what he was up to. We met behind the tree and had a clear view of what he was doing. Just as I suspected, he had half a bottle of whisky down by the side of his chair and he had emptied one glass so he was able to pour the Scotch into it and then add a nice drop of iced water from the other glass.

'You rascal,' said Mike, laughingly, as we both stepped out from either side of the tree, making him jump.

'What do you mean?' he said, trying to hide the bottle under the chair.

'You told us a few days ago that you were under strict orders from the doctor not to have a drink before 9 o'clock at night,' said Mike emphatically.

John looked at the pair of us, looked at his watch and calmly announced 'What's the panic? It's 9 o'clock back home!'

To that, Mike and I had no answer and we wandered off to get another iced beer. From that day on John Ireland always gave the same excuse when drinking – 'It's 9 o'clock in England.'

Having a nightcap with John Ireland in the hotel bar in San Francisco, the bartender was relating the time when all the crew who were making the film *Bullitt* stayed at the hotel. Obviously, the main star, Steve McQueen, did not stay there, but lots of the rest of the cast did.

'I'll bet that was fun,' said John Ireland, 'having all those cowboys in the bar. Did you slide the drinks along the bar to them, like they do in the films?'

The barman smiled politely, obviously puzzled as to what this English gentleman was referring to. While the barman was serving somebody else we tried to explain to John that just because it was called *Bullitt* it did not mean it was cowboy film. We did not bother to go into the fact it was spelled differently!

'Steve McQueen starred in it,' we said.

'Steve who?' he replied.

We gave up. It was late and he had had a few so there was not much point in pursuing matters. Next morning on the coach going to training we passed the famous cobbled zig-zag area that Steve McQueen drove down in the film. As the driver was explaining this the word '*Bullitt*' jogged the chairman's memory now he was sober.

'I don't quite understand this,' he said. 'They didn't have cars in cowboy films.'

We smiled and quickly changed the subject.

It was mostly on tours that we mixed with John Ireland, but there were other occasions in the Wolves Social Club, a place of which he was very proud, when we were in a position to have drink with him. If we had played away from home and arrived back at the ground with time for a couple of drinks before going home to take our wives out for the evening we would call in the social club, which was in Waterloo Road, right next to the ground. John Ireland was of similar habit and we knew that we would get a drink on his tab if we were in his company. The public never got to see this other side of him, his generosity and his dry sense of humour

Being the Wolves Social Club, there were obviously always a lot of supporters in there and they would come and ask for autographs and want to talk to you for a few minutes, which we were used to and did not mind. However, for John Ireland it was different because, being the top man in the club, people wanted to tell him how to run it, who to buy and other bits of advice. It was embarrassing for him, but he went along with it and then he would play his ace. 'I take on board your suggestions,' he would say 'and you have some good ideas, but just at this moment in time I'm having a drink and a chat with some of the players.' He would then produce his diary and proceed to tell whoever was giving him the third degree that he would be free on such and such a morning at 11 o'clock and would be delighted to take their conversation and suggestions further at that time. This always did the trick and even if the person tried to continue the conversation he would say 'Save it until we meet in the week' and that would leave him free to have his drink and a chat with the lads. I was witness to his ploy quite a few times and to my knowledge nobody ever turned up at the allotted time. He had made his point that most people who came to him telling him to do this and that and how to run Wolverhampton Wanderers were talking in drink and did not have the courage to turn up for a meeting or had forgotten that they had booked an appointment with him.

One night in the Social Club we were at a function and the drinks had just started flowing. The chairman was not even in our company that night and the drinks must have flowed a lot more for him. I had just walked over to see him when he announced 'Waggy, they've got me drunk.'

'Who were they?' I thought. I could not see anyone near him. Lofty Parkes and Willie Carr had just joined me to have a drink with him, but they could both see what a state John Ireland was in.

'David,' he said.

'He's called me David,' I thought, 'what's coming next?'

'I would like you to drive me home in my car.'

'Certainly, Mr Chairman,' I replied. 'No problem.'

I had only had a couple by then but there was a problem. John Ireland's car was an Aston Martin DB6 – a James Bond car – and I had never driven one before. Willie said that he and Lofty would follow me to the chairman's house and bring me back to the social club. We managed to get him into the passenger seat, then I looked at the dashboard. It looked like the cockpit of an aeroplane, there were that many dials.

'Push that button there,' he said, 'that's the starter. Just find a gear and stay in it till we get home.'

I did as I was told and then we were mobile. Down Newhampton Road and up Tettenhall Road. I was beginning to enjoy driving the DB6 but soon we were at his house. I drove him straight up to the front steps, and as I went round to the passenger side to help him out the light over the front steps came on, the front door opened and out came his wife.

'What's happened?' she asked, concerned that he might be ill.

'Nothing,' I replied, 'he's just had one too many and didn't want to drive home.'

She tutted. 'Not again, John,' she said to him.

'Oh, hello, dear,' he exclaimed, recognising his wife as I helped him up the steps.

'Come on, let's get you inside,' she said as I got him to the top step.

Suddenly, he turned back round, facing his car, and announced 'I shan't be long, dear, I've got to give Waggy a lift to the social club.'

'No, no, bedtime for you,' I said.

'I insist,' he stammered drunkenly.

'Look, Willie Carr and Lofty are in that car behind,' I explained. 'They're taking me back.'

He finally relented and Mrs Ireland ushered him inside.

'Goodnight, Mr Chairman.'

For an intelligent businessman, John Ireland did make some bumbling mistakes at times and make himself look a fool, but the lads were used to it and laughed along with him. They all thought the world of him.

On a pre-season Norway-Sweden tour somebody had arranged a fishing trip for us in one of the fjords. It was not fishing as we know it, with rods, but just dangling a hand line over the side of the boat trying to entice some young codling to take the bait. It was a pleasant afternoon and, of course, the chairman had come along just to be one of the lads. I think we caught only a couple of fish between all of us but it was a relaxing way to spend the afternoon. As we pulled alongside the quay to get off the boat it had become quite choppy and the vessel was bobbing up and down. The best way to get off was to wait for the boat to rise and jump off, but if that was easy for us players we just knew that it was going to be a problem for the chairman.

John Ireland stood on the prow like Captain Pugwash. The boat was bobbing and he was biding his time, waiting for the right moment to take off. 'Now,' shouted the lads but, his reactions being rather slow, he jumped as the boat was at its highest point and went overboard. He was soon fished out and his main concern, having hit the quay wall, was for his pipe, which was in with his tobacco. He feared that he had broken the pipe but all turned out well and he was back in the bar that night, puffing away at it with his whisky in the other hand.

Deep down, he was a very old-fashioned person. He dressed old-fashioned and some of his mannerisms were old-fashioned at times. He had not caught up with modern everyday things. After taking him to his room one night, having had a session in the bar, when I left he had put his shoes outside the door in the hotel corridor, expecting them to be cleaned and returned to him next morning. This practice in hotels had not been in operation for years and, consequently, when he got up next day his shoes had disappeared without trace. He thought that some of the lads had played a joke on him but I can assure you that they had not. Someone had taken a shine to the lovely pair of brown brogues and made off with them. He did not look the part next morning at breakfast dressed in a suit with a pair of sandals on his feet.

John always seemed to be mislaying or dropping things, or breaking things, and this was when he had not had a drink! I remember a time in Malta when we were all outside the hotel waiting for him, having been invited to an official lunch where he would naturally address our hosts to thank them. We were all sat patiently on the bus when he appeared from the hotel door. What a sight! His glasses had been stuck together with a piece of elastoplast and were balancing precariously at an angle on his nose, just like Jack Duckworth in TV's *Coronation Street*. Stuck to his face were four or five blobs of toilet paper. As he boarded the bus all the players were quietly smiling and also feeling sorry for the state he was in. As he took his seat, fellow director Wilf Sproson went mad at him. 'John, look at the state of you. You're the chairman of Wolverhampton Wanderers Football Club. You cannot represent the club looking like that. What's happened to you?'

John Ireland sheepishly explained. 'I dropped my glasses and while I was looking for them I trod on them, breaking them. It took me quite some time to mend them and realising that I was going to be late I had to shave in a hurry and you can see the result. These things happen, Wilf.'

'Well, you look an absolute disgrace,' said Wilf Sproson, lowering his voice, realising that everyone on the bus was listening intently. 'I suppose I will have to stand in for you on this occasion.'

As things turned out, neither of them had to make a speech. It proved to be an official dinner but a low-key one. We were taken to the other side of the island to a restaurant that specialised in a local dish, rabbit pie, and it was absolutely delicious. The only person who had to be thanked was the chef.

After an incident at a hotel in Atlanta he did not speak to me for a couple of days — until he found out the true story. The whole party was waiting at the reception desk of the hotel for our room numbers and keys when five very well-dressed young ladies breezed into the reception area, looking for all the world like the Supremes. They all seemed in a really jolly mood and one of the girls shouted over 'What are you guys, some sort of team?'

'Yeah, a soccer team,' replied somebody.

'From England?' she asked then addressed the other girls. 'Girls, a real live soccer team from England.'

'You're welcome to come up to our party,' said one of the other girls. 'We've hired suite number 1500 to celebrate a joint birthday so come on up and enjoy yourselves.'

They disappeared into the lift as we finished sorting out the keys and the rooms.

'Where did they say the party was?' John Ireland asked.

'Suite 1500,' I replied.

'Will the lads be going to the party?' he asked.

'I don't know. We'll probably meet in the bar and decide what we're going to do,' I told him.

About an hour later, after getting washed and changed, half a dozen of us met in the bar. After discussing it between ourselves we decided to show our faces at the party. After all, we had been invited. Hiring a suite to have a party was the 'in' thing at the time in America. You did not have to clean up the mess and wash up afterwards. The music was playing along with the chatter of all the people as we were welcomed into the suite.

'Help yourself to drinks,' said one of the girls, 'and there's food available in the other room.'

Everything was going along well when one of the girls by the telephone shouted 'Who's Dave Wagstaffe?'

'I am,' I shouted back amid the noise of the party. She came over to me and explained that there was a telephone call for me but because of all the noise I should take it in the bathroom, off the bedroom adjoining the suite. I picked up the receiver and, half-closing the bathroom door to cut out the noise, I heard the voice of John Ireland.

'Do you think it will be all right if I come up to the party?' he asked.

At that precise moment two men burst into the bedroom, arguing in very loud voices. I could see them through the gap in the hinge end of the door and they were about two metres from me. 'Hang on,' I whispered down the phone to John Ireland, wondering what was going on.

'I'm gonna kill you,' shouted one of the men, pulling a gun from his jacket. 'You've let me down badly.'

'You don't want me to come to the party do you?' John Ireland was saying to me on the other end of the phone.

'It's a little awkward at the moment.' I whispered back to him, worried that one man was going to shoot another right in front of me.

'No, I don't think I'm wanted there,' said John and put the phone down.

I was now in a very precarious situation, the only way out being the door on the other side of which these two men were still arguing. Suddenly, into the bedroom came three women. 'Are you two still arguing?' shouted one of them. 'Don't be so stupid.' With that she calmly moved in between them, snatching the gun. 'Now get in there and enjoy yourselves,' she ordered and off they went with their tails between their legs. I was out of there as fast as I could and the other lads followed soon afterwards, apparently following another altercation in the main suite. We settled for a little bar just around the corner.

John Ireland did not speak to me the next day, obviously still believing that I had not wanted him to join the party, but after I explained it all to him over a cup of coffee in the hotel lounge the following day he understood and was thankful that he had not been there. I must also point out that John Ireland would back his players, as I discovered when I had been sent off in a League match against Blackburn in January 1967. I had been getting some rough treatment from Rovers full-back Mike Ferguson, who used to be a winger himself. I was used to full-backs trying all sorts of things to stop me, but this time something snapped and I retaliated. Referee Keith Styles came running up, notebook in hand, and was going to book me. I just lost it and stupidly refused to confirm my name to the ref. The upshot was not a booking but a sending-off. Fortunately the team rose to the occasion to earn a 0–0 draw, but I had let myself and the team down. John Ireland rightly took me along to Keith Styles after the match to apologise. However, the chairman sprang to my defence when he talked to the *Express & Star* the following Monday.

'There is no excuse for Wagstaffe,' the chairman emphasised. 'In refusing to give his name he left the referee with no option but to send him off. On the other hand, I think he is entitled to expect some protection from the official against some of the treatment he is getting from opposing players. Provocation may not be an excuse – in this game he was blatantly kicked, tripped and hit in the face – but he was certainly provoked. At the time he was sent off he was in fact in considerable pain after being kicked on the leg and left on the ground beyond the field of play in an incident the referee apparently did not see.'

The chairman went on 'This "Stop Wagstaffe by any means" is not fair to the player and I feel both he and the club are entitled to more protection from referees than we are getting. If this sort of thing continues I am afraid one of these days Wagstaffe may be seriously hurt.'

Phil Morgan also came to my defence, writing 'I must say this season he has, until Saturday, shown remarkable patience after some pretty harsh treatment from opponents. I do not condone what he did at Ewood Park but I can understand how he felt.'

The sequel to all was that I was severely censured by the FA and fined £25. It could have been worse – I could have been suspended – and I will always remember how the chairman gave me his support. When I finally left Wolves to play for Blackburn Rovers I was disappointed because I did not get a chance to say goodbye to John and I had to wait quite some time before I met him again — when the Doog made him honorary president of Wolves, after taking over the club with the Bhatti brothers.

There were many other amusing tales involving John Ireland, but they are too numerous to relate. However, a story he told me many years later shook me rigid.

'I've never mentioned this before, Waggy, but I'm at liberty to tell you now,' he said. 'Several clubs made inquiries about you while you were playing for Wolverhampton Wanderers. In fact Manchester United made a bid for you.'

This stopped me in my tracks. I was a Manchester lad. Barbara was a Stretford girl. I had played for Manchester City for five years, always in the shadow of United, one of the most famous clubs in the world. What a dream move that would have been and I never knew a thing about it. I was not bothered about who the other clubs were because I was so shocked that I could have moved back to my place of birth.

To conclude my memories of our exploits with John Ireland I must emphasise that he was a very much respected and well-liked official of Wolves. On the one hand he was like the Frank Spencer character in *Some Mothers Do 'Ave 'Em*, full of mishaps which the lads all laughed along with and on the other he was the chairman of Wolverhampton Wanderers. A lot of fans remember him only for the sacking of Stan Cullis, which was before my time at Wolves, and the anger and resentment over his actions never really went away among the older fans who had watched the team during the highly successful Cullis days. We can only speak as we found John Ireland and this was, in our opinion, a man whose company we all enjoyed and who was a very generous person.

I was sad when his name was taken off the Molineux Street stand and it was renamed the Steve Bull Stand. Not that I have any grievance against Bully whatsoever. In fact, I have the greatest admiration for the part he played in bringing the name of Wolverhampton Wanderers back into the headlines for the right reasons. I was also an avid admirer of his goalscoring feats along the way. I totally agree that the name of Steve Bull should have been honoured by Wolves in some shape or form but, having known John Ireland all those years and travelled the world with him, it saddened me to see his name erased from the history of Molineux.

Semi-final Sadness

After the Asa Hartford hole-in-the-heart incident when having a medical at Manchester City, the authorities decided that before each season every professional at every club should have a complete medical examination before being allowed to play. We all duly had our medicals and it was found that Derek Parkin, one of the fittest players at Molineux, had some kind of problem with his heart and he would not be allowed to play until it was resolved.

Test after test was carried out by different specialists but nobody could come up with an answer about exactly what the problem was and, more importantly, how to cure it. This was really creasing Derek, because not only was he stopped from playing, but he was also banned from training. Derek was one of those players who loved his training as much as he loved playing, so it was a double blow to him. At first the problem was blamed on all the injections that we had had at RAF Cosford to enable us to travel to different countries and perhaps his condition was the result of a reaction to one of them. I personally could not have coped without knowing what was exactly wrong with me, but Derek just took it all in his stride. Eventually, after several months, it was decided that Derek be allowed back to training. Within a short time he was back to his best and was playing again as though nothing had ever happened. I don't think that to this day that there was ever an answer as what the specific problem was. Whatever it was, it did not stop Derek from clocking up 609 senior appearances for Wolves in his 14 years at Molineux, a fantastic achievement. I used to love to watch – and I mean watch, as I kept well out of the way – Derek's battles over the years with Mike Summerbee of Manchester City. No quarter was asked and no quarter given between two truly great players who at the end of the day respected each other.

Bernard Shaw, who had partnered Derek as the other full-back for the past couple of seasons, was to leave us at the end of the 1972–73 season after 150 senior appearances. It was a good move for Bernard because he went back to his native Yorkshire. The last I heard of him he was running a public house and eating establishment in the picturesque region of Bakewell and Matlock.

One incident involving Bernard always makes me smile but at the time it left Bill McGarry fuming. We were in Dallas and it was a stifling hot day with a match to play in the cool of the evening. Bernard had been for a walk around during the afternoon, looking in the shops and generally just meandering about. What he had not taken into account was the fact that on his feet were just a pair of sandals and the sun had burned the exposed skin. Much to the amusement of the rest of us, he had to report to McGarry that there was no way that he could take part in the match with burnt feet. The only thing he could bear near his feet were a pair of flip-flops. McGarry made an example of Bernard in the dressing room. 'Look what this stupid b*****d's done,' he bawled, pointing to Bernard's feet, which by then looked like two hot cross buns, with the cross where the sandal straps had been clearly showing up white against the red of the sunburn. The rest of us had to look away to contain our laughter.

During the close season, after the previous marathon campaign, Bill McGarry bought Steve Kindon from Burnley. Once again I felt that he was trying to replace me, because Steve had been playing number 11 for Burnley. I was injured at the start of the season so I do not know whether I would have been selected or not. Steve had been chosen as number 11 and Mike O'Grady was the substitute so I had two players that played in my position to contend with. After two games there was another person to play in the number 11 shirt — Steve Daley. He had stood in for me before when I had been injured and scored that all-important goal in the semi-final of the UEFA Cup. So all of a sudden we had four outside-lefts on the books — O'Grady, Kindon, Daley and myself. Mike O'Grady left the club shortly afterwards, but it still left three of us, and once again I felt that I might be on my way out of Molineux.

Steve Kindon was a great addition to the dressing room, another absolute character. He made us laugh as soon as we met him, as you would not think a great big strapping lad like him — we nicknamed him 'The Tank' — would talk with a lisp. If he reads this he will be thinking 'You've mentioned me being an addition to the dressing room, Waggy, but I did play on the pitch as well.' His exploits on the pitch I will come to later. Steve now has a career as an after-dinner speaker and if you get the chance to see and hear him, take it because he is one of the very best.

Steve was the biggest and fastest player in the team, but McGarry always had it in for him. If we were not playing well the first person he criticised was Steve. 'Kindo, what the f*****g hell were you doing?' or 'Where were you when Doog flicked the ball on?' It was as though McGarry had to take his frustration out on somebody and he always picked on Steve. His answer to every question McGarry threw at him was 'I don't know, boss' with a sheepish look on his face like a scolded schoolboy.

Steve was clumsy and he knew it and made us all laugh with his antics. He was also a bully, not a physical one but like the biggest lad in the school he would take liberties. He took great delight in walking past and pinching a handful of our sweets while we were playing cards on the team bus. Mind you, we soon cured him of that by substituting some of them with those red hot sweets you could buy from the joke shops. His clumsiness showed when during a kick-in session before a First Division game he hit one ball too hard and it hit the Doog full in the face, knocking him out. It was a complete accident, but no one had ever heard of anyone knocking his teammate out before a game, particularly when the person that knocked him out was the substitute. McGarry was foaming at the mouth with rage but Sammy Chung managed to bring the Doog round before the kick-off. Steve never did reveal to us what conversation transpired between him and McGarry when he went to sit on the bench with him after the kick-off. It would not have been about the weather. He got some stick off the lads after the incident. 'You'll try anything to get a game, Kindo,' we used to joke with him.

Not long after Steve joined us he managed to get on to our all-time keepy-uppy honours board. With all the hours of practice he had put in, he managed a magnificent total of six. So he is the proud owner of the lowest-ever total by any Wolves player and his name will be etched there forever because we cannot see anybody beating it – or wanting to!

I do not want to steal his thunder, but Kindo will tell you this himself if you go and listen to him speak. Bill McGarry, exasperated with him one day, called him over during a practice session. He said 'Steve, you've got the speed of a racehorse but the brains of a f*****g rocking horse.' That was not all. Steve could eat like a horse but that was quite restricted when McGarry was about. On the odd occasion that McGarry was not around it was time for Steve to take advantage. Staying in a Kuwait hotel one trip, Steve found himself in the situation of a kid in a sweetshop, Bill McGarry having flown back to England earlier, leaving the hotel menu at the mercy of Steve. John Richards, Steve and myself were having a quiet game of cards in Steve's room when he decided that he was hungry again! He had worked out that 'burger' on a menu in any country was the same word all over the world, so he could order this with complete confidence. He picked up the phone and ordered 'Burger, burger and chips' from room service. In other words, double burger and chips.

He chomped it down with a huge smile on his face, knowing that Bill McGarry was thousands of miles away with no chance of catching him. The cards were becoming sticky with tomato ketchup from Steve's fingers but Steve's mind was not on the state of the cards now that he had food in front of him. As soon as he finished his plateful he picked up the phone and ordered the same again – because he could. He wolfed the second lot down in record time and we had to abandon the card game because by now the cards had become unplayable with the amount of ketchup stuck to them. Steve sat back, beaming with satisfaction at having got one over on McGarry. Not only that, he had another two days in which to plunder the menu with our hosts picking up the tab.

Another player that McGarry signed early that season was Derek Jefferson, who had played under his management at Ipswich. Derek was a no-frills, no-nonsense player who was good cover for Frank Munro or John McAlle, his only problem being that he was as blind as a bat – the Mr Magoo of Wolverhampton Wanderers. He did wear contact lenses, but they did not seem to have any effect. I felt sorry for Derek during his stay at Wolves because the crowd never seemed to take to him for some unknown reason. Mind you, it must have been difficult standing in for the likes of Frank, probably the most skilful centre-half in the League. I never heard Derek moan about the stick he got off the crowd. He just carried on regardless.

Little did people know that the Jeffersons had a special needs baby who had to be given much love and attention and needed a parent to be there at all times. All credit to Derek, he never brought this situation into the equation. He could easily have said that he had not had much sleep when he had a bad game. He did not, however. His home situation was something he kept very low key, keeping his private life separate from his footballing life.

It was in this season that John Richards was knocking the goals in regularly and his partnership with Derek Dougan was as good as any in the Football League. We were also doing reasonably well in the Football League Cup, during which I was to fall foul of McGarry's petty unreasonableness. We had played Blackpool at home in the fifth round, drawing the match 1–1. The replay was the following Wednesday and it was decided that the team should stay at the seaside until the weekend. For some reason, that night I played in the number-eight shirt, with Steve Kindon playing in my usual number-11 shirt. I cannot even remember why so it could not have been that important. Anyway, we won a not very exciting game 1–0 with a humdrum performance putting us into the semi-final.

We were staying at the Norbreck Hotel on North Shore, Blackpool, so naturally the team coach took us back there. Before we could get off the bus, McGarry stood up and ordered 'Nobody leaves the hotel. You can have a couple of drinks in the bar but, I repeat, nobody leaves the hotel.'

I knew we had not played that well but we were in the semi-final and should have been pleased as punch. My mum and dad lived three minutes from the hotel and I had promised to go and see them after the game so I went to see McGarry and asked him if I could go.

'Go and phone them,' he said. 'We're here for another few days so you've plenty of time to see them.'

I could have lost my temper with him, but it would have only resulted in a fine so I had to accept his decision. So we were 'confined to barracks' and settled for a drink in the hotel lounge bar. Four or five of us were sitting round a table when Sammy Chung came over with his glass of pop and joined the company. Within minutes the sole topic of conversation was the game we had just played. There was a very important point that Sammy was trying to make so, using the table as the pitch – it was rectangular – he dipped his finger in his drink and drew the goals. We all picked our glasses off the table and when Sammy asked us all to indicate where we were at a crucial free-kick during the game we all dipped our fingers in our beer and indicated with a wet mark where we were. The scene was set.

'Now,' said Sammy, ' this is a very important point I'm going to make and I want you all to remember this.'

At that moment a voice said 'Excuse me, boys,' and a little old waitress leaned over the table and wiped it clean. 'There, lads, that's much better,' she said and off she went. As you can imagine, we all fell about laughing and to this day we never found out what that very important point was that Sammy was going to make.

The season was moving along quite nicely and by January we already had a good few points in the bag, but Spurs had once again dampened our spirits, this time knocking us out of the League Cup in the semi-finals, even though we took it to extra-time in the second leg at White Hart Lane. Two weeks later our hopes were raised after beating Manchester United in the third round of the FA Cup in front of 40,000 fans at Molineux, Mike Bailey scoring the only goal of the game. With a break in fixtures we were off on our travels again, this time to Kuwait to play their national team. Waiting at Heathrow Airport for the call for our flight, it suddenly struck me that it was going to be quite a boring week. Kuwait was a dry country — no drinking allowed — so there would not be any pleasant bars in which to relax and have a drink during the evenings. I decided to get myself a book to read and a thick one at that. Hurriedly looking through the book stand — our call was imminent — I grabbed one of the hardbacks simply because it said on the cover 'Soon to be made into a film by Daryl Zanuck.' I struck lucky. I had never heard of the author, Peter Benchley, but the title of the book was to become known all over the world — *Jaws*. My nose was in the book from the moment of take-off until we were the victims of another quite serious incident.

After landing at Beirut for refuelling we had still a few hours journey left before reaching Kuwait. By now it was dark and around an hour into the journey the familiar drone of the engines slowing down signalled that there was something wrong. We could not possibly be coming in to land in Kuwait, so what could be wrong? Eventually the pilot decided to enlighten us with a message: 'Ladies and gentlemen, in a few minutes' time we will be landing at Beirut airport.'

We had left Beirut an hour before, so this statement from the pilot left everybody with an uneasy feeling that things were not right. No further information came from the cockpit, so you can imagine the quiet and the tension as the plane was on its landing approach and all we could see were the runway lights. We touched down with a sigh of relief from all the passengers, then we were ordered off the plane and into the airport terminal. Everybody was concerned about the lack of information and the courier we had travelling with us decided to go and find out what was happening.

On his return he informed us that a plane had been hijacked and was somewhere in the surrounding air space. In this kind of situation, not knowing which way the hijacked plane would go next, every plane for hundreds of miles around had to be grounded. It was a relief at least to find out the reason for our return to Beirut, but for the moment we were stranded in a lounge at the airport. After a couple of hours the situation had still not been resolved and it was decided to put us in a hotel in downtown Beirut for the night. This turned out to be another shambles as the hotel was full, so the only alternative for us was to bed down on the settees and armchairs in the hotel reception. At that time Beirut was the trouble spot in the Middle East and in the background could be heard the sound of gunfire and the occasional explosion. It was common to see the troubles on television but we never dreamt that one day we would be in the vicinity. Several hours later we got the all-clear and completed our journey to Kuwait. Even though it was January, we expected a place like this on the edge of the desert to be red hot, but we did not need the summer gear we had brought with us because even though there were blue skies it was blowing an extremely cold wind. Much to my surprise, the population of Kuwait consisted of only 250,000 actual Kuwaitis. The rest were odds and sods, mostly labouring and working at the oil terminals. Most of these lived in tents alongside the main highways into the city. They certainly looked after their own, and even all those years ago their pensioners were given at least twice the equivalent of our pensioners' pay today.

There was not a lot to see really, but we were given a friendly tour around by a representative of the Emir. Asked why there was a continuous line of ships to-ing and fro-ing on the horizon, he told us that the only thing they produced was oil so, consequently, everything they wanted had to be imported, hence the vast array of ships coming in. Being such a rich state they could afford to do this.

Sammy Chung asked him what a huge odd-looking contraption sitting not far out in the sea was. Our guide told us that it was the biggest desalination plant in the world, turning sea water into drinking water. 'And the British installed it for us,' he was proud to state. We inquired why they should need such a plant when the mountains in the distance provided plenty of water. He explained that on the other side of the mountains was Iraq – a country they did not trust – and should the water coming off the mountains contain poison then that would be the end of the Kuwaitis. 'They want our land,' he said, 'and one day they will try to take it.'

Enough said. We know the rest.

Bill McGarry had gone home after the game, so Sammy Chung was left in charge. We approached him with a view to getting an early plane home because the lads were quite bored with sitting around playing cards. Sammy came up trumps, managing to get us all the odd seats on a plane from Delhi which was to stop at Kuwait to refuel. It was an unusual flight as we were the only Europeans on board. The rest of the passengers were the wealthier children of Indian families flying to London to start a new life in England. I found myself sitting next to two young Indian girls who spoke impeccable English. They explained to me that they had been taught by their own private tutor in India in readiness for their move to England. That was back in 1973 and one wonders how they fared in their new country. By the way, I finished my book on that journey home.

Danny Hegan kept putting himself on the AWOL list, and whenever he did not turn up for 24 hours or so Bill McGarry would be on the phone to Phil Parkes telling him to get a message to Danny in order that he get back into training. Apparently, McGarry had this notion that Phil would know the whereabouts of Danny's drinking place and would be able to initiate his return. Danny Hegan was a familiar name in the papers, but on one very unusual occasion it was his wife Patsy who stole the headlines. While driving on the motorway, making her way up north, Patsy was stopped by the police for speeding and consequently had to appear in court. Her explanation to the court was that she was running very low on fuel and was trying to get to the next services as fast as she could!

By the end of March we were handily placed in the League and were in the semi-final of the FA Cup with a date against Leeds United on 7 April at my former ground, Maine Road. It was a great chance to get to Wembley, but on the day we just did not perform to the best of our ability. I had a relatively poor game on my old stamping ground. I just could not get enough of the ball to get myself into the game. Near the end we were desperately trying to get an equaliser, and when Allan Clarke went down the back of my leg as I crossed the ball I lashed out in frustration with my fist as he stumbled at the side of me and caught him on the cheekbone. I was lucky not to get sent off. Fortunately, both the referee and linesman were watching where the ball had gone. We lost 1–0 and I was so disappointed, feeling that I had let my teammates down on a pitch that I had always loved to play on. It is an awful feeling at night, having lost a match in the afternoon. The game goes through your mind time after time – if only I had done this and if only I had done that – but you can never change the result. In football sometimes you have to wait a week to try to make amends for a poor personal performance. Not even the world's greatest players can perform well week in, week out.

That night after the semi-final I seemed to have been punished twice, once in the disappointment of losing our game and again, as the night wore on, through the pain in my hand that became worse and worse. Next day I had an X-ray in A & E and it was discovered that I had broken a bone at the base of my thumb and index finger. Hitting Allan Clarke had done me no favours at all. I always maintained that he was hard-faced! Even to this day, over 30 years later, when I do any painting that particular area of the broken bone starts to ache and ache. It's a permanent reminder of that losing semi-final day at Maine Road.

In the League we had finished the last furlong with a flourish, losing only three of the final 15 games to finish in fifth position. John Richards had a magnificent season, scoring 36 goals in first-class games.

No Melting

During the 1973 close season I received my usual notification of the terms and conditions of my next contract. Nothing new, no rise, no new bonus scheme. Not that I expected anything different, but one thing was puzzling me – the option period that I had been offered. I was not absolutely *au fait* with all the rules and regulations that covered our contracts, but I was sure that there was something amiss. So I decided to phone Cliff Lloyd, who at the time was head of the players' union, the PFA. Cliff was a very amicable person who always had time for a player with a problem. He got me to read to him over the phone the exact wording of the part that I was not so sure about so that he was able to write it down and consider it.

'Somebody has dropped a real clanger here,' he said, after reading through it. 'The option that you have been offered is not in line with the contract you have been offered.'

He explained further. 'Consequently, you do not have to accept this contract because you have not been offered what you are entitled to. You can, if you want to, become a free agent.'

In other words, somebody had made a serious error in putting the contract together and unless I pointed this out to them, enabling them to rectify the error, then after a certain date had passed I would become free of any contract binding me to Wolverhampton Wanderers. This was fantastic news – I could go to any club that wanted me with no fee involved and be able to negotiate my own signing-on fee. In other words, I was free to leave. It was certainly an attractive prospect.

One thing was for sure, whoever had sanctioned the terms that I had been offered was going to be in a whole lot of trouble because it was not just a typing error, it was huge mistake. I phoned Cliff back just to make doubly sure that I could, if I wanted to, become a free agent. During the conversation he mentioned something that I had completely overlooked.

'You're not too long away from your testimonial, are you?' he asked.

I suddenly went from elation to deflation and from my slightly prolonged silent reaction Cliff could tell.

'I'll leave that one with you to sort out,' he said. 'You'll have to decide which option is going to benefit you better.'

I was in a quandary; was it better for me to walk away from Wolves to get a better wage and an instant injection of cash from a signing-on fee, or should I wait a few years and have my testimonial? Which one would be more financially viable? I thought long and hard for a few days and eventually opted for the testimonial, mistakenly thinking I would make more money from that and secure a better financial future.

So the only thing left to do was take the contract back to the club and point out the mistake that had been made. It was with great delight that I knocked on McGarry's office door, secretly hoping that it was he who had dropped the clanger while dictating the terms to whoever had to type them out.

'Come in,' he said in his usual monotone voice, looking surprised to see me as I opened the door.

I chose my words carefully, not wanting to let the cat out of the bag. 'I need to talk to you about this contract that you've offered me.' I began but I did not get any further.

'My hands are tied,' he said. 'It's no use asking for more money. You're all on the same.'

'It's wrong,' I interrupted.

'Nothing f*****g wrong with that,' he snapped back again. 'Everybody's on the same money.'

'No, the contract's wrong,' I said.

'What's f*****g wrong with it?' he growled.

I explained to him that I had been in contact with Cliff Lloyd and told him that in Cliff's opinion I was a free agent because Wolverhampton Wanderers had not offered the correct option to me. It was at this point that I wished I had taken the 'free agent' choice. It would have given me the greatest of pleasure to have said 'Goodbye, Mr McGarry, it was nice knowing you!'

McGarry was livid. The mere mention of Cliff Lloyd did not go down well with him. He asked to look at the contract that I was holding in my hand, still in the brown envelope that it came in. He quickly began scanning through it and I pointed out the part of it that was incorrect.

'Leave it with me,' he said in the quietest voice I had ever heard him use. He was embarrassed and he knew that I could tell.

Some time during that afternoon, and I don't know by whom, a long brown envelope was posted through my letterbox containing a valid contract. To this day I have never found out who was responsible for the mistake that meant I could have walked away from Wolverhampton Wanderers a free agent, and I have often wondered which team I would have gone to. However, it was a case of 'Que sera, sera'.

The 1973–74 season was McGarry's fifth in charge and by then one would have thought that he would have in some way warmed to the lads a little more. After all, in the previous two seasons we had taken him to the Final of the UEFA Cup, the semi-final of the League Cup and the semi-final of the FA Cup, besides finishing both seasons in the top 10 of one of the best Leagues in the world. I am convinced that had he taken the trouble to get a bit closer to the players then we would have been able to achieve that little bit more. Other managers, even the big name ones, had fun with their players. It all helped break the ice and make for a better atmosphere.

Tommy Docherty, when manager of Manchester United, was not averse to a bit of fun, even though it was shortly before a game. We were walking up the corridor that housed the two dressing rooms at Old Trafford once when Tommy shouted 'Hey, lads!' adding with a laugh 'Have you seen our new secret weapon?'

He beckoned his new centre-half Jim Holton out of the home dressing room and into the corridor. Big Jim walked out wearing nothing but his jock strap, showing off his large muscular frame as Tommy paraded him like a prize bull.

'What a specimen,' Tommy said proudly. 'Our training this week was three times round big Jim and in the bath,' he quipped. 'Off you go, son, and get your kit on,' Tommy said to Big Jim, who immediately retreated to the United dressing room like an obedient schoolboy. It was funny but it was innocent fun. Even though we were to play against each other in 45 minutes' time it just showed that daggers did not have to be drawn at all times.

Malcolm Allison used to stand outside the City dressing room at Maine Road with the door open as the visiting team walked past on the way to their dressing room. He would say 'F*****g hell, lads, you want to see this one. He's a stone overweight, he won't be able to run. Here's another one, he looks as though he's been out all night. This one's only a kid, he'll be frightened to death.' So it went on, but this was just a little bit of psychological fun before the match.

Brian Clough would sometimes take his entire team out for a couple of beers the night before a game, just for a complete change of routine. Don Revie, when England manager, used to get the lads playing bingo while relaxing in the hotel, and guess who called the numbers out? He did! Lots of managers incorporated different techniques in order to try to ignite some spark of reaction in their players. Bill McGarry, however, never tried anything different from the norm and the last thing he would ever have done was shout out bingo numbers for his players. Even McGarry's hero and ex-colleague, Bill Shankly, a most revered and successful manager at that time, always took time to have a word with you if you happened to pass him in the corridor.

The aspirations of the Wolves players were quite high before the start of 1973–74 because of our achievements the previous season. Another young man, Alan Sunderland, had played himself into contention and looked a very good prospect. On a pre-season tour in Europe some of the lads and myself, who had not been selected, were watching one of the games that included Alan and saw him score a brilliant solo goal.

It started with a corner for the opposition and everyone was back in defence except for Alan, who was occupying two defenders in the centre circle. The ball got hammered out of our defence from the corner straight towards Alan. It looked as though he was going to chest it down, but at the last second he took his body away and dummied the first defender, leaving him for dead. Then there was a race for the ball with the other defender and Alan just managed to get his toe to the ball first and nick it past him. The ball was then running towards the goalkeeper, but Alan got there marginally before him and took the ball round him to roll it into an empty net. It was a stunning goal and received rapturous applause from the spectators.

Seconds later the referee blew for half-time and Sir Alf Ramsey, the England boss, who had been sitting on the same row as us, declared 'If any of you went into the dressing room now and asked him how he did it, he wouldn't be able to tell you. Everything that he did came naturally to him and he didn't have to think about it. That's the thing with professional footballers, it becomes second nature to them and sometimes it's as though they're on auto-pilot.' How right Sir Alf was.

The week before the season began we played a game that I never knew existed. It was a play-off to decide third place in the FA Cup between the losing semi-finalists. We were one of the teams and Arsenal were the other, but how they decided which ground the game would be played on I don't know. It just happened to be Highbury. The third-place game had been introduced in 1970 and each match had been on neutral territory until it was our turn — Manchester United beat Watford 2–0 at Highbury in 1970, Stoke beat Everton 3–2 at Selhurst Park in 1971 and Birmingham beat Stoke 4–3 on penalties after a 0–0 draw at the Hawthorns in 1972. Maybe there had been poor attendances when the game was on a neutral ground so the FA decided that having it at the home ground of one of the clubs involved might boost the gate.

Danny Hegan had not been on his best behaviour so — and I am only guessing this — Bill McGarry decided to make him captain for this game to give him some responsibility and make him knuckle down to the job in hand. It worked because he had a good game and we beat the mighty Arsenal 3–1 on their own pitch. Brian Hornsby scored for Arsenal and Derek Dougan (two) and Jim McCalliog hit our goals. Burnley won 1–0 at Leicester the following season, but after that the idea of a third-place decider was dropped. Even though it was at the home ground of one of the teams involved, only 4,000 turned up at Filbert Street. No wonder the FA saw sense and scrapped the idea.

Though Danny Hegan had done well at Highbury, within a couple of months he had been off the rails once too often and Bill McGarry decided to dispense with his services. It had got to the stage where his wife Patsy was having to go to the ground to pick up some of Danny's wages or, alternatively, somebody would go to the house and drop them off there. It was a very great pity because Danny was a very talented footballer, but he was never able to establish a position of his own in the team. Without being unkind to him, he was never going to wrestle the number-four shirt from skipper Mike Bailey and Jimmy Mac and Kenny Hibbitt were holding down the only other positions that he might have been able to play in. Players love to play, and it was no good for someone like Danny to be in and out of the side. He loved playing football and was the sort that needed to play continuously instead of in fits and starts. Danny was a cracking guy to have in your dressing room, with his sense of humour and his unusual sayings, and he was a lot of fun to go out and socialise with, except that he sometimes found it difficult to draw the line at the end of the night!

Right to the very end, Danny would look in his pocket and tell us that the great Helmut Haller was still in there, then remind us about that brilliant effort he had from almost the halfway line, which Pat Jennings managed to tip over the bar in our game against Spurs. The week that Danny was released from Molineux he had appeared in the UEFA Cup second round for us and it was ironic that his last League game for Wolves was against one of his, and Bill McGarry's, former clubs, Ipswich Town.

In the first round of the UEFA Cup we had been drawn against the Portuguese club Belenenses with the first leg to be played in Portugal. We won the game 2–0 but the sending-off of John Richards meant that he had to miss the return. His deputy for the Molineux leg was Peter Eastoe, who had gained his chance by scoring 23 of the 60 goals in total scored by the Central League team the previous season. Peter's only first-team appearances had been one Texaco Cup and two League games, but this was his debut in European football and he was duly rewarded with a goal in our 2–1 win.

Locomotive Lepizig were our opponents in the second round and once again we were drawn away from home in the first leg. As the curtain came down on Danny Hegan's career at Wolverhampton Wanderers the curtain came up for another aspiring young man – Geoff Palmer. They played together in the first leg of the tie in Leipzig, but there was no fairytale endings or beginnings as we lost the match 3–0.

For sheer excitement and goals the second leg was a feast for the spectators. We needed four goals to get us through to the next stage so, as you can imagine, we threw caution to the wind and played an all-out attacking game, simply because we had nothing to lose. We did get the four goals we set out to score but, unfortunately, when playing an attacking game like that we were always going to be susceptible to a sucker punch and that was exactly what happened. They scored and, on the away goals rule, went through to the next round. It was disappointing for both the players and the fans, the only consolation being that they got to watch a cracking game played at thrilling speed. In hindsight, I wish that we had been let loose to play like that many more times, but managers, not just Bill McGarry, always played with a certain amount of caution. With the attacking force that we had in our team I am sure that we would have been more successful if we had played to our strengths. Manchester City did it in the 1960s when Mercer and Allison were in charge, attacking every team they played against, and they finished up winning the League, the FA Cup, the League Cup and the Cup-Winners' Cup in that period. This was not long after I left Maine Road and they turned the club round, transforming the team from mediocrity to being one of the most entertaining sides around.

It was around that time that Mike Summerbee bought a huge, rambling house at Bredbury on the outskirts of Manchester. Before he attempted any renovations or decorating he had a house-warming party to which he invited all his City teammates and many of the United lads. I happened to be in Manchester that weekend and Mike invited Barbara and me along too. It was a cracking night and, as you can imagine, there was plenty of booze flowing. As I was standing talking to a few of the players, Malcolm Allison walked over. 'Hey, Waggy,' he said, looking deadly serious. I listened intently, thinking he was going to come out with something really interesting.

'It's a pity you left Maine Road when you did,' he continued.

'Why is that, Malcolm?' I asked.

'Well, if you had stuck around a little while longer I might have been able to make you into a player,' he said, laughing loudly.

Malcolm was well-known for taking the mickey, but I have often wondered how I would have fared in that team that he and Joe Mercer put together.

The first three and a bit months of the season had been very busy indeed for us. Not only had we played 17 League games and four European games, we had also been quietly moving along in the League Cup, having beaten Halifax, Tranmere, after a replay, and Exeter to reach the fifth round. Twenty-five games and we had not even reached the end of November. The players did not mind this at all because, as I have said before, players love to play and having two games a week relieved us of the boredom of the heavy training sessions that were employed when games were seven days apart. Some of the lads took these sessions in their stride, but for most of us it was a drag and we were mentally defeated before we started.

These training sessions were usually on Tuesday and if the balls did not appear on the team bus as we left for training I was absolutely deflated, knowing that we would be running all morning. Not only that, the running would be done up and down those hills on Cannock Chase and worse was still to come: we would be back in the afternoon to do some more running at Molineux. The morning session at Milford Common would start with some warming-up exercises, then a gentle jog for about half a mile. Then it would get serious. Sammy Chung would be the marker at the top of a long winding incline and it was around Sammy and back to McGarry a couple of times, then another half-mile run and again up the hills around Sammy and so on, each time getting further and further away from Sid Kipping's coach parked on the common.

After about an hour of this, and when McGarry thought we were far enough away from the coach, he would say, 'Everybody make their way back to the coach and anyone finishing behind me will have to make their own way back to Molineux.'

On one occasion Frank Munro and I, with our in-built radar, reckoned that if we went as the crow flies, through the trees and bracken, we might even be there before some of the good runners, who would be sticking to the main tracks among the pines, the bonus being that we would not have to do half as much running as the rest. Having gone five minutes into our journey like two explorers hacking their way through the jungle with their machetes — in truth we were treading carefully through the bracken — suddenly a wild animal jumped out on us and we ran like hell, much faster than at any time that morning. After 30 yards we plucked up the courage to look behind and see what this animal was. We could see it clearly now — a young deer running the other way!

Over the years, to my knowledge, there was only one person to be left behind on the Chase to make their own way to Molineux — Hughie Curran. He had somehow got disorientated among the trees while making his way to the coach, which was parked on Milford Common. 'Hughie's not on,' we shouted, as McGarry gave Sid orders to drive us back to Molineux. 'That's his look-out,' said McGarry as he reiterated his order to Sid, who was messing about with the gears, obviously stalling for time, waiting for Hughie to appear. 'On you go, Sid,' McGarry said once more and off we went. The rest of us had showered and changed by the time Hughie got back an hour later. Apparently he got a lift on a milk wagon returning to Wolverhampton. Good job it was not a milk float or he would not have got back before nightfall!

Tuesday afternoon would then be another running session, this time on the track and up the South Bank. The track work was difficult, running backwards and forwards with dumbbells, but the South Bank work was just as tough. Any of you who watched matches from that old terrace will know how high it was, and our task on the whistle was to hit the corrugated sheeting at the back of it to stop the watch inside 13 seconds. It does not sound that difficult, but the stairways we ran up every so often changed from large steps to small steps, causing a stutter in your sprint for the top. The punishment was that if you did not reach the top in 13 seconds you had to do it again until you did.

Chatting about the height of the stand before one of these sessions, Sammy Chung idly boasted that he could hit a golf ball over the South Bank stand from the North Bank goalline. Sammy was well known for hitting a high ball with his driver, but not one of us believed that he could possibly do what he boasted. Several of us had a little bet with him to push him into trying to prove it. Out came his clubs and he teed up his ball on the goalline at the North Bank end. He had a couple of practice swings and then, whack, he hit the ball. Standing there at the North Bank, looking towards the South Bank, it did not seem possible, but the ball sailed over the top and into the Molineux Hotel car park, never to be seen again. What made it more incredible was the fact that he did it at the first attempt. He had several more attempts but got nowhere near it. Next time you are at Molineux have a look at the height and distance needed to achieve the feat. I know that the Jack Harris stand is there now, but you will get some idea of what a mighty blow it must have been.

I have not written in much detail about Sammy until now, but I can tell you that he was respected by all the players as a person and as an excellent coach. His unenviable task was being the link between the players and Bill McGarry. He was the bearer of the bad news and very occasionally the good news that came out of McGarry's office. Bill McGarry determined what the training sessions would entail and Sammy's job would be to put his instructions into practice. Occasionally, when McGarry was not at the training session, Sammy was left to his own devices and was able to display some of his own coaching assets. At these he was very adept, making the sessions interesting and, as far as possible, enjoyable for the players. What he was like as a manager I have no idea because I had left Molineux by then, but I can tell you that even if you are the best coach in the world it does not follow that you will become a good manager. I am not being detrimental to Sammy, I am just stating the fact that management and coaching can be two entirely different things.

Sammy got on well with the players, but at times I suppose he had to report certain misdemeanours to the manager. As I have mentioned, it was an unenviable position to be in and there must have been times when he was left with the predicament of what to report and what not to report to Bill McGarry. Certain situations could have had serious consequences. I remember one particular incident on a pre-season tour of Sweden. Some of us, including Sammy, were having breakfast in the hotel restaurant which, unusually, was situated at the back of the hotel. A taxi arrived at the back of the hotel and out got two of the younger lads who had been included in the touring party. Nobody said a word, not wanting to draw Sammy's attention to the situation, but it was quite obvious that he had seen them and it was also quite obvious that they had been out all night – why else would they direct a taxi to the rear of the hotel so as not to be seen? Completely oblivious to the fact that they had been spotted they both appeared in the restaurant five minutes later, dressed in their track suits ready for a bit of breakfast before training.

'Morning, lads,' said Sammy. 'Did you sleep well?'

'Very well thanks,' they both replied, almost in unison, lying through their teeth.

'Good,' said Sammy, 'then you'll be ready for a hard training session, won't you?'

They were lucky on two counts – one, that McGarry had not been in the restaurant and, two, that Sammy did not report them to him. It must have been a very difficult decision for Sammy because reporting those two lads to McGarry could have had dire consequences for their future roles at the club. Fortunately, he chose not to say anything and the two lads in question became successful players in the years that followed.

On another occasion we were staying at a hotel in Southport for a few days relaxation. Bill McGarry was not in one of his better moods and on the Wednesday night declared that 'everyone will be in by 11 o'clock'. A few of us thought that this was unreasonable, there not being a game until Saturday afternoon. So we decided to report at 11 and then go out through the back door to the Kingsway Club, just 50 yards from the hotel. It was a club in which one had to wear a collar and tie so Frank Munro went off to his room and arranged to meet Bernard Shaw and myself, who were already wearing ties, in the club.

Frank was aware that Sammy was on the prowl along the corridor where the players' rooms were so he decided to wait five or 10 minutes before slipping out the back door and over to the club where Bernard and I were already enjoying a pint. He heard Sammy's voice in close proximity and then a knock on the door.

'Who is it?' shouted Frank, knowing full well who it was.

'It's me, Sammy,' was the reply.

'Come on in,' invited Frank.

Sammy entered the room and all he could see of Frank was his head sticking out from the bedclothes. Sammy smiled and said, 'Frank, do me a favour and go and get those two out of that club.'

'I don't know what you mean,' said Frank. 'Which two?'

'You know what I mean,' said Sammy, walking over to the bed and pulling the bed covers back to reveal Frank fully dressed in his shoes, suit, shirt and tie, all ready for the off. It was a fair cop and Frank had to hold his hands up.

'OK, Sammy,' he said. 'I'll go and get them for you.'

Of course, when Frank came to the club and told Bernard and me that Sammy had sent him to collect us we genuinely thought he was taking the mickey, even more so when he ordered himself a pint of lager. But when he almost downed it in one we began to take him seriously. Frank then gave us a choice. 'I'm going back now. I've passed the message on and it's up to you two whether you stay and suffer the consequences or come back with me.' We chose the latter and were glad we did. Sammy never said a word to us the next day, nor did he say a word to Bill McGarry or we would have been on the next train home with a hefty fine to follow. To this day he has never revealed how he came to know of our plan to go to the Kingsway.

I have made him sound like a soft touch but I can assure you he was not. There were many occasions on which he reported much less serious incidents to Bill McGarry but, deep down, I think he was a man who thought about the consequences and the effect on the team and the club before he made the decision as to whether certain incidents should or should not be reported. We remained friends after I left Wolves and, when he became manager, he and his wife, Heather, came to stay for a short break with Barbara and me at our small hotel in Blackpool. Needless to say, I pointed out to him that the house rules stated tea and biscuits at 10.30 and in bed for 11 o'clock.

Meanwhile, back on the pitch we had successfully progressed to a fifth-round confrontation with Liverpool in the Football League Cup. December 1973 was a very bad month for the players, with five away games, three home games in the League and this very important game against Liverpool, which was played at Molineux on a Wednesday afternoon as it was the time of the three-day week and the power cuts that went with it. Not surprisingly, only 16,000 spectators turned up for the game but, under the circumstances, it was a reasonable turn-out. John Richards scored a wonderful goal, with strength and speed and a perfect finish, to put us into the semi-final of the competition. It needed all the assets that John possessed and I would say that only he out of all the team would have been able to score it. Suddenly the dream – every footballer's dream – of a real chance to get to Wembley was in sight. It was only peeping over the horizon at that moment, but with a two-leg semi-final against Norwich to come we really fancied our chances.

Barry Powell had played himself into the side at the expense of Jim McCalliog, who for some reason had fallen out of Bill McGarry's favour. The semi-final was not far away, with Barry in charge of the number-seven shirt and Ken Hibbitt and Alan Sunderland playing tug-o-war with the number-eight shirt. The situation was quite uncanny, because it was not long after Bill McGarry had dispensed with Danny Hegan's services, yet now the particular positions that Danny could have played in were up for grabs after being unavailable for so long. Despite being so young, Alan Sunderland had played in the numbers two, three, four, seven, eight and 10 shirts and must have been a little alarmed at the fact that he did not have a settled position that he could claim as his own.

McGarry had the luxury of a dress rehearsal in the form of a League game before choosing his line up for the semi-finals. It was the seven and eight jerseys that he had been juggling with at that stage, picking any two from three – Barry Powell, Kenny Hibbitt and Alan Sunderland – and preferring to ignore the experience of Jim McCalliog. I never did find out the reason behind the rift between McGarry and McCalliog but, looking back, it was perfectly obvious that there was one. Jim was not the type of lad that brought his problems out into the open, so we never discovered what the issue was.

Anyhow, for the League game against Norwich McGarry chose to play Barry Powell and Alan Sunderland, with Ken Hibbitt as substitute. The game finished a 1–1 draw, Derek Dougan scoring after returning to the side following injury. The fact that McGarry stuck with exactly the same line up for the first leg of the semi-final suggested that he was reasonably happy with the result and the performance in the League game, but when the Cup game finished 1–1 he was more than disappointed. I would have guaranteed that any other manager whose team had gained a 1–1 draw in the away leg of a major semi-final would have been more than pleased, but it was just the opposite with McGarry. If anything John Bond should have been the more disappointed of the two managers but, as I have already told you, he was the one who came and had a drink with the lads after the game.

For the second leg McGarry had no choice but to change the team. An injury to Derek Parkin meant that the versatile Alan Sunderland played at left-back and Kenny Hibbitt resumed his normal position of right midfield. Winning the tie with a John Richards goal was a dream come true. It was probably the same for Bill McGarry, but still there was not a flicker of elation from him. Of course, he said 'Well done, lads' collectively, but any other manager whose team had got to Wembley would have praised each player personally and joined in the euphoria of the after-match atmosphere. Not McGarry. It was not in his make-up.

During the following week's team talk he impressed upon us that he would be watching carefully during the five League games before Wembley for anyone not giving 100 per cent in case they sustained an injury before the big day. To be honest, I had not even given that scenario a thought until he mentioned it but, ironically, I picked up an injury in the first of the five games. John's injury was a little more complicated and although he returned to the action as soon as I did, he had to miss the two games prior to the Final because of a recurrence of his problem. What happened next was quite extraordinary. McGarry brought back into the team Jimmy Mac, a player that he had discarded and who had not started a first-team game for three months. I did not think about it at the time but, looking back, it must have been very unsettling for Barry Powell, Alan Sunderland and Ken Hibbitt, wondering just who was going to be in the side at Wembley.

Anybody who plays football at any level – even schoolboys – dreams of playing in a Wembley Cup Final. Without being blasé about it, for the past three seasons or so the team, barring injuries, had virtually picked itself and I could not understand why earlier in the season McGarry had more or less dispensed with the McCalliog-Hibbitt combination in midfield. Anyhow, instead of picking any two from three, it was now a case of any two from four and the Final was only a week away. It must have been even more agonising for the four lads not knowing whether or not they would make the line up, as Wembley did not come up as a venue every week. I know I keep mentioning the word 'Wembley' but it really was the place to play. OK, some footballers were very fortunate and played there many times in their careers, but for those of us who did not it was still the ultimate goal to strive for.

To cover all eventualities, McGarry took a huge squad of players down to the south coast in the week leading up to the Final. The first two days' training sessions were more about fitness than tactics so there was still no hint of what the team was going to be. Wednesday was the game of golf that I have already told you about, followed by the ball work session that I still dread to think about, knowing the concerns it brought me.

Thursday was a cold crisp day, typical for that time of year, and after a rather light training session we were to move from the south coast to a country hotel near St Albans. I did not join in the training session because of my thigh injury and had to settle for an hour on the treatment table instead, followed by 10 minutes jogging. The injury was nowhere near right, but I tried not to think about it and told Toby Andersen that I was getting better when all the time I had a nagging pain in my thigh muscle. From St Albans we paid a visit to Wembley Stadium on the Thursday afternoon, where I was dealt another body blow. We were strolling about on the famous turf chatting to the groundsman, who said, 'The weather forecast isn't very good. There's going to be more heavy frosts again for the next few days, which will leave the pitch frozen. There's also a chance of snow should it cloud over.'

I was gobsmacked. I had waited 15 years to get a game on this hallowed turf and not only did I have a bad leg but there was a chance that the pitch might not be in its usual wonderful condition. I did some light training with Toby the day before the game and with the help of his treatment my condition improved somewhat, but I was still to have a fitness test on the morning of the game.

I did not sleep well the night before the game and I was continually looking out of the window to see if the dreaded snow had fallen. Exhausted, I finally dropped off, to awake the next morning with the sun streaming through the window, much to my delight. No frost, no snow, so I only had the bad leg to contend with, which was still a major problem to me. That morning I had a light work-out and kicked a few balls about with Toby, declaring myself fit to play. I was nowhere near 100 per cent but I was not going to miss this!

After our pre-match lunch the whole squad changed into our Wembley '74 tracksuits, specially produced for the occasion. Next on the agenda was the pre-match team talk in one of the hotel's smaller lounges. I do not know when Bill McGarry confirmed to Ken

Hibbitt and Alan Sunderland that they were in the team but it only became clear to the rest of us what the line up was as the team talk progressed. One very disappointed person in the room was Steve Kindon, who had been told by the manager the day before that he would be the substitute. It made sense because Steve was a natural replacement for John Richards or myself, having played in both our positions before. Steve accepted the decision, not having expected to be in the original line up and now having a chance of taking part at some stage of the proceedings, due to the injuries that John and I were carrying. However, during the team talk it emerged that Barry Powell was to be the substitute. Steve had no quarrel with Barry at all, but was bitterly disappointed after being told by the manager 24 hours previously that he would be on the bench.

It also emerged during the team talk that once again McGarry had a downer on Jimmy McCalliog. Having played him for the last two League games he was neither in the team nor named as sub. Jimmy hadn't expected to be called on anyway, but McGarry stopped the team talk to admonish him.

'If you don't go back to your room and have a shave,' McGarry said, 'you won't see one twin tower, never mind f*****g two.'

Jimmy's head went down. He was embarrassed and I was embarrassed for him. The manager need not have done that. He could have had a quiet word with him after the meeting. Anyhow, I do not see anything wrong with not shaving before a game. Next time you watch the interviews after the games at the weekend you will see that most of the players have not shaved before the match. Personally, I used to come out in a red blotchy sweat rash through shaving before playing.

Team talk over, Bill McGarry's orders were for the whole squad to have a stroll along the lane in order to walk off the pre-match meal. We set off en bloc in our nice new track suits – yellow bottoms, black tops with three Wolves and 'Wembley '74' embroidered on them – down the country lane to the end of the drive of the hotel. It was quite a narrow country lane, just about wide enough for two cars to pass each other. So when a car approached us from the opposite direction the driver virtually had to stop when confronted by 20 men in track suits. Steve Kindon, although still smarting from his disappointment, nevertheless found time to play a little joke on the unsuspecting driver. Steve had the driver open his window and said:

'Excuse me, I wonder if you could help us?'

'I'll certainly try,' said the driver.

'Are we on the right road for Wembley?' continued Steve.

Suddenly the driver looked quite concerned. He had obviously twigged that we were the Wolves team on our way to Wembley but wrongly assumed that we were walking there – all the way from St Albans.

'Yes, you're going in the right direction,' he said, 'but you'll never get there in time for the kick-off.'

He then proceeded to give us directions to the station. 'Catch the London train and then the tube and you'll be there in good time,' he said and shouted 'Good luck!' as he drove off.

It was Sid's coach that took us to Wembley, not the train and the tube, and it was a proud day for him being able to drive us up Wembley Way and into the stadium. Trying to describe to anybody what the whole occasion was like is impossible. It was one of those things that you had actually to take part in to know how it felt. It was a wonderful day, not only for the players and the officials, but also for the many fans who had made the trip from Wolverhampton and surrounding towns to support the team. The result put the icing on the cake.

I woke the next morning with a dreadful headache but it was not from the number of drinks that I supped while celebrating our win. It was the after-effects of the Champagne bottles hitting me on the back of the head when the bunny girl tripped and spilled them. I ordered breakfast for Barbara and me from room service and was gobsmacked when I saw the price on the menu card that was in the room. It was 1974, more then 30 years ago, and breakfast at the Hilton was £4.50 per head. It is difficult to equate it to today's prices but I do know that all these years later I would be able to get a full breakfast from any of the stores in Wolverhampton for less than that. Still, it was not every day we stayed in posh hotels and Wolves were paying the bill. At least I hope they were, because I certainly did not pay for it when checking out!

Little did we know, earlier in the season when some of us booked our tickets for the PFA awards dinner, that we would already be in London that day, the proud owners of the League Cup, but we were duty bound to travel back to Wolverhampton to parade the Cup at the Town Hall to our victorious fans. We received a fabulous reception from the huge crowd when we arrived back at the town centre. Personally, I had had an uncomfortable ride back as a result of my leg injury and was in so much discomfort that there was no way I was fit enough to travel back down to London that evening for the awards dinner. For the rest of the lads who were going it was a case of a hasty parade of the Cup, tea and sandwiches, then a dash down the M1 to the PFA dinner. It was a measure of the respect that the players had for the fans of Wolverhampton Wanderers that each and every one of us made the journey from London, many knowing that they had virtually to turn around within hours to make the return journey. It was the first major trophy that Wolves had won for 14 years. However, as everyone knows in football you have to get on with the future, not bask in the glory of the past. So the following week it was back down to earth and a return to the bread and butter of League football.

March was the month that Jimmy Mac left us to join a struggling Manchester United team. I thought that Jimmy was still a good enough player to warrant a place in the team, but Wolves had decided to sell him. In over 200 first-class games for Wolves he could be proud of the contribution he had made to the success of the team during that period. He was a tireless worker on the field and a very unselfish player.

Jimmy played in United's last 11 games that season and scored four goals, but he could not help them avoid relegation. Yet he would prove that Wolves's loss was Manchester United's gain by playing a big part in their gaining promotion back to the First Division at the first attempt. He played 20 League games for them in 1974–75. The very next season his success reached even greater heights when, having moved to Southampton, he laid on the winning goal for Bobby Stokes against his old club Manchester United in the FA Cup Final. It was as though he wanted to be able to turn round to Bill McGarry and say 'Jim's not finished yet, by any means.'

I missed the next two League games after Wembley while recovering from my thigh injury but, looking back, I had not really recovered sufficiently and returned to the team too early. After only three more games I had to return to the treatment table and miss the remaining games of the season. Sitting out, watching, it became obvious to me, seeing the Doog on the subs' bench, that Bill McGarry did not consider him to be a major player any more. He made him sub for seven of the last eight games. So with Jimmy Mac recently gone, both Doog and I over 30 and with him out of favour and me having a long-term injury, was this going to be the beginning of a break-up of the team that had served McGarry so well for four or five seasons?

With nothing to lose during the latter part of the season, McGarry was able to experiment a little and he chose to partner Alan Sunderland with Steve Kindon up front, as John Richards was also sidelined with injury after the Wembley game. Actually, it was quite a successful experiment. The team lost only one of the last eight games and the new pairing scored eight goals between them. So at least the manager knew that should JR be out for any considerable time then he had a ready-made pairing. When JR was fit again he could play either of them alongside him. Finishing 12th in the League with the League Cup in the bank, the season had been reasonably successful.

Ground for Concern

I had been at Molineux 10 years when the 1974–75 season began, and while the ground had not been in the best of condition when I arrived it was now absolutely falling to pieces. In the early days I had seen a model of a stadium that John Ireland wanted to build on the Dunstall Park racecourse, but it never came to fruition. Molineux did not look pretty from the outside, but the inside was even more of a disgrace. If, for any reason, you had to call in at the ground after dark following an away trip you could see the cockroaches scurrying for cover when you switched on the lights. The bathroom, which housed one toilet between all the players, shed tiles daily, not weekly, and was in a dilapidated state – a state that would have meant closure under today's health and safety regulations.

Despite all the money that had come into Molineux over the years and the fact that the players' pay packets were probably bottom of the League, nothing, except for everyday essential repairs, had been spent on ground improvements. Billy Pilbeam, the groundsman, was a very important member of staff, but the headquarters for him and his colleagues was the boiler room. Billy always provided us with a decent playing surface, weather permitting, and was proud of the job he was doing. He was well thought of by all the players and it was a good job he had a sense of humour because he came in for plenty of ribbing and friendly banter from them.

Billy was quite a character, who preferred the banter and the company of the players but had to lean towards the management side because of his job, although he was only paid a pittance for the hours that he put in at Molineux and had to have the boiler room as his base. He was very protective of his pitch and woe betide anybody who set foot on it during the week when he was preparing it for a game. He had been known to remonstrate with the opposing 'keeper for marking the centre of goal on the six-yard box. Some mornings I would sneak up the empty stand for a crafty fag before training and Billy, knowing my little hideaway, would come up and tell me when Bill McGarry was on the prowl. 'He's mooching about,' he would say, 'and he's not looking at seat numbers.' That was my cue to retreat down the back stairs and off to the dressing room.

When Billy cut the pitch in the usual striped pattern he was in the habit of dropping off mounds of grass at intervals at each end of the ground, ready to be bundled up by his mate Fred and some of the apprentices. On one particular occasion before the start of a new season, the time of the year when the turf was in pristine condition, Billy was cutting his grass with tender care and as usual leaving the heaps of grass cuttings at the ends of the playing area. It was a Sunday morning and the squad of players were having a jog around the pitch — a warm-up session prior to leaving that day for a small pre-season tour. A small group of us were jogging along the corner-to-corner stretch in front of the South Bank when skipper Mike Bailey began sneezing, probably due to the effects of the newly mown grass cuttings. Nothing unusual about that, but as we rounded the corner to run down towards the clock Mike let out a gasp of 'Oh, no!'

'What's wrong?' somebody asked.

'I've lost the cap off my tooth,' he replied, exposing a hideous fang as he spoke. 'I must have lost it when I sneezed going along that back straight.'

So we decided that the best chance of finding it would be to walk back in a line along the red shale track — like the police do at a crime scene — and one of us should be able to spot the white cap against the red shale. Twice we carefully scrutinsed the shale stretch in front of the South Bank but the cap was nowhere to be found. By this time Mike was getting a little distraught.

'I can't go abroad like this,' he said. 'I'll be a laughing stock.'

I had to admit that the rest of us were finding the whole incident quite amusing, seeing Mike with this hideous bit of tooth hanging down in the middle of his top teeth. We had searched the track and the grass in between Billy's mounds of cuttings without success so there was only one place the cap could be — in one of the piles of cuttings. Talk about the proverbial needle in a haystack, this was the equivalent. There were several mounds to search because nobody could remember at which point Mike had started sneezing, so we split into pairs and began what looked an impossible task. After five minutes it looked as though Mike was going to have to make the tour and keep his mouth shut if he was not to feel embarrassed. However, just when all seemed lost the cry of 'Here it is!' came from one of the lads. Even though the cap had been found the problem for Mike now was how to get it fitted back into place, because there was no chance of seeing a dentist on a Sunday. Jack Dowen came to the rescue with a couple of packets of chewing gum, which he gave Mike to take on tour to keep the cap in place until we returned home and he could see the dentist.

I was not fit enough to start the 1974–75 season. In hindsight, playing in the League Cup Final with an injury was a big mistake and now I was paying the price. In fact, I was to miss the first 14 games of that season with the troublesome thigh injury. Quite often, when a player incurs a niggling long-term injury, the management eventually try to convince the player that most of the problem is in the mind. Unfortunately, in those days, they could not X-ray muscles and there was no such thing as a scan, which would have enabled the medical profession and the management of clubs to see the amount of damage to my muscle.

Consequently, it was intimated that the majority of the problem was mental and that I should be able to play through the pain of the injury. I can assure you that this was not the case and my injury was too restricting to play through. After several games with the reserve team I eventually played in the 15th game of the season against Aston Villa but, alas, the injury let me down and I was sidelined once again. By this stage of the season the Doog had started only twice, which showed he was still clearly out of favour with Bill McGarry.

Ten years at the club meant that I was entitled to a testimonial and a chance at last to make some money for the future — or so I thought. My basic wage at this stage was £80 per week, hardly enough to save for my eventual retirement from the game. I had one or two good money-making ideas for my testimonial year so I went to see McGarry to put him in the picture in order that he could sanction them, but the response I got was not exactly the one I expected.

'Come in,' he growled, as I knocked on his door. I could tell he was in a bad mood by the tone of his voice. 'Yes,' he went on in a monotone voice as I entered his office. I was not offered a seat so I stood there looking down at him.

'Boss,' I began, 'you know that it's my testimonial year?' I did not get any further. He was straight into a fury.

'F*****g testimonial year? What do you mean by year?' he shouted.

'Well, the normal procedure is to have a few functions to raise money then finish off with a testimonial game,' I replied.

'Listen here,' he continued, 'there's two of you having testimonials this year and I don't want my players distracted by functions and testimonial games. So you get one f*****g function and a match and that's it.'

There was no point in protesting or arguing because he was the boss and his word was law as far as us players were concerned. To say that I was disappointed was an understatement. This was to be my reward for 10 years of loyal service, my only chance to accumulate some money for the future. Suppose the function did not do as well as I expected, suppose the weather was horrendous on the day of the match? Something I'd waited 10 years for could all be blown away and there was no second chance.

By the time I was fit enough to warrant a place in the team again McGarry had been experimenting with several different players in the number-10 shirt to partner John Richards. Alan Sunderland, Steve Kindon, Steve Daley and Peter Withe had all worn the shirt that the Doog had filled so successfully for the past seven or eight years. After another couple of games I had to pull out again and John Farley, whom McGarry had bought to be my successor, took my place once more. Steve Kindon, Steve Daley and Alan Sunderland had also played in the number-11 shirt and it was noticeable that all this chopping and changing and lack of continuity was not helping the team.

Players hate being injured and I was no exception. The season was almost half over and I had played only three games. So far it had been a fairly mundane, unexciting season, being knocked out of the FA Cup, League Cup and UEFA Cup in the first round and hovering around mid-table in the League. McGarry had been experimenting with several different permutations in midfield and up front but with injuries also complicating the situation he had not been able to field the same team more than two or three times consecutively. I could not understand why he would not give Peter Withe an extended run as John Richards's partner and play Steve Kindon wide on the left. It was perfectly obvious that Peter was more of an orthodox striker than Steve, who was used to playing on the wing.

After another couple of games I was back on the treatment table and was beginning to think that I would never recover entirely, but I did manage a sustained run of seven games later in the season. The middle game of the seven was probably the highlight of that boring season and one of the most exciting for the spectators. We beat Chelsea 7–1 with our new signing Willie Carr scoring his first goal for the club and yours truly scoring the seventh. Willie Carr must have thought he had joined a super team as he walked off at the final whistle and must have felt well pleased with himself, scoring on his debut and playing a huge part in the rout of Chelsea. The rest of us felt good too as we nonchalantly trooped off the field into the dressing room only to be shot down by a furious Bill McGarry.

'That was f*****g diabolical,' he roared. 'Pussyfooting about, you scored seven but it should have been 12. When are you fellas going to learn?'

That certainly wiped the smug smiles off our faces. He certainly did not fill us full of confidence because we lost the next two games.

One function, one game – that's what he was allowing me for my testimonial, so as the season was nearing its end I had plenty of arranging to do because the date for the game was to be 6 March and the social club had a vacancy a few weeks before that. *The Comedians* had been a very popular television show and one of the best and funniest was the controversial Manchester comedian Bernard Manning. Bernard was an avid Manchester City fan and I knew him from my days at Maine Road. He had two clubs in Manchester at that time. One was the famous Embassy Club and the other was a small night club in the centre of the city called the Wilton Club. It was the Wilton where Barbara and I spent many Saturday evenings when I was playing for Man City and consequently got to know Bernard. So it was natural that I thought I might stand a chance of getting him to top the bill at the social club.

My next problem was getting in touch with Bernard, so I phoned Johnny Hamp, who was an agent for many of the comedians, with the date of the function in the hope that he might be able to arrange something with Bernard. Johnny called me back to say that he had spoken to Bernard, but on the night in question he was booked at another venue. The good news was that the other venue was Jolly's night club in Stoke and Bernard had very kindly suggested that he could do first spot at Jolly's, drive down to the Wolves social club to do a spot for me, then drive back to Jolly's for his second spot. He would do the show for free with one proviso — everyone else on the bill was also to give their services free of charge. It was a wonderful gesture from Bernard and I hurried off to organise the printing of the tickets. Two other people whom I had booked to appear were up-and-coming artistes, only too glad of the publicity and being on the same bill as Bernard Manning. They readily agreed to waive any fee. The posters were put up — Bernard Manning plus supporting acts at the Wolves social club. Tickets were on sale at the club for £1.50 each.

I expected to sell about 300 tickets and, with raffles and things on the night, I was hoping to make in the region of £600, which would have been a great start to my testimonial fund. After a few days I inquired at the social club as to how many tickets had been sold only to be told that the total was — nil. That night I went around putting up more posters a little further afield, on the outskirts of Wolverhampton. However, after a few more days I got the same reply that not one ticket had been sold. I had sold 30 or 40 tickets to my own circle of friends but I could not let Bernard come and perform to such a small audience. It was getting very close to the date of the function by then and the sales were still zero, so I had no alternative but to call a halt to the whole affair. To this day I still have no idea as to why no tickets were sold. I could have accepted the fact if only three, 10, 20 or 30 had been bought, but not zero.

I phoned Johnny Hamp and, embarrassed, explained the situation. Johnny was sympathetic and was of the same opinion as myself that somewhere along the line somebody had got it in for me. There was no slight on Bernard, because no matter who it had been at the top of the bill the result would have been just the same. Johnny kindly explained the situation to Bernard and thanked him on my behalf for the wonderful gesture he had been prepared to make. So the first part of my testimonial, the thing I had served Wolves 10 years for, had actually cost me money in expenses instead of making me a profit. With one down and one to go I was not feeling very confident of a good attendance at the match that was being arranged.

At this juncture, I sat down and pondered how ludicrous the situation was. A player serves a club for 10 years and is rewarded with a testimonial, but who is it who rewards the player? It is not the club. That player has to rely on the generosity of the public, many of whom have already spent money over the years watching the player and his teammates. He also has to rely on the services of famous players from within the game to give up their own to time to come and play in a game for him. Fortunately, in my case the players who had been contacted had all agreed to play so all I had to hope for was a fine night and a good attendance.

Robert Plant, of Led Zeppelin fame, was, and still is, a staunch Wolves supporter and came up with a great idea for a fun game before the main match involving many names from the world of showbiz. 'Don't worry, Waggy,' he said to me, 'I'll arrange all the showbiz side of it.' It was very kind of him and I really appreciated it. 'Don't worry' Robert had said, but I was worried, not about Robert's side of it but the fact that I might not even be fit enough to play in my own testimonial game. However, I need not have worried because Toby Andersen had me fit before the end of the season.

Of course, when people play in your testimonial game, none of them expects any payment, so the usual practice is to give everybody a keepsake to remember the occasion. After hours of deliberation I finally decided to give everybody a small piece of Wedgwood. Since close on 50 people were involved I thought it necessary to pay a visit to the Wedgwood shop adjacent to the Wedgwood factory on the outskirts of Stoke. The shop was like Aladdin's cave, filled with all kinds of different Wedgwood pieces. I wandered around and made a list of the various smaller pieces that I wanted to buy. It was 48 in all. I approached the saleswoman and showed her the different items I wanted to purchase. At first she was under the impression that I required one of each, but when I quoted what was on my list — so many of these, so many of those — she exclaimed. 'Let me stop you right there. Even though this shop is attached to the factory we get a delivery just like any stockists of Wedgwood.'

'So you can't just pop into the factory and pick them up?' I asked hopefully.

'No chance,' she replied. 'And another thing — I have already sent my orders in and even on the next delivery there wouldn't be the quantities of the items that you require. It would take at least three weeks to get everything of yours in stock,' she said sympathetically.

'I'm afraid I haven't got that amount of time,' I answered with dismay.

'Just bear with me for five minutes or so,' said the very helpful assistant. 'Give me your list and I'll make a few phone calls to some of our stockists and we'll see what we can muster between us.'

Off she went into her office and I sat there patiently, thinking what else I could do as an alternative when suddenly she reappeared exuberantly from the office, obviously bursting with good news.

'You're in luck,' she said. 'I've found a store that has every item you require in stock. Not only that, they have got a 10 per cent discount on all Wedgwood items for one week. The bad news is this store is over 30 miles from here'.

'I don't mind that,' I said, 'as long as they've got all the items. In any case, I've already driven about 30 miles to get here.' I then asked, 'Where is this place?'

'It's a store called Beatties, based in Wolverhampton,' she replied.

She frowned as she saw me laughing out loud until I explained that I lived in Wolverhampton and then she saw the funny side of it. She was so helpful and so were the staff at Beatties. She phoned them again to say that I definitely wanted to buy all the items and I should be there within the hour. When I arrived at Beatties, everything had been parcelled up and all that was left for me to do was to pay the money, less 10 per cent of course!

The week before the testimonial game I spent every evening after dark driving around Wolverhampton putting up posters wherever I could in order to try to get as many spectators to the game as possible. One night I even climbed on to the railway bridge that spans the end of Compton Road to display one of the posters advertising my big game.

The day of the match arrived and I just had to hope that it was going to be a fine temperate evening, which, fortunately, it was. Robert Plant had done me proud by getting such names as Jeff Lynne and Bev Bevan from ELO, Roy Wood (Wizzard), Clifford T. Ward and Jasper Carrot to appear in a fun game before the main one, alongside some old-time Wolves favourites. It amazed me to see how nervous the stars were. After all, they had performed in front of millions of people, never mind just thousands. A bottle of whisky was passed along as they lined up to go out on to the pitch and each in turn took a slug to calm the nerves. Anyway, they all seemed to thoroughly enjoy it and Jasper even did a short skit about it on his next record.

The main game of the evening was a Wolves team against an International XI, which included some big names in football — Peter Shilton, Trevor Francis, Colin Bell and Mike Summerbee, to name a few, with the Doog guesting for them as well. George Best had promised to play but at the 11th hour decided to withdraw. Those of us who knew George always knew there was a possibility of this happening. The evening went off as well as could be expected and a crowd of 14,000 turned out to watch. It was as much as I could have hoped for, seeing that the average League gate for that particular season had been around 23,000.

But for those 14,000 spectators I would have got nothing at all for the 10 years of service that I had given Wolverhampton Wanderers, because what did the club contribute? Nothing money wise. They lent me the pitch, that was all. Why was it that loyal players had to rely on the generosity of the public? It was something that I have never been able to understand. It was a totally unfair system to my mind. Take, for example, three players who have all served 10 years. They have got to be good players, otherwise they would not have been in the team for that amount of time. Player A may be the most popular of the three and gets the best attendance at his testimonial match. Player B, unfortunately, has his match on an horrendous day weather-wise so gets a very poor attendance. Player C struggles to get an opposition together because of their club commitments. Three different scenarios, but the fact remains that they have all served 10 years and deserve equal reward. In fact, there could even be a situation where the player who receives the least amount of money has played far more games in those 10 years than had the other two. There are all sorts of different permutations but, in my mind, every one should be treated the same.

The gate receipts for my testimonial game came to around £6,500 but, as I was to find out, that figure would diminish quite a bit. The club charged me for the floodlights, the turnstile operators and the tea ladies. Then came another blow. I was told that I had to pay for the policemen who had been on duty inside and outside the ground. Then there was a small matter of VAT, which I had not taken into consideration. The £6,500 had now shrunk to less than £5,000.

Some time later I went to see Bill McGarry to find out when and how I would receive the money that was due to me. I should have known better.

'Boss,' I began, 'this money that I'm due from my testimonial.'

'What about it?' he snapped.

'Well, I was wondering if I could see the accountant with regard to the most economical way that I should be paid the money.'

That was it. His desk nearly went over as he stood up in a complete rage. 'Don't you come in here asking for this club to go f*****g bent for you. You'll gate the f*****g money when and how I say,' he roared.

McGarry had taken everything I said completely out of context. All I wanted to see the club accountant for was to get some advice. I did get the money how and when he said. It came on my next payslip, added on to my wages, so you can imagine how much income tax I had to pay on that little lot. Some 16 months later, when Mike Bailey had his testimonial, he was allowed to pay all his moneys into a pension fund specially designed for professional footballers. It went into the scheme tax free and he was allowed to draw it out, with profits on his investment, when he was 35. This was the kind of thing that I wanted to see the accountant about, but Bill McGarry was convinced that I was trying to pull off some underhand scheme.

By the end of the season, Derek Dougan had quietly retired from Wolverhampton Wanderers. The Doog had arrived at Molineux in March 1967, his sixth move in nine years.

I do not think any of the team at that time had played with him or even knew him personally. However, we all knew of him and, to be fair, we all expected a real rabble-rouser when we heard that he was on his way to Molineux. When he swept into the dressing room for his first day's training with us he surprised us all. He was not the brash character we all expected but was Irish charm itself.

Doog's first appearance for Wolves was at Plymouth, just about as far away from Molineux as you could get, and he acclimatised himself and slotted into the team with ease. We won the game 1–0, but it proved to be merely his dress rehearsal. The command performance was to follow. That win at Plymouth was our fifth in a row, keeping us well in the promotion race, so it was not surprising that with promotion on the horizon and a new centre-forward to show off, 30,000 people, our best home gate of the season, turned out to watch Doog's first home game, against Hull City. What happened next was one of those occasions where you could not have written the script, unless, of course, you were writing an episode of *Roy of the Rovers*. Our hero entered the arena to a fanfare of trumpets and left after scoring a hat-trick with the cheers of the crowd ringing in his ears, an occasion now embedded in the history of Wolverhampton Wanderers. The Doog scored nine goals in the last 11 games of the season as we duly regained our place in the First Division. That is not to take anything away from the rest of the team. We had worked hard to get within striking distance of promotion and, as it turned out, Derek was the final piece in the jigsaw.

All credit to manager Ronnie Allen. He had hooked the big fish, but was he going to be able to keep him? With Derek's track record for moving about, nobody was sure that he would settle down at Wolves for any sort of prolonged period. He was to prove every doubter wrong because, as you probably know, he stayed at Molineux for the rest of his playing career. His record in European games was incredible. To score 12 goals in 18 appearances against European defences was as good, if not better, than any other top striker before or since. His record in the League, 95 goals from 244 games, was a considerable contribution to our successes. John Richards, in the early days, must have learned a lot from Derek and, once he became his own man, a gifted striker in my opinion, they were as good as any strike pair in the League.

Derek was at arm's length with the management because of his PFA connections but was a popular lad in the dressing room. Although he liked a drink, it was very rare that he joined the rest of the lads at the Moreton or the Mermaid. That is not to say there was anything wrong with that, but he was always one for playing hiscards close to his chest. He was a good player to have in your team, always kept himself fit and was always willing to make runs for you or make himself available as a target to hit or flick the ball on to John Richards. He was certainly a character on the field of play and the opposition knew they had been in a game when the Doog was around.

I travelled the world with the Doog in the eight and a half years that we were in the team together and I do not think we ever had a wrong word — except maybe about to whose turn it was to get the drinks when we were on planes! In all seriousness, Wolves were good for the Doog and the Doog was good for Wolves. He could be more than proud of his efforts over those eight and a half seasons. It was no surprise that so many glowing tributes were paid to him after his sudden death at the age of 69 in June 2007.

So Derek called it a day at the end of 1974–75 and, although I didn't know it when I lined up against Manchester United for the opening game of the 1975–76 campaign, this was also going to be my last season as a Wolverhampton Wanderers. Little had I dreamed in 1964 that 11 seasons later I would still be a Wolves player. As a professional footballer, you tend not to count the seasons as each one, in principle, is the same as another. As one ends, it is only a matter of weeks before the long slog of pre-season training — the worst part of player's life, in my opinion — starts for the next one. Then there is a pre-season tour and the new season is upon you. So it goes on.

While the club had made a significant signing in the experienced Willie Carr during the latter part of the previous season, I think it was a big mistake to sell Peter Withe to Birmingham, leaving the club with only one out-and-out striker, John Richards. Steve Kindon had been partnering John up front and the same pairing kicked-off the 1975–76 season, but it was always felt that we lost Steve's skill of being able to run at speed at people by playing him with his back to the opposing goal. We were treading on thin ice if one or both of them was injured. The only other person with any experience of playing striker was Alan Sunderland, who had not been a regular for some time. Having said that, Alan could have come into the side in almost any position and done more than a reasonable job. The Doog had gone, I was injured and Bob McNab had come in, meaning Derek Parkin had to switch to right-back, so the side had a slightly disjointed look about it and only two games of the first 15 that season were won.

It was around this time that Sammy Chung came into the dressing room and announced, 'Waggy, the boss wants to see you in his office. Now.'

I had a quick wander around my memory to see if I had done anything wrong or been anywhere I should not have, and with two negative answers I meandered down the corridor, full of confidence and wondering why I had been summoned before the manager.

'Sit down, Davy,' he said in the friendliest tone I had ever heard from him.

'Davy? Something's wrong here,' I thought. 'He doesn't call me that.'

'Jim Smith, from Blackburn Rovers, has been on the phone to me with a view to taking you on loan. How do you feel about that?' the manager explained.

'When do I leave?' was my excited reply, which took him by surprise.

'No need to be hasty about it,' he replied. 'It was only a tentative inquiry.'

'Tentative or not,' I said, 'ask him when he wants me to start.' By now I was brimming with confidence, knowing that he wanted to be rid of me and I was being given the chance to get out of his clutches. I wanted to grab the chance with both feet, as it were.

McGarry had not expected my reaction to be so positive and it took him a second or so to give me his answer. 'I take it you're interested in his proposal and I'll contact him later to tell him. Come back and see me after training,' he said.

It suddenly hit me while I was training. I had never met Jim Smith. I did not know anything about him. He could be as bad as McGarry to work for. He might be worse. Had I dropped a clanger? Had I been too eager? McGarry would just love it if I was out of the frying pan and into the fire! Anyway, I was soon to find out. After training, McGarry told me that Jim would like to see me the following afternoon at Ewood Park.

Driving up the M6 the next day to Blackburn I was trying to remember the last time I had played there. How could I have forgotten? I got sent off there in our 1966–67 promotion season. I arrived at Ewood and, parking in the cobbled street outside the ground, I set off to find Jim Smith's office. I discovered that it was not at the ground but in a terraced house on the opposite side of the cobbled street. Yes, Jim had the luxury of a converted bedroom in a terraced house. As I walked up the stairs I did not know what to expect, having never met the man before. I need not have worried because the moment he opened his office door it was just like meeting an old friend. No airs and graces. 'Thanks for coming. Do you want a cup of tea?' he said, as he put the kettle on.

My fears had gone now that I had met Jim and from the very start I knew that we would get on well together and understand each other so I agreed to a loan period of two months with Rovers. Jim explained that Rovers were skint and that was why he was having to take players on loan. At that time the club could just not afford to buy anybody.

'Right,' said Jim, 'we can't afford to put you into a hotel so we will fix you up with some digs.'

'I think I might be able to solve that problem,' I replied. 'My mother and father live in Blackpool, which is only 30 miles from here. It's virtually all motorway and wouldn't take much more than half an hour to get here. So if that's OK with you, I'll stay with them.'

'That's fine by me,' said Jim. So we had got off to a very amiable start.

We had a really good chat and I felt that even if I was not offered a permanent position with Rovers at the end of the loan period, playing in a lower division might help me get some confidence back and the change of environment would be good for me, having started the last 11 seasons for Wolves. It was as though a weight had been lifted off me – a new lease of life, a fresh challenge.

Jim gave me that fresh challenge. Before I ran out on to the pitch for my first game for Rovers his only words to me were 'Play it as you see it', giving me carte blanche to play how I wanted to play and deal with any on-field situations as they came along. The more games I played the more my confidence came back. I was really enjoying playing in the Rovers team. Being the elder statesman, I was looked up to by the younger players as they realised that I could still play a bit. Actually, dropping down a division gave me that few extra seconds to do things and made life a little easier. The more I played the more I enjoyed it and I became a bit of a favourite with the Rovers crowd.

Staying in Blackpool with my mum and dad gave me chance to read the local papers and I could not help but notice how cheap, compared with the Midlands, the property was in Blackpool, especially guesthouses. I knew that Rovers wanted to sign me permanently so I earmarked one of these guesthouses for that eventuality. There was a seven-bedroom property for sale on the promenade at Bispham, the north part of Blackpool. It also had a rear building that could easily be converted into two more bedrooms. The beach and the sea were, in effect, the front garden, a view that could not be taken away. All this for £17,500. I phoned Barbara to tell her about it and asked her to put the house in Compton up for sale. She thought I had gone mad. She had not even seen this place on which I was about to make an offer.

As the weeks rolled on the solicitors were interacting on both properties and I was becoming a very busy person, travelling between Wolverhampton, Blackpool and Blackburn, not to mention the away trips. However, the main thing was that I was really enjoying playing football. The mere fact that I had peace of mind made the amount of to-ing and fro-ing seem insignificant. Yes, everything was rolling along nicely until Jim Smith called me into his office with some news that put a dampener on it all. Bill McGarry wanted me back.

I travelled down to Wolverhampton and immediately confronted him about why I had been recalled to the club. 'You're only on loan,' he said, 'legally you belong to this club and I can recall you any time I like.' I had no answer to that, so I had to retreat with my tail between my legs and join in the training session. I was totally bewildered. The game that he had recalled me for was a fifth-round FA Cup tie against Second Division Charlton Athletic and when I saw the team that he had selected I was even more confused – John Richards was substitute.

No wonder I was confused. I was preferred to Steve Daley, John Farley, Steve Kindon and Jimmy Kelly, all of whom could play in a natural outside-left position. Furthermore, why was JR sub? After all, McGarry could have played all three strikers in a 4–3–3 formation. It was all beyond me, but I managed to resolve the situation not long after the game began – not by choice, I might add. Attempting to block a cross from one of the Charlton players, I raised my left leg and felt the electric shock-like pain down the back of my thigh which meant I had pulled my hamstring. I left the field to the blackest of black looks from McGarry and John Richards took to the pitch, where he should rightfully have been from the start.

John went on to score a hat-trick as Wolves won 3–0 and triggered his goalscoring exploits for the rest of the season, finding the net another 12 times in 15 League and Cup games. The club also benefited from a lucrative sixth-round tie against Manchester United, which was replayed at Molineux after a 1–1 draw at Old Trafford, watched by a total of over 103,000 fans. Wolves, incidentally, did in the replay what, during my time with them, they had twice before done against United in Cup games – lost after being two goals up.

The only real loser in the Charlton Cup tie was me, with a torn hamstring and a dilemma as to which club was going to treat the injury. As usual, McGarry did not want to know because injured players were no use to him and I do not recall that we ever exchanged words again until an occasion 10 years later. In fact, the last time I heard his voice was when Jim Smith turned on the intercom in his office on deadline day when McGarry asked him to pass on his threat to make me play in his third team if I did not sign for Rovers.

It became a farcical situation on that deadline day with McGarry wanting me to sign for Rovers but still wanting a fee of £6,000 for me, money that Rovers just did not have. I knew that I was going to be the one to miss out, because there was no chance of my getting a signing-on fee due to Rovers' financial problems. It did not seem fair to me that Wolves could unscrupulously demand £6,000 for me after I had given them 12 years' loyal service. What made me more annoyed was the fact that they would be raking in more than I had made from my testimonial.

Deadline day became very hectic for Jim Smith. Not only was he negotiating with Wolves as to how and when they were to receive the £6,000, but he was also negotiating the signing of Gordon Taylor, who, as you know, went on to be top man at the PFA. It was obvious that Jim was not an office-type football manager and he would have much preferred to be out on the training pitch with the lads. Anyhow, he negotiated his way through the proceedings and I duly signed forms to become a Blackburn Rovers player.

My career as a Wolverhampton Wanderers player had finally come to an end after a period of 12 years. It had been a long and, for the most part, enjoyable journey, with many more ups than downs. I had had the privilege of working with a fantastic set of lads, enjoying many great times on and off the field. There had been a lovely family side to it with all the wives socialising together and most of us watching each others' children grow up in the time that we were together. On the field I was grateful for the wonderful support that the Wolves fans had given me over the years. The encouraging roar when I got the ball was a tremendous fillip and I hope that I was able to provide them with their just reward.

Just to put the record straight — many people thought that I was susceptible to too many injuries in my career, but if you compare my record with the other two elder statesmen of the team, Derek Dougan and Mike Bailey, you will get a surprise. Our average League games per full season were; Mike 33, myself 33 and Derek 29. So it seems that I was not injured more than the norm.

I have some wonderful memories of my Molineux playing days. At a football club there are many people involved behind the scenes and I can honestly say that I had a great rapport with Billy Pilbeam and his men, all the office staff, the tea ladies and many more unsung heroes who went about their duties in the background. This was goodbye to my footballing days at Molineux, but little did I know that it was only 'au revoir' as far as my relationship with the club was concerned.

A Rover in Clover

The playing staff at Rovers consisted mainly of Lancashire and Yorkshire lads so I did not feel out of place, having been born in Manchester. It was a financially struggling club but what it lacked in monetary terms was overshadowed by the friendliness of the players and staff alike. It was just right for me and I felt completely at home now that I had signed permanently.

The property deals that I had mentioned had both gone through and Barbara and I became the proud proprietors of a small private hotel on Blackpool's prom. The name of the place was Beachholme, but we soon changed that because it sounded like on old folk's residence. We renamed it Queenscliffe and as we proudly put up the new sign a smaller one went up in the front window. It said 'Vacancies'. This was a chance to supplement our income because joining Rovers had not provided me with a signing-on fee nor a rise in wages. The directors had been very helpful and Billy Bancroft, the chairman, had promised that the club would help out with my moving expenses. One of the directors, a Mr Brown, who had a wallpaper factory, supplied me free of charge with enough wallpaper to refurbish every room in the hotel. There was an advertising board behind one of the goals at Ewood Park and on it was written 'Walker's Steels'. I purchased some steel girders from that firm, owned by the man who would eventually rebuild the ground and finance the purchase of players to win the Premiership title. That man was, of course, Jack Walker.

It was an old-fashioned, friendly, homely club to be part of and the manager's name certainly summed him up. Jim Smith, plain Jim Smith, what you saw was what you got — no airs and graces with Jim, it was straight to the point and if it hurt, then tough. He was a lot closer to the lads than any other manager that I had known, but he did not get too close. He knew how far to go and the good thing was that he was not afraid to have a laugh with the lads. Some of the players were so laid back and were just happy to have a game of football on a Saturday. What had gone on before Jim became manager I do not know, but it seemed that these lads took nothing seriously and just went along with everything. I'll never forget the first team meeting that I attended. One Friday morning after training Jim Smith announced, 'OK, lads, have a bath and we will have a meeting in the first-team dressing room at 11.45.'

At 11.45 I was sitting next to Gordon Taylor and the rest of the lads were spread around the dressing room. The door opened and in walked Jim.

'Right, lads,' he said, only to be interrupted by one of the players.

'Mecca's not here yet. He won't be a minute. They open at quarter to.'

'What opens at quarter to?' inquired Jim, who was then interrupted again by the dressing room door opening to reveal Stuart Metcalfe (Mecca) carrying a cardboard box.

'Sorry about this, boss,' he said, 'there was a bit of a queue.'

He put the box down and took out a piece of paper to scrutinise.

'Now then,' he said as he reached inside the box, 'Smigga, yours is sausage and chips with a buttered bap,' he added as he passed a white paper parcel to Smigga. 'John, yours was pudding and chips. Oh, sorry, here's your bread and butter to go with it.'

As this went on Jim Smith looked at Gordon and me with an expression of disbelief. He was gobsmacked and so were we. We had never seen anything like it. Jim let things progress.

'Fish, chips and peas,' announced Mecca and, looking at his list, passed them over to another one of the lads. By this time Jim had sat down with his head in his hands, totally perplexed. After all the food was dished out, Jim stood up.

'What the f*****g hell's going on?' he said, not in a nasty tone but one of disbelief. 'You're supposed to be professional footballers, not a gang of navvies, having their dinner in the portacabin.'

The room went quiet. Then Mecca broke the ice. 'Would you like a chip, boss?' he asked.

I thought that Jim was going to explode but, to my amazement, he walked over to Mecca, picked a chip out of the paper and said 'Thanks very much.' Then he exploded...

'This will never f*****g happen again,' he roared. 'It was the most unprofessional thing I've ever seen in football.'

Jim then carried on with the meeting and I can assure you that it did not happen again during his reign at Rovers. Once Jim made his point, it was carried out to the letter. The lovely part about all this was that the lads in question did not think they were really doing anything wrong. All they wanted was a game of football and everything else was just a part of their normal life. Stuart Metcalfe was a wonderfully skilful midfield player and in some respects had the same attitude as young Peter Knowles – nothing else mattered as long as there was a football at his feet and the climax of the week was that game on Saturday afternoon.

Life after Molineux was certainly different. Every day was a long day for me, but I was still fit enough to cope with the running of the hotel and the training and playing for Blackburn Rovers. I was up early in the morning, giving Barbara a hand to cook breakfast for the visitors. Then I would serve the breakfasts before having to leave for Blackburn, not forgetting my sandwiches made of any eggs broken in the course of cooking breakfast. Forty minutes later I would be at Ewood Park ready for training. After training there was another bonus – just over the road was the best pie shop I have ever been to, Lever's, a family-run business which made the finest pies I have ever eaten. Apparently, even though Ewood was rebuilt, the pie shop is still there to this day. I would eat my pie on the way back to Blackpool and in the afternoon would help Barbara prepare the vegetables for the evening meal and then help with the serving of the meal. I drew the line at all the washing-up afterwards and instead prepared my small bar in the lounge, which I would open at around 8 o'clock and close when the visitors were ready to go to bed.

Most football clubs work along the same lines but the more affluent ones can afford better facilities all round. Rovers, unfortunately, were not one of the affluent clubs and Jim Smith had to ring around in the mornings to find somewhere to train, Rovers not having a training ground of their own. Sometimes it was a school or the local park or any old place that could accommodate us. One of the places where we used to train was in the grounds of a brickworks overlooking the rundown remains of the Accrington Stanley ground. A tall chimney stood in the brickworks with the word 'Nori' in white letters on the side of it, which people could see from miles away. Rumour had it that when it was built the bricklayer who incorporated this into his brickwork had somehow got his wires crossed and it should have read the 'Iron' brickworks! Another place where we used to train was the playing fields of a mental institute on the outskirts of Blackburn. The fields were rarely used by the inmates and it was always in fine condition. All sorts of weird and wonderful characters used to come and watch us train and collect the balls from behind the goal. When Jack Walker took over the reins at the club many years later he actually bought the institute and its grounds after it had closed down. It is still to this day Blackburn Rovers's academy and has been made into a wonderful place.

The whole of the club was a team at Rovers and everybody did their bit whenever they could. It was not unusual to find directors forking the pitch to drain the water away before a game. The directors were the friendliest bunch of people that you could wish to meet and the boardroom, a wonderful original oak-panelled room, had the reputation for the best food in football, most of it home-made by the tea ladies.

When we had a Saturday fixture in London we would travel down on the Friday afternoon after training, but before we left we were all invited to Mr Brown's wallpaper factory for lunch in the works canteen. It was a basic menu but the food was absolutely lovely! Mr Brown's factory was a converted mill on the side of the recently-restored canal and it had been changed into an impressive place that all the lads enjoyed visiting.

The Rovers chairman, Mr Bancroft, or to give him the name everyone knew him by, Billy Bancroft, was still in the cotton industry and was a very ordinary down-to-earth guy. He was impressed with my prowess on the field and if I had a good game he would wait at the end of the tunnel as I left the field to give me a cigarette, already lit. Jim Smith could never work out how I could come off the field and into the dressing room after a game with a lighted cigarette.

Rovers still owed me some money for my moving expenses and also some travelling expenses and every time I saw Billy Bancroft he would whisper to me, 'I'll try to get your money for you this week.' The amount in question was £400. I learned to take this promise of payment with a pinch of salt, but I knew that one day it would come to fruition. Sometimes, on away trips, Gordon Taylor and I were allowed to be picked up by the team coach close to junction 31 of the M6 and this was the case one time when we had a midweek fixture in London against Fulham. Gordon boarded the bus first and as I climbed up the step behind him, Bill Bancroft, who was sitting on the front seat, pointed to his inside pocket, opened his jacket slightly and revealed the corner of a brown envelope, at the same time mouthing to me, 'Got your money.' It was good news for me as I had been waiting quite some time for it.

George Best played for Fulham that night but at this stage of his career he was not the George that we knew and loved. At one point in the game I was brought down from behind and, looking up, could see George stood there with his hands on his hips. 'Sorry, Waggy,' he said, 'I knew I wouldn't be able to catch you.' In his heyday it would have been very different.

I cannot remember the result of the game but I can remember what happened later in a London club. Ex-squadron leader Joe Mercer, who was an avid Rovers supporter – he travelled to away games from Newquay in Cornwall – had arranged to meet Graham Hawkins and a couple of the lads after the game to go for a drink. I tagged along too and Joe took us to a small club that was completely run by women – most of them topless. It cost you money if they sat at your table and even more money if you bought them a drink because they drank only champagne.

'Don't worry,' said Joe, 'I know the madam and she won't let any of the girls bother us, so we can have a nice few drinks while we watch the floor show.'

He was right. None of the girls badgered us and we were left in peace at our table. Very surprisingly, later into the night Billy Bancroft and Jim Smith came into the club. 'Move over, lads,' Billy shouted as he and Jim pulled a couple of chairs up to our table. It was quite obvious that he had been drinking and was in a very merry mood.

'What are we all having?' he asked as a waitress came to take the order and he proceeded to buy us all a drink.

'Who's in charge here?' he asked the waitress. Joe stepped in and called over the madam, introducing her to Billy.

'That girl there,' said Billy, pointing to one of the topless barmaids, 'the one with the biggest knockers. I'd like her to come and sit on my friend's knee,' he added, pointing to me.

'No problem, sir,' she replied, 'but it will cost you and you will have to provide champagne.'

'Carry on,' he said and the madam went off to get the girl and the champagne.

Billy insisted the girl sit on my knee, yes, the girl with the big knockers, and proceeded to order more drinks. What was I doing? I had a topless girl on my knee and a glass of champagne in my hand and I had only come out for a few beers after the game — but I could not argue with the chairman, could I? After more champagne it was time to go and Billy Bancroft shouted for the bill. The madam came over with the bill in her hand. 'How much?' asked Billy. Even in those days it was expensive in London clubs. '£375,' answered the madam.

The next thing, my eyes nearly popped out of my head — and not at the girl's large chest but at the brown envelope that Billy took out of his inside pocket. 'There's four hundred in there,' he mumbled, feeling the effect of the drinks. 'Keep the change.'

'F*****g hell,' I whispered to myself, 'there goes my money.'

Many hours later, when the coach pulled off the M6 at junction 31 to let Gordon and me collect our cars, the chairman was sitting in his usual position on the front seat and as I passed him to get off he quietly said, 'Waggy, don't go without this' and he pointed to a brown envelope on the seat next to him. I had got my money at last.

End of the Line

There was never a dull moment at Blackburn Rovers under the management of Jim Smith and his assistant Norman Bodell, whom I had known from my days at Wolves. Naturally, the football was taken seriously, but off the field we had bundles of laughs and one low point when I managed to get myself into the *Guinness Book of Records*, not intentionally, I might add.

On 2 October 1976 we were playing Orient at Brisbane Road. Jim Smith had asked me to play in midfield that day and I found myself in direct opposition to Alan Whittle, a small and very tricky ex-Everton player. Alan managed to foul me four times in the first 15 minutes. They were not bad fouls, but just enough to put me out of my stride. Minutes later he completely wrong-footed me and I had no alternative but to obstruct him. The referee raced over and immediately reached for his top pocket, leaving me in no doubt what was coming. I was quite incensed by this because it was the first foul that I had committed. This was the first day that red and yellow cards had been issued to referees in the Football League and as usual the League management committee had made a hash of it. They had not instructed referees on how to administer these cards. This referee took the yellow card from his top pocket then for a few seconds he was transfixed. He had not been told the procedure, so he showed the card to all four corners of the ground like a referee in boxing giving a public warning. Then he pointed to me as if to say 'Yellow card for this man here.' This got the crowd bawling and shouting and made me even more incensed.

'F*****g hell, ref,' I snapped. 'Talk about players inciting the crowd, look what you've just f*****g done!'

With that he reached for the red card and, incredibly, he did exactly the same, showing it to all around the ground. I gave him a few more expletives and went for an early bath. If the referee had been instructed properly as to the correct procedure when showing these cards then the whole innocuous incident would have merely resulted in my having to accept the yellow card and then get on with the game — and that would have been the end of it. Unfortunately this incident left me with the unenviable record of being the first player ever to have been shown the red card. Being the first, it is a record that can never go away. While on the subject of discipline I will tell you about a couple more incidents.

Rovers were playing Nottingham Forest, who were pushing for promotion and had the late, great Brian Clough at the helm. Cloughie was a great manager and also a very good psychologist. Over the period of my career I had played against Cloughie's teams many times and for half a game — the half when I was close to the dugout — Cloughie would try to put me off with comments and insults. Being part and parcel of the game, I did not let it get to me and as many people said to me he would not have tried to get to me if he did not rate me as a player. With that in mind I carried on with my game, but on this particular occasion it was not his comments that caused a problem — it was his actions. Forest were leading 1–0 with maybe 10 minutes to go and we were pushing forward desperately for the equaliser. The ball was put out of play by a Forest defender and it rolled into their dugout, the old-fashioned type which was sunk into the ground. I ran over to retrieve the ball in order to take a quick throw-in but Cloughie and his two companions in the dugout seemed to have difficulty in locating the ball down among their feet. I wonder why? Eventually, after what seemed an age, Cloughie, with a big smile on his face, threw the ball out to me. By this time all chances of a quick throw-in had disappeared and the Forest defence were nicely back into position, just as Brian had intended. I was furious and, stupidly, lost my temper as the ball bounced in front of me. I half-volleyed it back into the dugout, fractionally missing Cloughie's head. The ball rebounded back into my arms and before I could take the throw-in the referee had come over to book me for ungentlemanly conduct, as it was then called. I turned to the dugout to glance at Cloughie, who by this time had an even bigger smile on his face. He had won our little battle of wits and, incidentally, his team went on to win the game and gain promotion that season.

To all football fans throughout the country Bobby Moore was the epitome of tranquility on the pitch. Unruffled under pressure, unruffled on the ball, I doubt that many of his fans ever saw him lose his temper — but I did. Playing for Manchester City against West Ham as a 17-year-old, my instructions from coach Jimmy Meadows were to hustle and harry Bobby Moore every time he got the ball. Bobby was playing in the right-half position that day and, to the detriment of my own game, I put more emphasis on Jimmy Meadows's instructions. Eventually, Bobby snapped after one of the incidents and kicked me on the back of my thigh as I walked away. The linesman spotted the altercation and alerted the referee, who had no hesitation in sending Bobby Moore off. This was the only time that the great man was sent off during his career and although over the years I was in his company many times he never mentioned the incident to me. However, he wrote about it in one of his books, putting it down to 'impetuous youth'.

So not only am I in the 'Hall of Infamy' for being the first player to be shown the red card, but I am also the player responsible for Bobby Moore's one and only sending-off.

Over the years I did receive many bookings. I would not in any way class myself as a dirty player and the excuse for the majority of my bookings was simply the fact that I could not tackle. A mistimed tackle from a forward looks twice as bad as it is because it is half an hour late! Just look back at how many times Paul Gascoigne and Paul Scholes were booked for what I call 'forwards' tackles'. Unfortunately, if it is not in your make-up, it is something you cannot learn.

Meanwhile, back at Ewood Park, the young lady who was responsible for the programme notes came to see me with some statistical news that had escaped my attention. My next home game would be my 500th League appearance. Had she not done her homework I would not have known, because there was no chance at all of the Football League informing me. Milestones like that were just not on their agenda.

The minimum time in which any player could have achieved 500 League appearances would have been 12 years and that would have been virtually without missing a game. So in reality, taking into account injuries and loss of place, I would estimate that 14 to 15 years would be a more realistic time to appear in this number of games. I guess the point that these were League games — not FA Cup, League Cup or anything else — was what made me so annoyed that the Football League did not, and still does not, recognise the significance of this achievement. It was a proud moment for me when I was presented with the plaque by the Rovers chairman on the pitch in front of the home crowd prior to the game and it is something that I cherish to this day. It would not have cost the Football League a fortune to produce a tie or maybe a blazer badge with '500 Club' incorporated into it. After all, it was not every day that players passed this milestone.

Some years later Bill Fox, who had become the Rovers chairman and also the president of the Football League, invited me to have lunch with him in one of the boxes before a game between Wolves and Blackburn Rovers. During a conversation I mentioned to him about there being no recognition from the League when players reached 500 games. He was very surprised to learn of this and assured me that he would do something about it to make sure that the occasion did not pass without being celebrated. Knowing Mr Fox, I was confident that he would do everything in his power to bring it to fruition, but sadly he passed away a short time after our meeting. So perhaps the 500 Club was never meant to be, after all.

As you can tell from my previous comments about the Football League, I did not hold the body in much esteem. They always had a figurehead, a president who would speak for them and answer questions on their behalf, but the rest were nameless, faceless people. I have never been able to find out how they got on the committee to begin with and how much they knew about our game of football, which they were allowed to make momentous decisions about. Very, very rarely did you ever get to meet any of these people, but I would like to tell you about one farcical occasion when I did.

I was asked by John Sillett, then an official of Chelsea Football Club, if I would appear on behalf of Alan Hudson to help with an appeal against a booking he received while playing against Wolves. This booking had taken Alan over the points limit and he was facing a ban so I had no hesitation in offering my services to help out a fellow professional. At the time of the incident between Alan and myself I thought that he was unlucky to be booked and said as much to the referee.

From the word 'go' the whole affair was comic cuts. Alan played for Chelsea and I played for Wolves, but where was the hearing to be held? Sheffield. I duly arrived at the hotel in Sheffield on the designated day and Alan and I went through the incident again, both in total agreement as what happened. I will now try to describe the incident to you and see what you think...

Wolves were kicking towards the North Bank and Chelsea towards the South Bank. Alan Hudson and I were exactly on the white line of the halfway line facing each other, he looking towards the Waterloo Road stand and me looking towards Molineux Street. We were approximately five yards apart and the ball was bouncing midway between us. Naturally we both went for the ball and I got there fractionally before him. I dragged the ball with my left foot into my own half and Alan unfortunately clipped the bottom of my left foot. The referee promptly ran over and booked him.

'It doesn't warrant that,' I protested to the ref.

'Keep it shut or you will be in the book as well,' he replied.

That was it, the end of the incident. I have already mentioned what I call 'forwards' tackles' and this was another example. He was a little late and it looked worse than it was. Alan was called into the hearing and after about 15 minutes he came out looking completely befuddled. Then it was my turn. I entered the room to be confronted with what looked like half a dozen bespectacled pensioners seated behind a huge table which was covered with a Subbuteo board and a full complement of players – reds and whites.

'OK, Mr Wagstaffe,' please give us your version of events using the Subbuteo players to pinpoint your position,' said the gentleman who was obviously chairing the meeting.

I pushed the red players into one half and the white players into the other half to denote which team was defending which goal. I picked up a red player and a white player, placing them facing each other on the white line of the halfway line just outside the centre circle.

I began ' We were kicking this way and they were kicking that way' indicating to the panel with a pointed finger. 'This is Alan Hudson and this is myself,' I went on, pointing to the two players that I had positioned facing each other on the halfway line.

I placed the plastic ball in between the two players and then proceeded to describe the incident as I have described it to you but with the added visual aid of the Subbuteo players and the Subbuteo pitch. As it got to the point where I dragged the ball away from Alan Hudson into my own half I was abruptly stopped by one of the panel as I was demonstrating with the white Subbuteo player.

'You've got hold of the wrong player,' he said, 'the whites are kicking the other way.'

I then proceeded to explain that because I was left-footed I would in that situation try to pinch the ball with it and consequently take it towards my own goal. Another one of the panel then chipped in to ask why I was going that particular way when I should have been attacking the other goal. I again tried to explain about me being left-footed and that there were many times when you needed to be running with the ball towards your own goal, but by now they were totally confused and were not sure who were the reds and who were the whites. I could not believe it. These were some of the committee who had input into the running of our game and they could not comprehend what I was trying to explain to them. I tried to defuse the situation by saying that it was just an innocent incident in which Alan meant no harm. He was fractionally later than myself getting to the ball and it looked worse than it was.

'Did the referee tell you that I said so at the time?' I inquired.

'Conversations between the panel and the referee are strictly confidential,' I was sternly told.

Before I left the room I informed the panel that Subbuteo sold players in the colours of every club and that maybe using the correct team colours during my demonstration would be helpful in explaining on-field situations to the panel. Surely it was a small price to pay in order to simplify matters? But even this suggestion was frowned upon. Needless to say, Alan's appeal failed and he was hit with a fine and a ban.

After my first full season at Rovers I had a wonderful surprise. I had been voted 'Player of the Season' by the fans. This was a great compliment to me and the statuette that I was awarded stands alongside the other awards that I received at Blackburn. Alas, all good things come to an end and during the next season Jim Smith decided to move on to pastures new, leaving us all with some fond memories of the happy times that we spent with him at Rovers. Jim Iley then took over as manager, but at the end of the season I decided to join Bob Stokoe, who was in charge at Blackpool.

After a season with Bob Stokoe at Bloomfield Road in 1978–79 I had a message from Blackburn, asking me to return to Ewood Park. I was almost ready to quit football but could not resist the challenge of going back to Blackburn. Unfortunately, in my second game for Rovers I split my shin open and was sidelined for a good few weeks. It was such an awkward injury that any knock would open up the wound and I was back to square one. In the meantime, Howard Kendall had joined the club as manager and I was looking forward to playing for him but, to my dismay, when I started full-time training again I found that I had lost a yard of pace. That yard of pace was so important to my game and at 34 years of age no amount of training was going to get it back. I made up my mind that was it. I was not going to play any more. I went to see Howard and told him of my decision. He kindly offered to send me on holiday to Spain for a week to think it over,

I declined, telling him that I had made my mind up. I walked out of his office and did not enter a football ground or watch football on television for three years until I had got it all out of my system.

So that was the end of my football career of almost 20 years and the best part of 600 League games. Now for another swipe at the Football League! Blackburn Rovers obviously informed them that there was no longer a contract between them and myself and that I had decided to retire from the game. A few days later I received a letter from the Football League. It was one of those standard letters, already printed with just the blanks to fill in before it was sent to me. It read:

'Dear Sir (not Dear David or Dear Mr Wagstaffe, we had not been together long enough to be that familiar!), As from this day forth your registration as a professional footballer is hereby cancelled.'

In almost 20 years that was the only correspondence that I received from them. No words of thanks, no record of my appearances, just those few stark words to confirm that it was all over and I was no longer a professional footballer.

By this time Barbara, the children and myself had already moved from the guesthouse into a private house. We had both agreed that our relationship with the children had been suffering due to our workload looking after the guests and although the guesthouse had been doing well and we thoroughly enjoyed it, we decided that it was not the ideal situation in which to bring up a family.

With football over and the guesthouse gone, it was time to find a job. After a spell in the building trade I finally decided that a job behind the bar would be the best for me and, after doing a few relief spells at different pubs and clubs, Barbara and I became steward and stewardess of Bispham Conservative Club. Situated on the north side of Blackpool, 200 yards from the sea, it was a well-patronised club with live entertainment on Wednesday, Saturday and Sunday. There was a bowling green at one side of the club where I was able to pursue my new-found hobby of crown green bowls, and although it entailed long working hours we thoroughly enjoyed the whole atmosphere. The kids were settled and we would probably have stayed there for a very long time, but for a telephone call from Wolverhampton.

Back to Molineux

In 1982 Wolverhampton Wanderers (1923) Ltd were in serious financial difficulties. Roger Hipkiss, a staunch Wolves supporter all his life, called an extraordinary general meeting when it was revealed by two people in control of the club, Doug Ellis and Malcolm Finlayson, that they had been unable to get the backing of Lloyds Bank to enable the club to continue. As a result of the meeting it became clear that Wolverhampton Wanderers (1923) Ltd would have to be put in the hands of the receivers and consequently the club was put up for sale.

Nobody came forward to buy the club and even an approach to Jack Hayward proved fruitless, as he was unwilling to purchase the club at that time. As the deadline approached, Doug Hope, a local businessman, contacted Mike Rowland, a prominent figure in the Allied Properties company, with a view to the company buying the club. As a result, owners of Allied Properties, the Bhatti brothers, showed an interest and agreed in principle to take it on, but only after an assurance from Wolverhampton Council that they would be able to sell some of the land with planning permission to a major supermarket in order to finance the building of a new stadium and units in a surrounding complex. It was only at the 11th hour that the deal was done and Wolverhampton Wanderers (1982) Ltd was formed.

Doug Hope, the instigator of the whole thing, and Roger Hipkiss became directors of the new company and Derek Dougan became the chairman. During the 1982–83 season Derek sold his strike partner John Richards to Maritimo, the Portuguese club. John had finished a loan spell at Derby County, but his transfer to the island of Madeira left many quite disconcerted. John himself had a major falling-out with Derek that never got resolved.

Early in 1984 I was contacted by Derek Dougan at the Bispham Con Club to see if I would be interested in coming back to Wolverhampton to work for Wolverhampton Wanderers (1982) Ltd. Consequently a meeting was arranged between Derek, Doug Hope, Barbara and myself. We had lunch with Derek and Doug at the Goldthorn Hotel in Wolverhampton where they told us of the plans for the football club. The plans that they outlined sounded good to us and we listened with interest, but at the end of the meeting we decided to go back to Blackpool and discuss it with the rest of the family – Gary, Scott and Mandy – before making a decision.

The family decision was to return to Wolverhampton and initially manage the Wolves Social Club, which stood next to the ground on Waterloo Road, until the proposed new ground and complex were built. We had been promised by Derek and the Bhatti brothers that once the new stadium and surrounding complex had been built that I would be given a senior management position in the new buildings. The social club was in a dire state, with repairs needed wherever you looked and a distinct lack of furniture. Upstairs in the gymnasium, the wooden block floor was listing in patches due to the rain coming in from a dilapidated roof and none of the showers or toilets worked in the changing rooms.

Barbara, the kids and I rented a house on Cannock Road, and a couple of days after moving in we set about the task of trying to make the interior of the social club presentable. It was an unenviable task because most of the jobs needed skilled tradesmen. Then came a bolt from the blue — Roger Hipkiss came to see me and asked if anyone had told me about a wedding reception that had been booked in for a few weeks hence. There were to be 400 gypsies for a sit-down meal from 4pm on Saturday, with another 200 guests arriving in the evening, and worse was to come. It was to be a free bar and they had also booked the big room for Sunday night for an after-wedding celebration, also with a free bar.

My mind was buzzing. Where was I going to get an extra 300 chairs from? Where was I going to get the tables from? How many glasses were there? There were so many questions to be answered and so much preparation to be done. I was pleased to discover that an outside caterer had been employed to cook the meals in our kitchens and that their own catering staff would serve the meals.

With the catering out of the way I was able to breathe a little more easily, but there was still a lot to do when I did a stupid thing. An Indian family came to see me with a view to booking the big room and using the kitchens for a wedding during the Sunday daytime in the space between the two gypsy celebrations. Thinking this would be good financially, I took the booking on the understanding that they would come in to organise the room on Saturday night after the gypsies had gone, be in at 8am Sunday and then be out, leaving me time to get the room ready for Sunday night.

Round about this time a gentleman came to see me and asked if there were any job vacancies. He told me that he was a keen Wolves supporter and that he had been to the ground to look for work but to no avail so he thought he would ask at the social club because he dearly wanted to work for Wolverhampton Wanderers.

'What kind of work are you looking for?' I asked him.

'I'm good at most odd jobs,' he replied, 'and I used to be in the plumbing game so I think I would be useful in here and around the ground.'

I was really looking for somebody like this but doubted that I would be able to employ him because of the financial situation. There was to be a board meeting the next day and I was going to ask the brothers if I could employ this man.

'Come and see me in two days' time,' I said to the fella, 'and I will let you know whether there is a job available.'

I had to be at these very frequent board meetings with Keith Pearson, the club accountant, in order to give the Bhattis a financial run-down on the social club. My part took no more than two minutes, but I was obliged to sit with Keith for the duration of the meetings, which sometimes took up to two hours. The only plus side of this was that I heard from the horses' mouths everything that was going on. The worst part for me was learning of the poor financial situation that I had brought my family into by leaving a good job in Blackpool. I realised what a mistake I had made, but there was no turning back now and I had to try to make the best of it for the sake of my family.

After I had given my report I told the brothers about the Wolves fan who so desperately wanted to work at Wolverhampton Wanderers. At first they did not want to know, but when I mentioned that he was good at odd jobs and plumbing and might be a good man to have around they became quite interested.

'Offer him a job. If he's that keen to work for Wolves he would probably work for nothing, but as an incentive offer him £10 a week. Tell him that's all we can afford,' said one of the brothers.

This was a miserly mercenary statement, but I could not say so. I had to accept it. The man was so keen that he was waiting for me outside the social club the next morning. I was dreading telling him the news.

'I've got some good news and some bad news,' I said to him, trying to play the whole thing down. 'The good news is I can offer you a job, the bad news is I can only pay you 10 quid a week.'

'I'll take it,' he said in a flash.

I was absolutely amazed, but I am glad he did and so was he. He has been a friend of my family and myself to this day. He stuck with Wolves through all the bad times and worked his way up to become the official Wolves historian. Who would have thought all those years ago when he took that job at £10 a week that one day he would have a stand, albeit a temporary one in the corner of the ground, named after him. His name? Graham Hughes.

The gypsy wedding was imminent and I found a place to get some chairs — the boxes in the John Ireland Stand. The Civic Hall was kind enough to lend us some trestle tables and the brewery had supplied us with as much drink as we thought we would need. Roger Hipkiss had offered to help behind the bar, but we were going to need all the bar staff that we could muster.

The big day came and, just as I thought, every bar was swamped with throngs of guests demanding drinks. We managed to get a little respite when the food was served but soon there was food being thrown about and they were back at the bar knocking drinks back as fast as they could. It is difficult to describe, but the whole place soon became a shambles. Friends of ours who came to see us even finished up helping behind the bar. Roger Hipkiss had been told to phone the Bhatti brothers every so often throughout the evening to inform them how much we had taken or rather how much the bride's father owed us as the free drinks flowed. I had never seen so many drunk people, but strangely we had no problem getting them to vacate the place. For some reason the bride's father, just after 10pm, decided that it was time to go and within 15 minutes the place was empty.

As you can imagine, the whole place, including the toilets, was like a war zone. I keep saying that it was difficult to describe but it really was. You had to be there to believe it. It had taken the caterer and his staff hours to wash all the crockery and get the kitchen back to normal and now it was our turn to get the club back to some sort of normality ready for the Indian family to come in and organise the room how they wanted it.

It was after 2am when I knocked on the door of the terraced house in Whitmore Reans, where the Indian family were waiting for me to tell them that the rooms were available for them to prepare for the following day's wedding. It had been a long, long day, and by the time that they had finished and I had locked up the club it was 4am. I was back again at 8am to let them in to cook their food, ready for the 300 guests who were expected to arrive at around 11.30am. As they had paid room hire and corkage on the drinks they had brought with them, it was not necessary for me to arrange any bar staff so I was looking forward to a restful time before the next celebration that evening.

Roger Hipkiss had called in to see me and we were sat having a cup of coffee in the front bar as the Indian wedding party arrived. The Indian band started up and everything seemed to be going according to plan. In hindsight, I should have locked the bar door because 10 minutes later in walked the father of the gypsy bride with two or three of his pals. Roger was hoping that they had come to pay the previous night's bill, so when they asked for a drink he was only too pleased to oblige, going behind the bar and serving them.

'Put it on my bill,' he said, and immediately Roger realised that he should not have served them. Within minutes there were over 100 gypsies in the bar and the father of the bride told us to put all the drinks on his bill. It was not long before some of them were worse for wear, and I whispered to Roger that it would be better if the gypsies left — after all, they should not have been there. The Asians had hired the club for the daytime.

It was getting late in the afternoon so I said to the father of the bride 'I'm closing this bar so that I can go and help the Asians to clear up ready for your party tonight in that room.'

'We'll get them out,' said the father of the bride.

'It's OK,' I replied. 'If you get your party off home, Roger and I can clean up in here, then help clear up in the other room. You do want everything to be just right for your guests tonight, don't you?'

'I do, I do,' he said and promptly shepherded his pals to their cars on the car park.

The party kept their word and vacated the premises just after 4pm. The family and I cleaned up the concert room and went home to have our tea and get ready for the evening . I made sure there was a full complement behind the bar ready for the evening rush. Roger Hipkiss was also coming along in the hope that at the end of the evening the bride's father would settle up with him.

Spot on 7pm the rush started, not as many as the night before but at least 300. There was a strange atmosphere that night, something told me that everything was not as it should have been. There was a thick-set tough gypsy guy strolling about, hell bent on causing trouble. He had already had a scuffle by the bar and twice he went on stage and challenged anybody in the room to fight him. It soon became clear there was friction between some of the families and with the amount of free drinks flowing it was surely going to end in trouble. Round about 10pm a car was set on fire in the car park, causing a gang of people to rush out to the scene. Suddenly a shotgun was heard and people were running everywhere. Roger called the police and they were there within minutes — a whole squad of them.

The police entered the club and the inspector immediately ordered me to close all the shutters on the bars. The bride's father asked Roger to let him out the back door, saying that he was in danger. Suddenly, within minutes, the place was empty and all that was left in the car park was a burnt-out car and a new Volvo that had been turned over on to its roof. It was a harrowing experience and shook everybody up.

Roger phoned the Bhattis to tell them what had happened and they instructed him to get the two cars removed immediately. They were also concerned that the man who owed all the money had slipped out the back door, but Roger assured them that he would know where to find him next day. Eventually that night the cars were taken away and we all had one or two nightcaps and headed off home to bed. That was the end of that — or so we thought.

The next evening I arrived at the social club to open the bar at 7pm. Driving on to the car park — it was pitch black — and in the gloom I could make out four or five figures standing at the top of the steps to the social club. As I approached the steps I could see that they were men.

'Evening gents,' I said, trying not to show that I was uncomfortable with the situation.

'Are you the manager?' one of them replied, and as soon as he spoke I realised they were gypsies.

'I am,' I said as I reached up and opened the locks.

'Where's the Volvo?' he demanded in a threatening tone.

'Hang on a minute,' I said, stalling for time, 'let me put some lights on.'

I put the lights on in the foyer and saw that I was confronted by five rough-looking gypsies.

'Where's the Volvo?' the first man repeated.

'I don't know,' I said, which was an honest answer. I explained that it was not me that had arranged for it to be taken away, but that I would try to find out for him.

'You have half an hour to find out,' he said, menacingly, and off they went down the steps.

I went in search of the Yellow Pages, prepared to ring every local number in order to find out where the Volvo was being stored. I was lucky. The Yellow Pages was in my office on the desk, still open at the relevant page. I was lucky again. Mandy, who had contacted the company, had put a small asterisk next to the name of one of the companies. I rang the number and got even luckier. It was the same young lady who had been on duty the previous evening and had taken Mandy's call. She particularly remembered the call because at the time the company she worked for could not deal with it so she gave Mandy the name and number of the company who could. Relieved, I thanked her and scribbled down the information. By the time the gypsies returned I had opened up the bar and did not feel so uncomfortable as there were one or two people in the place. As I passed over the piece of paper with the information on that they required they left the premises.

The next evening I was reading the *Express & Star* and a headline on the front page caught my attention. It read 'Garage owner threatened at gunpoint.' The story said that a garage owner was threatened at gunpoint after a group of men refused to pay a towing-in fee for a Volvo that he had recovered. I did not have to read any more. A shiver went down my spine as I wondered what would have happened to me had I not found the number.

In the next edition of the *Express & Star* there was another headline which read 'Gypsy site hit by food poisoning.' The article went on to say that a number of gypsies with food poisoning had attended a wedding some days earlier. It had also affected gypsies from another site who had attended the same wedding. So it was quite obvious where the source was. Thank goodness we had nothing to do with the catering.

Later that week I was sitting in my office catching up on some paperwork when I became aware of somebody standing in the open doorway.

'My husband is still in hiding,' she said.

Then I realised who it was. It was the mother of the gypsy bride. She came to the desk and leaned over, looking down at me. 'I owe you eight grand,' she said. She slowly put her hand down her low-cut sweater. I held my breath. I did not know what was going to happen next. 'Here you go,' she said, pulling out a large wad of money from down her bra. Then the other hand pulled out another wad of notes. 'Count it,' she said. 'It's all there, eight thousand pounds.' I counted it in front of her and then she went.

At the end of that week I had to sit down and take stock of the situation. The football club had no money, and the social club was not breaking even. OK, we had just taken £8,000 behind the bar, but that was a one-off. We were living in rented property and the only transport we had was the club van, which was not always available.

The social club began to struggle. We were relying on match-day takings and the letting of the concert room for different functions, but this was hardly keeping the place afloat. Very few people came in during the evenings and lunchtimes, but I did have one quite frequent visitor during the lunch hour – Mrs Clamp, who came in for a chat and a drink, always sitting in her favourite chair near the bar.

At the next meeting things were looking up. The Bhattis had decided to turn the social club into a sports centre with five-a-side football, badminton, tennis and aerobics, aerobics being a big thing at that time. They picked a girl named Sally to be the aerobics teacher, who was photographed and became the main subject in a two-page advert for the sports centre taken out in the local paper. Sally did not need any special equipment to do her aerobic classes, but what the Bhattis had not taken into account was that to play tennis or badminton in the gymnasium the appropriate nets and equipment had to be there, so, consequently, I had to refuse anyone phoning up to book a tennis or badminton session. One good thing had happened – the 'Doog' had managed to get me a small car to drive about instead of having to rely on the availability of the club van.

Even though Graham had fixed the showers upstairs in the gym, these were primarily for the lads playing five-a-side, and we could hardly expect any of the ladies who had taken part in one of the aerobics sessions to use them, so I had a key for the away team dressing room which I could access from Waterloo Road. It was a bit of a pain, but at least we were providing the facilities. The whole thing was farcical really, and I often regretted leaving the Conservative Club in Blackpool, but, on the plus side, all the family were involved and they were happy about it – and we did have some damn good laughs with the lads who helped us behind the bar on match days and at functions, namely Casey, Tic and Brady.

Having access to the visitors' changing room was also a bit of a bonus for me because whenever the ground was empty I could go and have a nice long soak in one of the baths. Early one Sunday morning, after bottling up at the sports centre, I had found time for a hot bath at the ground before opening the bar. Lying there soaking and reminiscing about how many famous players must have used the baths and showers since 1923, I became aware that somebody had opened the dressing room door that led from the corridor inside Molineux. The familiar creak of it gave it away.

Suddenly, a figure brandishing a large sweeping brush came running into the bathroom. It was Mrs Clamp. 'Got you, you swine,' she shouted. By this time I had jumped out of the bath ready to defend myself. 'Oh, it's you, Waggy,' she stammered as she recognised my Tarzan-like physique. This was my second naked encounter with Mrs Clamp. We just had to stop meeting like that!

'I though it was one of those hard-faced buggers that was out on the pitch earlier,' she said.

She told me that a dozen or so people were having a game on the pitch when she arrived that Sunday morning. They had broken into the kit room and were playing with a brand new ball.

'I soon chased the cheeky sods off,' she said, 'but we've lost half the kit and a new ball.'

'Never mind, Mrs Clamp,' I said, 'you did your best. Come up to the club when you've finished at lunchtime and I'll buy you a double to calm you down.' With that I got back into the bath and Mrs Clamp went about her business.

The Bhatti brothers were very secretive people in everything that they did, and there were very few people from Wolverhampton who managed to catch a glimpse of them, never mind meet them. I don't think they realised the significance of their intervention before the receiver closed the door on Wolverhampton Wanderers. In other words, they saved Wolves from extinction and, had they gone public, showing their intentions to the Wolves fans, I am sure that they would have got plenty of encouragement.

There was no input in the running of the club from the Bhattis at all and they even gave us the task of feeding the young players at lunchtimes – a task that we thoroughly enjoyed, I might add – but it was all a drain on the resources of the social club itself. These young lads were the possible future of the club, and I was told that I had to organise a sportsman's dinner to raise funds to send the youth team to a European tournament without any help or input. It was little wonder that I had not been surprised when the Doog had fallen out with the brothers and left his post as chairman. Knowing Derek's temperament, I was amazed that the association had lasted that long.

By this time, Tommy Docherty was the manager and he was anxious for me to get on with the arrangements for the dinner so that the itinerary for the youth team could be put into place. Comedian George Roper was to be the guest speaker and, much to my relief, the tickets were sold in no time at all. An outside caterer provided the meal and the evening turned out to be quite a success, raising enough to send the youth team on their way. At the end of the evening I found myself left with Tommy Doc and George

Roper having a nightcap at the bar. One nightcap led to another and another and before we knew it the clock seemed to have raced around to 3am. George and Tommy disappeared into the night and I called a taxi to take me home after a long day and equally long night.

At 9 o'clock the next morning I was going about my daily chores in the social club, albeit quite bleary-eyed from the session with George and Tommy hours before. Sid Kipping, our jovial ex-coach driver, had a little part-time job at the ground tidying up the boardroom and making tea for the office staff and any of the board who might have called in, but this particular morning he surprised me by coming up to the social club looking rather pale.

'Hello, Sid,' I said. ' What's up with you? You look as though you've seen a ghost.'

'I thought I had,' he stammered.

'Come on then, tell me all about it,' I said as I could see that he was a little shaken up.

Sid then went on to tell me how he had opened up the ground as usual, tidied up the kitchen, put the cups away and then decided to make sure that everything in the boardroom was shipshape.

'I went in and froze,' he said. 'There was a body on the boardroom table. I tried not to panic because I couldn't see the face, so I sidled round to the other side of the table to get a better look. As I got round the other side the body moved and grunted. I could see who it was then — it was Tommy Doc!'

'What did he say?' I asked.

'He didn't say anything, he was still asleep,' said Sid. 'So I came up here out of the way to get over the shock.'

While trying to calm him down I could not help but have a good laugh at the thought of poor old Sid finding a body on the boardroom table. I would have given him a brandy to calm him down but Sid was strictly teetotal, which was more than I could say for Tommy Doc, George Roper and myself!

The writing was on the wall for the social club by then. Every time I had a conversation with Keith Pearson he reminded me that the place was losing money. I used to put this to the back of my mind, trying to put off the inevitable, and struggled on with the facilities we had. After a little over 12 months with Wolves, Tommy Docherty left us and Sammy Chapman bravely took over the sinking ship. Sammy knew he was going to fight a losing battle financially and even to this day still tells the story of how he and the players had to have a whip-round to pay the milkman. He was the manager for the next few months, but then I heard a rumour — and I must admit at the time I thought somebody was winding me up. It could not be possible that Bill McGarry was coming back to Molineux, could it? However, the rumour was true. He did return. Walking down the corridor at Molineux a few days later, Greg Fellows, the coach, collared me. I should have known what he was going to say.

'Waggy, the boss wants to see you in his office.'

How many times had I heard that at Molineux? Not being part of the playing or coaching staff, I was not really duty-bound to heed the request, but I did so, more out of curiosity than anything else. Bill McGarry was not very happy, having realised that he had dropped a clanger in taking the job and I was probably the only person that he could have a good moan to. Anyhow, he only lasted 61 days and poor old Sammy Chapman had to hold the fort again.

Back at the social club things were not getting any better and a visit from the bailiff was very ominous indeed. Apparently, none of the bills had been paid and it was the bailiff's job to make a list of the club's assets – not that there were many – which would be sold off to pay the creditors. I knew this visit signalled that the end was in sight for the Wolves Social Club.

Although Derek Dougan was no longer anything to do with Wolves, he came to see me to take away the car that he had provided me with some time back. There was a lot of controversy about who the club cars actually belonged to, but I had no alternative and handed over the keys to Derek. It was not long before Keith Pearson came along to give me the bad news – the social club would close the next day. The family and I were given 24 hours to remove our personal possessions before handing the keys in at Molineux. That lunchtime Mrs Clamp came up for her midday livener and I had to break the bad news to her that this would be her last daytime visit before we closed down. She had known for some time that this day would come, but she came to me with a strange request.

'That chair that I always sit in is the most comfortable chair that I have ever sat in,' she began. 'Seeing as you're closing down is there any chance I could have it?'

'Of course you can, Mrs Clamp,' I said without hesitation.

'I'll send our Eddie round for it tonight,' she replied.

Eddie Clamp came round that evening and told me he had parked his van round the back. He wanted to strip the place of all the tables and chairs, but he was really disappointed when I told him that the bailiff had been and listed everything that was in the place. I explained about the old chair, but I could not let him fill his van with the furniture. Reluctantly he had to accept this, but I think that he had already got a buyer for all the stuff. All he went home with was his mother's favourite chair.

I borrowed the club's van that night to take home all our personal belongings from the social club and returned it the next morning when I went to hand in the keys. I gave

Keith the keys and what little cash we had taken the night before and set off for our rented house two miles away up Cannock Road. I cut through up the hill to the bus stop 30 yards past the Elephant and Castle pub. I did not know what number bus I was to catch, but I had worked out that if it stopped there it would be going up Cannock Road. A bus came along and stopped for me to get on, but what I did not know was that you were supposed to tender the right change and when I showed the driver a £5 note he looked at me as though I was daft. As a result I had to get off again and start to walk. As I set off, it suddenly hit home to me what a dire situation I was in. I had no job, no transport and no prospects.

I walked down under the bridge and up the slope towards the Wagon and Horses pub, wondering what was in store for us. There was a sign on the right — Mitchells & Butlers Brewery. Something clicked. I was sure I knew somebody there. I remembered who. So I set off down Grimshaw Lane with the intention of finding out how I could contact the person who was district manager. I walked into the reception and was just about to speak to the young lady behind the counter when an adjoining door opened and out walked the man himself. It seemed that my timing had been impeccable. I explained my situation to him in the hope that he could maybe fix me up with a pub or find me some relief work.

'There is nothing going at the moment,' he said 'and also the rules have changed. All future licensees, no matter what their experience, will have to attend a six-week course here at the brewery. There is such a course starting next week and if it's not fully subscribed there's a possibility that Barbara and yourself might be able to attend.'

At least there was a glimmer of hope, and I almost ran back to the house to tell Barbara and the kids. The very next day we learned that we could start on the course. It was long and, at times, tedious but it had to be done, the incentive being that there would be a very good chance of managing a pub afterwards.

On completion, each couple was allotted a pub to manage in various districts of Wolverhampton, and Barbara and I were given the Butlers Arms at Bushbury. We were no strangers to the Butlers because we used to have after-hours drinks there many years before, when Freddy Lavender and his wife Barbara used to run the place. Freddy and Barbara eventually moved from there to the Tavern in the Town in the centre of Wolverhampton, and when Danny Hegan used to do his disappearing act that was where he was usually found.

The Butlers was definitely not your run-of-the-mill pub. It was full of characters and we made friends with some grand people there. They were all down to earth, no airs and graces, and we had some great times with them. From the Butlers we moved to the Old Wulfrunians Club at Castlecroft on the outskirts of Wolverhampton. It had a contrasting clientele. They were the old boys of Wolverhampton Grammar School. This was more of a sporting environment with football, hockey and cricket teams. After several years there Barbara and I separated and the committee decided that because it had been a joint appointment, and Barbara and I were no longer together, I would have to relinquish my position and move out of the bungalow.

So once again I had no home, no job, no transport and no prospects.

At Molineux Again

With the rebuilding of Molineux after Sir Jack Hayward finally became owner of the club, it was decided by him and the architects to incorporate two function rooms in the belly of the Stan Cullis Stand. There were to be two bars in one room and one bar in the smaller room, with a centrally-situated kitchen to serve both rooms. John Hendley, who worked in the press office, came to see me with a message from Molineux about the possibility of me managing this particular area of the Stan Cullis Stand. After discussions with Wolves' commercial man David Clayton, I was asked to manage the rooms, which were later named the Stan Cullis Suite and Waggy's Lounge Bar. As you can imagine, I was pleased and rather proud to have been asked back to Molineux in the 1990s after service there in the 1960s, 1970s and 1980s.

My job specification was to be the same as any pub or club manager: hire the staff and door security, order from the brewery, clean the lines, serve behind the bar, take bookings, do the banking and all the rest. I would be on duty seven days a week and was to be paid £150 — just over £20 a day. It was not a lot, but I was happy to be back in employment and at a place I knew well. I was taken on board before the project was finished in order to liaise with the construction manager as to where I wanted certain things to be situated, particularly behind the bars, and to be a general go-between, relieving David Clayton of the task of meeting him every day. Sir Jack popped in quite often to see how things were progressing and to check that the materials being used were of English origin — after all, it was his money that was being spent. Obviously, one of the first things that was to be decided was which brewery was going to supply the bar and the rest of the stadium. After contacting several breweries to see what kind of discounts or deals we could get, it was Bass who came up with the best offer.

David Clayton was in overall charge of the ticket office, club shop, the gymnasium, the lottery, as well as my department and others, and it soon became clear to me that he knew very little about the licensed and catering trade, except percentage profits. Initially he came over as a very nice guy, easy going and amiable, but as time elapsed it became apparent that first impressions can be very deceptive.

Although I was manager of my department, I did not have the authority to order anything, except the beer, or pay for anything. All this was to be done by David Clayton, so imagine my despair when I found out that nothing had been ordered for my department before the opening night. He gave me permission to order some things on the condition that I would show him a list of what I had ordered so that he could sanction payment. Fortunately the workmen were still on site and managed to plumb in some glass-wash machines behind the bars.

Finding David Clayton to sanction the orders, which were running into thousands, was difficult as he was always otherwise engaged, and sometimes I would have to wait a full afternoon to see him, especially if he had been in one of his many meetings. Next came another blow. After the specially-made carpets, with Wolves emblems woven into them, were laid the place was looking amazing, and David Clayton came over to see the room so I asked him when I could expect the furniture.

'I thought that you had taken care of that,' was his reply, although he knew full well that I did not have the authority to order it. My heart sank.

In the beginning we had no set format and we decided to just open the doors and see how things went. We knew that match days would take care of themselves and Gary Leaver's tours of the new stadium would also bring in extra revenue. I had already booked in a few private functions, but because there had not been a chef assigned to our kitchen I was having to take care of the buffets myself. This was where my partner Val Williams came in. Val had been working for a private company in the John Ireland Stand and was transferred to the Stan Cullis Stand once it had been completed.

When I was introduced to Val, who knew nothing about football, the person who introduced us said 'This is Dave who used to play for Wolves.'

Val's first words to me were 'Do you still keep it up?'

To which I replied 'I don't train any more, if that's what you mean.'

Val later became my partner and to this day still is, and we often laugh about that first conversation.

In the early days Sir Jack became quite a frequent visitor to Waggy's Bar, normally at lunchtimes and almost always with Billy Wright, Jonathan, Jack's son, and another director Jack Harris, the former chairman. Sir Jack always put his hand in his pocket to pay for the drinks and the sandwiches, and Billy Wright was a perfect gentleman, always the same, even when he was not in the best of health.

Around that time Graham Taylor had become the manager of Wolves. He had received a large amount of mail from people who did not agree with his appointment. Many of the protesters were not happy at his treatment of Steve Bull, who had been in the England squad when Graham was manager of the national side. Graham came to see me and asked whether he would be able to use the room in Waggy's Bar for a couple of hours. He got in touch with as many of his critics as he could, either by phone or by post, inviting them to meet him face to face. He was a very brave man, as he had no idea how many of them were going to turn up or what kind of attitude they were going to take towards him. He arrived early that evening and we sat in my office chatting as the people filed in and took their seats. When everybody was in the room – there were at least 150 people – Graham faced them all. As he walked in you could almost feel the hostility towards him. He welcomed everybody, thanked them for coming and then he began:

'I don't need this job, but I want this job and the board of Wolverhampton Wanderers want me to have this job. If, after this meeting, we become a millimetre closer together I shall be over the moon because every one of us in this room has one thing in common – Wolverhampton Wanderers.'

He went on to give a wonderful résumé of his career and his plans for the success of Wolves. In conclusion he did a question and answer session in which he did not dodge any issues. He answered every question with complete honesty. After the session, which had lasted well over an hour, he walked towards the door where I was standing and looked at me as if to say 'Phew! I'm glad that's over,' but it was not over. He was pursued to the door by people wanting autographs and pictures taken with him. He had certainly won over the vast majority.

Graham Taylor earned my respect for the way he handled the whole situation. After all, they did not demand to see him, he invited them to meet him. I still think it was a grave mistake for Wolves to dispense with his services. I did fall foul of Graham once, though, but he did see my point of view at the end of it. The players had asked me if they could have a Christmas bash, a private one, in Waggy's Bar one afternoon in December. It was no problem for me, but Graham got wind of it and came to see me.

'I'm totally against these Christmas parties, especially when it's just the lads. They always seem to end with trouble and bad press,' he said.

I assured him that there would be just the lads, no outsiders and definitely no press. From the moment the party started the doors would be locked and it would be totally private. The afternoon kicked-off at 2 o'clock and, as you can imagine, all the lads were in party mood – after all, it was their Christmas do and they were entitled to let their hair down. At 6 o'clock it was time to wrap up the party. I had kept my end of the bargain with Graham. No strangers, no press and no nonsense from the lads. However, the players decided to go up town to carry on with the celebrations, and this was where the problems began. Apparently, certain things went wrong and there was a big splash in next day's *Express & Star*.

'I told you what would happen,' Graham said.

'I kept my end of the bargain,' I replied, 'and what chance did I have of persuading 20 grown men – footballers at that – not to go up town?'

Graham was fuming because, being a very astute man and football manager, he more or less knew what the end result would be, and he was right.

Initially Waggy's Bar had been running as an eaterie at lunchtime and as a normal public bar in the evenings, but I always felt that it just needed an extra spark to make it something special and worthy of its new surroundings. I decided to apply for a late licence and enlisted the help of an old pal – DJ Charlie Watson – to run a late-night disco on Saturdays. As it turned out, this was the spark that was needed, and the discos were so successful that we did one on Sunday nights too. Waggy's Bar quickly became one of the hottest night spots in Wolverhampton. It was certainly a great atmosphere, with a good mix of Wolves fans and the general public enjoying themselves together.

At the height of its popularity, I decided to leave, and writing this book has given me the opportunity to dispel any rumours of misdemeanours that abounded at the time I left. I must stress that I left of my own accord because of a clash of personalities between me and my immediate boss, David Clayton. I found that I could no longer work with him, which left me with no option but to leave my position as manager of Waggy's Bar.

I was really sorry to leave Waggy's Bar. I had made some really good friends there, and we enjoyed some great times together. It was 'our' bar – everybody who worked there or regularly frequented the place made it what it was, and I really appreciated that. My old friend DJ Charlie Watson died some time ago and deserves special mention. He made a huge contribution to the success of Waggy's Bar. I look at the old place now with sadness because it is only used to its maximum on match days. Gone are the days when there was a queue on the stairs every Saturday and Sunday night.

Final Thoughts

On Sunday 24 June 2007 I received a telephone call from a distressed Merlyn, the partner of Derek Dougan. 'Waggy,' she began, 'something terrible has happened.' From the tremor in her voice and the distraught manner in which she spoke I immediately knew what she was about to tell me – the Doog was dead. He had called her that morning with a desperate cry for help, but when she arrived by his side minutes later it was all over. Being understandably deeply upset and shocked, Merlyn entrusted Phil Parkes and myself to contact the other lads of our era to inform them of the bad news. The Doog was the first ex-colleague we had lost.

The next day Merlyn contacted me and asked if I would do her the honour of being one of the pall bearers. I immediately accepted and was very proud to have been asked, but I became incredibly nervous. I am a naturally nervous person, but this was to test me to the limit.

I mentioned how nervous I was feeling to my old pal Frank Munro. His reply certainly put things into perspective. 'I would give anything to get out of this chair and help carry that coffin,' he said, making me realise how lucky I was, being fit and able enough to do what I had been asked. Frank was later to play his part at the funeral by distributing the order of service booklets to all the mourners as they entered St Peter's Church in the centre of Wolverhampton.

Some days before the funeral I saw John Richards at Tettenhall Green, raising money for charity with the Round Table. Naturally we spoke about the Doog and I asked if he would be attending the funeral. His reply was 'Waggy, if I went to his funeral I would be a hypocrite.' A straight and honest answer. I have already mentioned that there had been a major rift between John and Derek many years before. I do not think that the real reason for this will ever be revealed but, knowing John's personality, I can tell you it must have been really serious for him to have given me the answer that he did. I have been bombarded with questions since Derek's death as to why no comment was made in the press by John and why he did not attend the funeral. It is not for me to reason why, and I have too much respect for John to ask him point blank.

Arriving at the Jennings funeral parlour at 11.30am on the day of the funeral, I was naturally feeling nervous. Derek's relatives were very nice people and the atmosphere was markedly on the relaxed side – something Derek would have approved of – which calmed me down considerably. I met up with Jutta and the two lads, Nicholas and Alexander, for the first time in over 30 years and they too were taking a more positive, rather than downbeat, attitude towards the proceedings. After the coffin had been sealed, the co-ordinator announced that it was time for the pall bearers to have a rehearsal at the rear of the funeral parlour where the hearse and other cars were parked under cover.

'This is Rod,' he said, as he introduced us to one of his colleagues. 'Rod will instruct you as to how you will handle, lift, walk and turn with the coffin.'

'Follow me, gentlemen,' he said as he set off down the corridor, and we followed in single file as though we were going down the tunnel and on to the pitch. Entering the room at the rear of the building, I saw the coffin sitting on two trestles with the hearse parked 20 yards away.

'Gather round, lads,' said Rod, just as we would for a pre-match talk. 'Once I have explained to you the procedure for handling the coffin I would like you to take it off the trestles and place it in the hearse. Then I would like you to take it out of the hearse, walk back to the trestles and replace it there. The next thing we need to do is decide which positions you will take up to carry the coffin.'

'I would like to be outside-left,' I requested, walking to the front left-hand corner of the coffin, which brought a smile from the rest of the pall bearers.

'Of course you can,' he replied. 'After all, that's where you spent your career, on his left-hand side.'

This broke the ice and instead of being a morbid rehearsal it was conducted with a certain amount of humour but still within the bounds of dignity. Rod instructed us on how to pick up the coffin from the trestles and we walked with it to the hearse, placing it in the back.

As the cortège drove to St Peter's I was amazed at how many people had turned out on the streets and by the church to pay their respects to Derek, and after a beautiful service I was equally amazed at the crowds outside Molineux, where the cortège naturally stopped for a few minutes on the way to the crematorium.

It was a short, family service at the crematorium, and Phil Nicholls and I decided to sit on the back row while the family occupied the front rows. As the curtains slowly closed around the coffin, for some reason I glanced at my watch. I nudged Phil and showed him the time. It was exactly 3 o'clock — kick-off time, and the time that had played a major part in Derek's life.

Back at Molineux, where the rest of the congregation from St Peter's had gathered, I managed to catch a few minutes with ex-colleagues Denis Law and Gordon Taylor before they left for Manchester. Denis remarked that he had been to more than a dozen funerals in the past 18 months. We are all in our sixties now, and I suppose it its inevitable that funerals become more commonplace in our lives. It was great to see my old friend and colleague Les Wilson, who had flown over specially from Canada to be at Derek's funeral.

Les was one of the original 'Tea Set' with the Doog, John Holsgrove and Bobby Thomson. It was a fitting tribute to Derek that people had travelled from all over the United Kingdom and, in Les's case, from much further away, to pay their respects to him. I have already written about Derek's career as a player at Wolverhampton Wanderers, but talking about the Tea Set has reminded me of one more tale that I am sure Derek would have loved me to tell you.

From day one, Derek and McGarry had been at arms' length for two reasons, one being the fact that Derek was chairman of the PFA and the other that Derek was a household name and McGarry had never had to deal with a big star before. They avoided each other like the plague, and in all the time that Derek played for him I never heard or saw a confrontation. Bill McGarry could not afford to have one, just in case he came off worse and lost face in front of the rest of the players.

I should point out that Derek could not stand sterilised milk and always drank pasteurised. After one morning's training session old Jack Davis had left the usual white enamel jug full of tea and a trayful of mugs on the bench in the middle of the dressing room. By chance, Bill McGarry just happened to pop into the dressing room as we were pouring out our mugs of tea. At that moment in walked old Jack, carrying a cup of tea in a nice china cup on a nice china saucer. McGarry must have thought what a nice old boy he was for bringing him in a cup of tea and stretched out his hand to accept it from Mr Davis. However, Mr Davis was completely oblivious to Bill McGarry and continued walking over to the corner where the Doog was taking off his training kit.

'Here's your tea, Mr Dougan,' he said.

McGarry's eyes bulged out of his head as he bawled, 'What the f*****g hell's this? F*****g waiter service?'

Mr Davis turned round with a start. 'Sorry, Mr McGarry, I didn't see you there,' he said. 'Er, Mr Dougan doesn't like the milk we use in the big jug of tea so I make him a separate cup.'

'Get that f*****g cup and saucer out of here,' growled McGarry, through gritted teeth, 'and throw the tea down the sink. Mr Dougan will have to make do with the same f*****g tea that everybody else drinks.' With that he followed Mr Davis out of the dressing room and we could hear him still growling down the corridor.

Getting older makes me look at things that have happened over the years in a more philosophical and meaningful light. We lost the Doog in 2007, the only player that we have lost from our original squad of the 1960s and 1970s, a squad that played together in the top flight, plus European and world trips, enjoying some magical times and memorable games together. Our squad has been very fortunate to have been able to work and socialise together for all these years, especially in our playing days, doing something that we all enjoyed.

Personally, when I look back I realise what a lucky person I was to have played football for 20 years, visiting some wonderful places in the process – and always with a cracking set of lads. As with every profession there are always ups and downs, so, believe me, the game is not always a bed of roses. Sometimes you can train and feel good all week then get out on the pitch on a Saturday afternoon feeling lethargic, heavy legged and completely out of sync.

Nevertheless, as I mentioned earlier, the good things far outweighed the bad and there was no finer exhilarating feeling than hearing the crowd roaring you on when you were having one of your better games. I must admit that I took a lot of my career for granted. I was fortunate that I did not have to work too hard at my game and I am not being conceited about the fact. Obviously, the fitness side of it had to be worked on, but most of my game relied on natural ability and that was where I was lucky because I was able to play my game without thinking about it. It just came naturally to me.

It is over 30 years since I represented Wolves on the football pitch and even after all this time I still get people shaking my hand and thanking me for 'all the enjoyment' that I gave them. Even though I get a little embarrassed it is a wonderful feeling to know that I was appreciated in that way and to know that I gave something back to the fans who paid to watch Wolverhampton Wanderers. I was lucky that my game was based on skill. I could make a hash of it a couple of times then make a run with the ball that had the fans on the edge of their seats and all would be forgiven. Goalscorers and skill players were the ones to get all the plaudits because they were the ones that excited the crowd, but let us not forget those who did all the staunch work of getting the ball for us in the first place. It is only when your playing days have finished that you really appreciate how good it was and how much you miss it. Lucky, lucky me to have had a job that let me share my thrills with the people that watched me performing.

Well, that is the end of my tales from the four decades – the 1960s through to the 1990s. I have tried to give you some insight as to what goes on behind the scenes and also the humorous side of my time at Molineux. I hope you have enjoyed it.